Clifford A Kiracofe, Jr, teaches political science at Washington and Lee University and history at the Virginia Military Institute. He was formerly a Senior Professional Staff Member of the US Senate on Foreign Relations and has extensive inside experience of American federal government. His previous books (in collaboration with Pierre de Villemarest) are a history of Soviet military intelligence (1988), and a history of the STASI (1991), both written in French.

Clifford A Kiracofe provides a highly readable and welcome analysis of the important subject of Christian Zionism as he traces the origins, development and ideology of this controversial movement. His nuanced discussion of the complex relationship between Christian Zionism and nineteenth and early twentieth century British imperial policy in the Middle East is both well presented and insightful. A detailed and provocative examination of the impact made by Christian Zionism on US foreign policy, *Dark Crusade* makes essential reading for all those with a serious interest in the prospects for peace in the Middle East and in Western policies in general toward the region.

Edmund Ghareeb, Professor of Middle East History and Politics,
American University, Washington, DC

INTERNATIONAL LIBRARY OF POLITICAL STUDIES

Series ISBN 978-1-84885-226-6

See www.ibtauris.com/ILPS for a full list of titles

19. *Choosing the Tory Leader: Conservative Party Leadership Elections from Heath to Cameron*
Timothy Heppell
978 1 84511 486 2

20. *The British Labour Party and the Wider World: Domestic Politics, Internationalism and Foreign Policy*
Paul Corthorn and Jonathan Davis (eds)
978 1 84511 401 5

21. *Harold Wilson and Europe: Pursuing Britain's Membership of the European Community*
Melissa Pine
978 1 84511 470 1

22. *The Greek Idea: The Formation of National and Transnational Identities*
Maria Koundoura
978 1 84511 487 9

23. *Conservative Suffragists: The Women's Vote and the Tory Party*
Mitzi Auchterlonie
978 1 84511 485 5

24. *The Contested Countryside: Rural Politics and Land Controversy in Modern Britain*
Jeremy Burchardt and Philip Conford (eds)
978 1 84511 715 3

25. *Liberals in Schism: A History of the National Liberal Party*
David Dutton
978 1 84511 667 5

26. *Communist Women in Scotland: Red Clydeside from the Russian Revolution to the End of the Soviet Union*
Neil C. Rafeek
978 1 84511 624 8

27. *Richard Crossman and the Welfare State: Pioneer of Welfare Provision and Labour Politics in Post-War Britain*
Stephen Thornton
978 1 84511 848 8

28. *Reunifying Cyprus: The Annan Plan and Beyond*
Andrekos Varnava and Hubert Faustmann (eds)
978 1 84511 657 6

29. *An Irish Statesman and Revolutionary: The Nationalist and Internationalist Politics of Sean MacBride*
Elizabeth Keane
978 1 84511 125 0

30. *Flood Planning: The Politics of Water Security*
Jeroen Warner
978 1 84511 817 4

31. *Dark Crusade: Christian Zionism and US Foreign Policy*
Clifford A. Kiracofe, Jr
978 1 84511 754 2

32. *Philosophy, Politics and Religion in British Democracy: Maurice Cowling and Conservatism*
Robert Crowcroft, S. J. D. Green and Richard Whiting (eds)
978 1 84511 976 8

33. *British Conservatism: The Philosophy and Politics of Inequality*
Peter Dorey
978 1 84511 352 0

34. *Global Russia: Eurasianism, Putin and the New Right*
Dmitry V. Shlapentokh
978 1 84885 036 1

35. *The Path to Devolution and Change: A Political History of Scotland Under Margaret Thatcher*
David Stewart
978 1 84511 938 6

36. *Democracy, Citizenship and Youth: Towards Social and Political Participation in Brazil*
Itamar Silva and Anna Luiza Salles Souto (eds)
978 1 84885 048 4

37. *Choosing Slovakia: Slavic Hungary, the Czechoslovak Language and Accidental Nationalism*
Alexander Maxwell
978 1 84885 074 3

38. *Khatami and Gorbachev: Politics of Change in the Islamic Republic of Iran and the USSR*
Zhand Shakibi
978 1 84885 139 9

39. *Critical Turns in Critical Theory: New Directions in Social and Political Thought*
Séamus Ó Tuama (ed.)
978 1 84511 559 3

DARK CRUSADE

Christian Zionism and US Foreign Policy

Clifford A. Kiracofe, Jr

I.B. TAURIS
LONDON · NEW YORK

Published in 2009 by I.B.Tauris & Co Ltd
6 Salem Road, London W2 4BU
175 Fifth Avenue, New York NY 10010
www.ibtauris.com

Copyright © 2009 Clifford A. Kiracofe, Jr

The right of Clifford A. Kiracofe, Jr, to be identified as the author of this work has been asserted by the author in accordance with the Copyright, Designs and Patents Act 1988.

All rights reserved. Except for brief quotations in a review, this book, or any part thereof, may not be reproduced, stored in or introduced into a retrieval system, or transmitted, in any form or by any means, electronic, mechanical, photocopying, recording or otherwise, without the prior written permission of the publisher.

International Library of Political Studies, 31

ISBN: 978 1 84511 754 2 (HB)
        978 1 84511 755 9 (PB)

A full CIP record for this book is available from the British Library
A full CIP record is available from the Library of Congress

Library of Congress Catalog Card Number: available

Typeset in Warnock Pro by Sara Millington, Editorial and Design Services

*To the memory of my great-grandfather
Reverend John Wesley Kiracofe (1841–1914)
of Virginia*

Circuit rider, pastor, educator

...a passionate attachment of one nation for another produces a variety of evils. Sympathy for the favorite nation, facilitating the illusion of an imaginary common interest in cases where no real common interest exists, and infusing into one the enmities of the other, betrays the former into a participation in the quarrels and wars of the latter without adequate inducement or justification. It leads also to concessions to the favorite nation of privileges denied to others which is apt doubly to injure the nation making the concessions; by unnecessarily parting with what ought to have been retained, and by exciting jealousy, ill-will, and a disposition to retaliate, in the parties from whom equal privileges are withheld. And it gives to ambitious, corrupted, or deluded citizens (who devote themselves to the favorite nation), facility to betray or sacrifice the interests of their own country, without odium, sometimes even with popularity; gilding, with the appearances of a virtuous sense of obligation, a commendable deference for public opinion, or a laudable zeal for public good, the base or foolish compliances of ambition, corruption, or infatuation...

George Washington, Farewell Address, 1796

These believers are convinced that they have a personal responsibility to hasten this coming of the 'rapture' in order to fulfill biblical prophecy. Their agenda calls for a war in the Middle East against Islam (Iraq?) and the taking of the entire Holy Land by Jews (occupation of the West Bank?), with the total expulsion of all Christians and other gentiles.

Jimmy Carter, 'Our endangered values', 2005

...you can imagine a world in which these extremists and radicals get control of energy resources. And then you can imagine them saying, we're going to pull a bunch of oil off the market to run your price of oil up, unless you do the following. And the following would be along the lines, well ... give up your alliance with Israel...

George W. Bush, remarks 4 November 2006

Contents

Acknowledgments		*viii*
Abbreviations		*x*
Preface		*xii*
Introduction		1
Part I	**Christian Zionism and Nineteenth-Century Imperialism**	
1	The Eastern Question and Imperialism	8
2	The Early American Republic and the Muslim World	27
3	Christian Zionism: Construction of an Ideology	45
4	Christian Zionism on American Shores	62
Part II	**Christian Zionism and American Foreign Policy, 1917–48**	
5	Fundamentalism, the First World War, and Palestine	72
6	Christian Zionism from the First World War to the Second World War	87
7	Zionism from the Second World War to 1948	104
Part III	**Christian Zionism and American Foreign Policy, From the Cold War to Bush**	
8	The Christian Right in the Fifties and Sixties	120
9	The Christian Right in the Seventies and Eighties	136
10	George W. Bush and the Dark Crusade	155
11	Christian Zionism and the Next War	174
Notes		183
Select Bibliography		225
Index		247

Acknowledgments

Alex Wright, my editor at I.B.Tauris, suggested I write this book. Given my academic research interests, and my experience on the senior professional staff of the Senate of the United States, it was natural for me to accept the invitation from I.B.Tauris to write on the ideology of Christian Zionism. I am grateful to him for his suggestion and also for his patience over the past three years. Sara Millington was meticulous in the copy edit and made a splendid job of the typesetting and design.

A number of colleagues have been kind enough to offer comment and support. In particular, I would like to thank Professor Eugen Weber at the University of California at Los Angles (UCLA) for his encouragement, courtesy, and hospitality when I visited the university on several occasions to consult important archival materials relating to European fascism located in the Charles E. Young Research Library. This earlier project, which is ongoing, deepened my interest in, and concern about, extremist ideologies and their impact on the modern world.

Vladimir Reisky de Dubnic, my late friend and professor at the University of Virginia in the Woodrow Wilson Department of Government and Foreign Affairs, first sparked my interest in political ideologies through several courses he offered on 'Ideological Influences in International Relations', which I took in the early 1970s. At that time, during the Cold War, we focused in particular on Marxism-Leninism in its Soviet Russian and Chinese forms.

The late Pierre Faillant de Villemarest (1922–2008), French journalist and decorated hero of the Second World War French Resistance, was a steady friend and mentor for some three decades and inspired my work and my own spirit of resistance. We collaborated on several books and various research projects concerning the Soviet Union, Nazi Germany, and Fascism.

The late Ambassador Adam Watson (1914–2007), former British Assistant Under-Secretary of State, who taught at the University of Virginia, inspired my thinking on international relations and international society.

My brother, Dr James Bartholomay Kiracofe, gave discerning critique and steady encouragement.

My cousin, Dr Jean Dunbar, generously gave me an essential hand through her judicious copy edit of the manuscript.

During our travels together to North Africa and the Gulf, my friend Dr Edmund Ghareeb has deepened my understanding of the Arab world.

Jeffrey Steinberg and Norton Mezvinsky offered encouragement and insights over not a few glasses of red wine in various favorite haunts in Washington, DC. My friend Marvine Howe, veteran *New York Times* foreign correspondent and bureau chief in Morocco and Turkey, was encouraging from the beginning of the project.

My late parents, Clifford Attick Kiracofe (1907–87) and Elizabeth Augusta James Kiracofe (1916–2001), emphasized civic engagement and religious toleration in our home. They inspired me to take my path of public service and education.

Abbreviations

ACCC	American Council of Christian Churches
ACPC	American Christian Palestine Committee
AFSI	Americans for a Safe Israel
AIPAC	American Israel Public Affairs Committee
AJC	American Jewish Committee
APC	American Palestine Council
ARP	*Anti-Revolutionaire Partij* (Anti-Revolutionary Party)
AZEC	American Zionist Emergency Council
CACC	Christian Anti-Communist Crusade
CCP	Christian Council on Palestine
CDM	Coalition for a Democratic Majority
CEF	Christian Economic Foundation
CFF	Christian Freedom Foundation
CLI	Committee for the Liberation of Iraq
CNP	Council for National Policy
CPD	Committee for the Present Danger
CSFC	Committee for the Survival of a Free Congress
CSP	Center for Security Policy
CUFI	Christians United for Israel
ECZA	Emergency Committee for Zionist Affairs
GOP	Grand Old Party (Republican Party)
HUAC	House Un-American Activities Committee
IASPS	Institute for Advanced Strategic and Political Studies
ICCC	International Council of Christian Churches
ICEJ	International Christian Embassy Jerusalem
IFCJ	International Fellowship for Christians and Jews

various research projects concerning the Soviet Union, Nazi Germany, and Fascism.

The late Ambassador Adam Watson (1914–2007), former British Assistant Under-Secretary of State, who taught at the University of Virginia, inspired my thinking on international relations and international society.

My brother, Dr James Bartholomay Kiracofe, gave discerning critique and steady encouragement.

My cousin, Dr Jean Dunbar, generously gave me an essential hand through her judicious copy edit of the manuscript.

During our travels together to North Africa and the Gulf, my friend Dr Edmund Ghareeb has deepened my understanding of the Arab world.

Jeffrey Steinberg and Norton Mezvinsky offered encouragement and insights over not a few glasses of red wine in various favorite haunts in Washington, DC. My friend Marvine Howe, veteran *New York Times* foreign correspondent and bureau chief in Morocco and Turkey, was encouraging from the beginning of the project.

My late parents, Clifford Attick Kiracofe (1907–87) and Elizabeth Augusta James Kiracofe (1916–2001), emphasized civic engagement and religious toleration in our home. They inspired me to take my path of public service and education.

Abbreviations

ACCC	American Council of Christian Churches
ACPC	American Christian Palestine Committee
AFSI	Americans for a Safe Israel
AIPAC	American Israel Public Affairs Committee
AJC	American Jewish Committee
APC	American Palestine Council
ARP	*Anti-Revolutionaire Partij* (Anti-Revolutionary Party)
AZEC	American Zionist Emergency Council
CACC	Christian Anti-Communist Crusade
CCP	Christian Council on Palestine
CDM	Coalition for a Democratic Majority
CEF	Christian Economic Foundation
CFF	Christian Freedom Foundation
CLI	Committee for the Liberation of Iraq
CNP	Council for National Policy
CPD	Committee for the Present Danger
CSFC	Committee for the Survival of a Free Congress
CSP	Center for Security Policy
CUFI	Christians United for Israel
ECZA	Emergency Committee for Zionist Affairs
GOP	Grand Old Party (Republican Party)
HUAC	House Un-American Activities Committee
IASPS	Institute for Advanced Strategic and Political Studies
ICCC	International Council of Christian Churches
ICEJ	International Christian Embassy Jerusalem
IFCJ	International Fellowship for Christians and Jews

IFRI	Institute Français des Relations Internationales
JINSA	Jewish Institute for National Security Affairs
LJS	London Jews' Society
NAE	National Association of Evangelicals
NATO	North Atlantic Treaty Organization
NUCI	National Unity Coalition for Israel
PLO	Palestine Liberation Organization
PNAC	Project for a New American Century
PPF	Pro-Palestine Federation of America
UCI	Unity Coalition for Israel
UNSCOP	United Nations Special Committee on Palestine
USCN	United States Committee on NATO
WCC	World Council of Churches
WJC	World Jewish Congress
YFC	Youth for Christ
ZOA	Zionist Organization of America

Preface

Diplomatic historian René Albrecht-Carrié once said of the Middle East, 'The Eastern Question is a hardy perennial which, in changing shape, appears throughout the nineteenth and the twentieth centuries.'[1] The Eastern Question, a competition among major powers for influence in what is today the Middle East, appears in a particularly thorny form in the present century. Britain's Palestine policy in the nineteenth and twentieth centuries set the stage for a deadly new rephrasing of this old and recurring question.[2] This book examines the radical answer advocated by Christian Zionism, an ideology long used to mobilize political support for imperial foreign policy in the Holy Land. Born again, it now powers Washington's counterproductive imperial crusade in the Middle East.

This book resulted from a suggestion by Alex Wright, my patient editor at I.B.Tauris in London. The challenge was to produce a concise book accessible to the general reader but also useful in an academic setting and to make it even-handed. I have received no funding from any outside source.

As a student of international relations and political history, I have long observed the ways that Christian Zionist ideology has supported political Zionism and the modern state of Israel. It has affected the USA's foreign policy with respect to Russia, China (and Taiwan), Syria, Iraq, and Iran. Its 'End Times' eschatology – its obsession with a deeply pessimistic vision of an imminent Battle of Armageddon – began as a nineteenth-century doctrine quite outside traditional Protestant, Roman Catholic, and Orthodox faiths. It is not found in the kindred ancient Christian faiths of the Middle East such as the Coptic Orthodox Church, the Syriac Orthodox Church, or the Armenian Catholicosate of Cilicia.[3] Yet, though Christian Zionism is, in fact, rejected by all these churches, its influence is – and has been – significant.

This book addresses Christian Zionism as an ideology motivating and shaping the viewpoint of the Christian Right, a growing political force in the USA, which seeks to influence legislation and foreign policy. The evangelical movement in the USA includes both socially concerned liberal evangelicals and conservatives; Woodberry and Smith note that defining 'conservative Protestantism is difficult because conservative Protestants (CPs) belong to such a jumble of different denominations and movements and they do not agree on any one label or set of beliefs'.[4] They estimate that about one quarter of the US population embraces conservative Protestantism.[5] Paul Charles Merkley arrives at an estimate of the Christian Zionist population in the USA from a consideration of the reach of mass television evangelism. 'The whole constituency of Christian pro-Zionists is therefore many times larger than the membership lists of the Christian Zionist organizations,' he says, 'and should be numbered in the tens of millions.'[6]

The deep pessimism of Christian Zionists stands in stark contrast to mainline and evangelical Protestants in the USA who have traditionally embraced amillennial, preterist, or postmillennial eschatologies marked by optimistic outlooks on life. Amillennialism sees the kingdom of God present in this world, which Christ rules through his Church and his Spirit. Under this view, at the Second Coming there will be no literal kingdom, or physical kingdom, on earth. Biblical prophecy such as found in Revelation is interpreted in a metaphorical, not literal, way.[7] Preterism sees prophetic events as being concluded by the destruction of Jerusalem in AD 70 or by the fall of the Roman empire in the fifth century.[8] Postmillennialism sees a long period of peace and prosperity on earth that comes before the Second Coming of Christ.[9] In this view, biblical prophecy such as found in Revelation is interpreted in a symbolic, not literal, way.

Such traditional optimism, together with a belief in human progress, lies at the core of the American psyche. Optimistic religious belief sustained Americans during the colonial era, supported the American Revolution and War of Independence, and saw the country through the Industrial Revolution, the Progressive Era and two World Wars.[10] Over the past three decades, however, the deeply pessimistic Christian Zionist outlook, based on a new and idiosyncratic interpretation of 'biblical prophecy' and promoted by a rapidly growing conservative evangelical subculture, has swept part of the nation into a belief in an apocalyptic End Times scenario.

Scholarly investigation and polling data suggest that the conservative evangelical community in the USA contains perhaps 30 to 45 million adherents, representing between 10 and 15 per cent of the population. These numbers, like this book, include members of Fundamentalist, Pentecostal, and Charismatic sects under the conservative evangelical umbrella. For simplicity's sake, I also use the term fundamentalist generically, to describe the conservative evangelical community.

Many scholars have concluded that Christian Zionism is the predominant eschatology within the conservative evangelical community in the USA. This book focuses on the dominant ideological current within Christian Zionism, which is known as dispensationalism. Dispensationalism, or dispensational premillennialism, is an eschatological belief system and ideology, based upon distinctive interpretations of biblical prophecy. This ideology arose in the UK in the early nineteenth century and migrated to the USA in the mid-nineteenth century.

Dispensationalism holds that human history is divided into seven periods and that 'signs of the times' today indicate that mankind has entered the final period, the Last Days, or End Times. The dispensationalist world view interprets current events and the world situation in light of biblical prophecy. Contemporary Christian Zionists believe that the End Times are marked by the birth of the modern state of Israel in 1948.[11] This book focuses narrowly on dispensationalism because doctrinally it specifically requires the physical and political restoration of the entire Holy Land, geographic Palestine, to the Jewish people as an exclusive possession, in order to advance the eschatological scenario just outlined. Those holding dispensationalist beliefs form a militant doctrinal theopolitical pro-Israel faction within American Protestantism.

Denominations in mainline American Protestantism, as well as the Roman Catholic Church and Orthodox denominations, take a strikingly different position. They generally deplore the Israeli–Palestinian conflict and support a just peaceful settlement acceptable to all sides, without presuming that peace must be scripted in a particular way. Such Christians commonly support a so-called two-state solution consisting of a sovereign Palestinian state side by side with Israel, but would also welcome a bi-national state in which Jews, Arab Christians, and Arab Muslims could all live together under one roof, in a single state.[12] Dispensationalist doctrine rejects solutions like these, making it an obstacle to peace in the region and a challenge to US foreign and national security policy.

In the USA, mainline Protestant denominations such as the United Methodist, Presbyterian Church (USA), Evangelical Lutheran, Episcopal, Disciples of Christ, United Church of Christ, and American Baptist have been losing members since the 1960s, while conservative Baptist and independent and separatist churches have been rapidly gaining members. Data from 1995 to 2004 indicate the persistence of the trend. For example, *USA Today* reported in 2006 that

> total membership in the seven largest mainline Protestant denominations – United Methodist, Evangelical Lutheran, Episcopal, Presbyterian Church (USA), Disciples of Christ, United Church of Christ and American Baptist Churches – fell a total of 7.4 per cent from 1995 to 2004, based on tallies reported to the *Yearbook of American and Canadian Churches.*

However, this statistic does not reflect a drop in church membership generally:

> The total membership count for Roman Catholics, the ultra-conservative Southern Baptist Convention, Pentecostal Assemblies of God and proselytizing Church of Jesus Christ of Latter-day Saints (Mormons) reported to the *Yearbook* is up nearly 11.4 per cent for the same period.[13]

The United States Religious Landscape Survey of 2008, by the Pew Forum on Religion and Public Life, presents current church membership as: evangelical Protestant churches, 26.3 per cent; Roman Catholic churches, 23.9 per cent; mainline Protestant churches, 18.1 per cent; historically black churches, 6.9 per cent; and unaffiliated, 16.1 per cent.[14]

The views of extreme Zionists pose a threat to a peaceful solution in the Middle East, as does extremism on all sides – whether Jewish, Christian, or Muslim. Such extremism is an obstacle to a just and comprehensive solution to the Arab–Israeli conflict generally and the Palestine Question in particular. George Antonius once noted the difficulty posed for students of Palestine: 'The passions aroused by Palestine,' he said, 'have done so much to obscure the truth that the facts have become enveloped in a mist of sentiment, legend and propaganda, which acts as a smoke-screen of almost impenetrable density.'[15]

The Eastern Question in its contemporary form presents many dangers to regional and world peace, at the very time when the Christian Right with its Christian Zionist ideology has become a growing and influential force in US politics. I hope this book will cast, in historical context, some useful light on contemporary American politics and will strengthen those forces at home and abroad committed to peace and justice in the twenty-first century.

Clifford A. Kiracofe, Jr
Washington, DC

Introduction

Contemporary politics in the USA preclude peace and regional stability in the Middle East because the Israel lobby (all those supportive of the geopolitical and religious claims of the nation state of Israel) plays a key role in Washington's imperial foreign policy.[1] While the Israel lobby draws its strength from the American Jewish community, another powerful pro-Israel element in American politics sways US policy: Christian Zionism. In the twentieth century, this movement radically transformed America's traditional policy of constructive commercial and cultural engagement in the Middle East. Today, many in the Arab and Muslim world believe that the USA, influenced by Christian Zionism and encouraged by Israel, has launched a dark crusade to dominate the region and its hydrocarbon resources.

Christian Zionism and the Israel Lobby

This book examines Christian Zionism as an ideological component of the overall Israel lobby. In American political terms, this lobby demonstrates how a highly successful interest group, albeit one comprising different factions, operates within the pluralist American democratic system. In this book the terms Zionism and Zionist follow the definitions sketched by American political scientist Earl Huff, who stated that Zionism is 'a complex of beliefs aimed at the promotion of a Jewish nation-state in accordance with the Basle Program of 1897. A Zionist can be defined simply as anyone who regularly, consciously, and actively promotes the aims of Zionism.'[2]

The Basle Program referred to in this generally held definition was adopted by the international Zionist conference held in Basle, Switzerland, in

August 1897. The conference also created the World Zionist Organization, a transnational political lobby, and its political program.³ As Mearsheimer and Walt define it in their recent book, *The Israel Lobby and US Foreign Policy* (2007), the phrase 'the Israel lobby' has become a 'convenient shorthand term for the loose coalition of individuals and organizations that actively work to shape US foreign policy in a pro-Israel direction'.⁴ Huff recognizes the diverse nature of American Zionism, saying, 'there are many organized interest groups within the United States which have actively promoted the aims of Zionism either openly or covertly'.⁵ For the analytical purposes of his paper, however, he treated American Zionism as a monolithic entity.

Huff is persuasive in his argument pertaining to the issue of interest group cohesion as a significant defining factor of monolithic unity. He argues that while at times the diverse Zionist organizations appeared fragmented structurally, nonetheless, 'as a result of an influential, well-placed leadership and the reinforcing influences which were prevalent within the Jewish community, Zionists were, in fact, a highly cohesive group'.⁶ The same may be said of Christian Zionists, who united in their advocacy of Israel and support for the Israel lobby as a whole. This book, accordingly, will treat Christian Zionism as part of the Israel lobby, which is considered a monolithic entity.

Christian Zionism, given its millions of devotees and its political influence, poses a structural political challenge to the American constitutional order, as well as to a just and peaceful international order. It is bi-partisan: both major political parties in the USA have been penetrated by, and are subject to, the political influence of the well-organized and well-financed Christian Zionist lobby. Since the days of the American Civil War, Christian Zionism has been embedded in various denominations in both the North and the South. Christian Zionists supported the Carter administration and, during the Reagan years, fundamentalist Protestant organizations such as the late Jerry Falwell's Moral Majority and Pat Robertson's Christian Coalition penetrated the Republican Party. Both televangelists' organizations, though based in Virginia, notably found their core support in the southern Bible Belt.

Kevin Phillips, a leading conservative Republican Party strategist, warns that Christian Zionism's blend of ideology and theocracy constitutes 'a gathering threat to America's future'.⁷ He warns against the Christian Right dominating the Republican Party (the 'Grand Old Party', or GOP), and, as a 'Lincoln Republican' and a son of the prairie born in the Chicago area, I share his concerns. Phillips estimates that it is 'Christian evangelicals, fundamentalists, and Pentecostals, who muster some 40 per cent of the party electorate'. Moreover, he warns that:

> strong theocratic pressures are already visible in the Republican national coalition and its leadership, while the substantial portion of Christian America committed to theories of Armageddon and the inerrancy of the Bible has already made the GOP into America's first religious party.[8]

Phillips is not the only leading Republican to voice this criticism. Former US Senator John Danforth, a prominent Republican from Missouri and an ordained Episcopal minister, penned a widely read column for the *New York Times* in which he said, 'Republicans have transformed our party into the political arm of Conservative Christians.'[9]

Leading voices in the Democratic Party also warn against the dangerous influence of religious fundamentalism and extremism in American politics. Former President Jimmy Carter forthrightly addresses this issue in his recent book *Our Endangered Values* (2005):

> Beginning about 25 years ago, some Christian leaders began to form a union with the more conservative wing of the Republican Party. Such a political marriage is in conflict with my own belief in the separation of church and state – I would feel the same even if the marriage were with the Democrats.[10]

President Carter's warning on Christian Zionist foreign policy is stark, powerful, and accurate. 'Their agenda calls for a war in the Middle East against Islam (Iraq?),' he says, 'and the taking of the entire Holy Land by Jews (occupation of the West Bank), with the total expulsion of all Christians and other gentiles.' He is emphatic on the influence of Christian Zionism on significant aspects of US foreign policy: 'Some top Christian leaders have been in the forefront of promoting the Iraq war, and make frequent trips to Israel, to support it with funding, and lobby in Washington for the colonization of Palestinian territory.'[11]

The USA first developed diplomatic and commercial relations in North Africa and the Middle East over two centuries ago and these relations have continued, unbroken, since that time. American specialists have long known what Professor Ephraim A. Speiser, a Middle East expert teaching at the University of Pennsylvania, put so plainly in his 1947 book *The United States and the Near East*:

> The political divisions which prevail in the Near East today should not blind us to the underlying cultural and psychological unity of the region as a whole ... The far-reaching interdependence of the local states and territories imposes on the interested foreign power the obligation to approach the entire region as a unit ... any foreign policy in the Near East which is not a comprehensive regional policy is an invitation to bankruptcy.[12]

Rami Khouri, editor-at-large of the *Beirut Daily Star*, recently explained the rise of anti-Americanism throughout the Middle East:

> Many people in the Middle East see themselves still engaged in a battle against Anglo-American–Israeli domination and colonial subjugation. The Anglo-American–Israeli push for war in Iraq and their continued pressure on Iran, Syria, Hamas and Hizbullah have sparked a whole new level of collective political resistance throughout the Middle East. In part this parallels global criticism of the USA, but it is also a distinct Middle Eastern historical process of mass self-expression and self-determination in the face of local and foreign powers that have never allowed such processes to occur.[13]

This book critically examines the phenomenon of Christian Zionism, and its influence, in historical context. Chapter 1, 'The Eastern Question and Imperialism', examines in historical context the imperial policies in the Middle East of the French under Napoleon and the British under Palmerston. The role of religion in foreign policy with respect to the 'restoration' of Jews to the Holy Land is assessed within this framework.

Chapter 2, 'The Early American Republic and the Muslim World', examines the eighteenth- and nineteenth-century constructive engagement of the USA in the Middle East from initial commercial relations with Morocco through to the establishment of educational institutions in Beirut, Istanbul, and Cairo.

Chapter 3, 'Christian Zionism: Construction of an Ideology', explains the construction of the Christian Zionist ideology in England during the early nineteenth century. The ideology of premillennial dispensationalism is considered, with particular reference to the lives and influence of John Nelson Darby and Edward Irving. The reader will be shown how this ideology was a departure from traditional Christian doctrine as expressed in the major traditions of the faith.

Chapter 4, 'Christian Zionism on American Shores', examines the transfer of the Christian Zionist dispensationalist sect to the USA via the missions of John Nelson Darby to North America that began in 1859. This chapter also explains the institutionalization of dispensationalist ideology in the

USA during the late nineteenth century through a ministerial network of Darbyites.

Chapter 5, 'Fundamentalism, the First World War, and Palestine', explains the rise of dispensationalist ideology, particularly its promotion via the Scofield Bible and its impact on US foreign policy with respect to the Palestine Question. An overview of American 'fundamentalism' is also presented.

Chapter 6, 'Christian Zionism from the First World War to the Second World War', explains the rising influence of dispensationalist ideology and its promotion via ministerial networks, seminaries, and organizations in the USA.

Chapter 7, 'Zionism from the Second World War to 1948', explains the effects of the activities of international political Zionism on US policy toward Palestine. The chapter considers the activity of Christian Zionists in lobbying for US recognition of the state of Israel and its significance within the sect's belief system.

Chapter 8, 'The Christian Right in the Fifties and Sixties', examines the early Cold War Christian Right. The relationship between the Christian Right and the radical political Right is examined, as is the establishment of conservative evangelical operations in Washington, DC.

Chapter 9, 'The Christian Right in the Seventies and Eighties', traces the development of the fundamentalist Christian Zionist subculture in the USA during the period and how the 1967 Six Day War confirmed for fundamentalists the eschatological 'End Times' belief system.

Chapter 10, 'George W. Bush and the Dark Crusade', examines the accelerating penetration of national politics by the Christian Right. This chapter discusses how the alliance between the Christian Right and George Herbert Walker Bush during his 1988 presidential campaign laid the foundation for Christian Zionist support of George W. Bush in the elections of 2000 and 2004.

Chapter 11, 'Christian Zionism and the Next War', considers the activities of Christian Zionist leader John Hagee on behalf of Israel and in support of continued war in the Middle East, with Iran as the next necessary target, and the associated implications.

This analysis of Christian Zionism, as a powerful factor within the overall Israel lobby in the USA, takes into consideration its historical and current impact on US foreign policy. I hope this book can contribute to peace in the Middle East by casting light on a heretofore obscure doctrine and subculture operative in the US body politic for over a century and a half.

Part I

Christian Zionism and
Nineteenth-Century Imperialism

1

The Eastern Question and Imperialism

Any examination of current US Middle East policy should consider it in the context of two key nineteenth-century imperial projects undertaken to exploit 'The Eastern Question', the vexing question of what to do with the rambling Ottoman Empire.[1] Whether French or British, the main protagonists played the religion card to mobilize support and to justify their intervention. France and Britain made official 'biblically based' appeals to both Jews and Christians, asking them to rally behind policies that promised to restore the Jews to Palestine and Palestine to the Jews. The French effort of 1798 under Napoleon was followed three decades later by an all-too-similar British project under Henry John Temple, the third Viscount Palmerston, the formidable British Foreign Secretary. The notion of Christian Zionism thus began in the modern period as an instrument of imperial policy.

European imperialism of the eighteenth and nineteenth centuries profoundly affected the vast region from North Africa across the Middle East to India. After the Second World War, the American foreign policy establishment felt obliged to assume the mantel of the British Empire. Consequently, the Palestine Question fell to Washington, as did the legacy of British efforts to restore Jews to the Holy Land. In fact, some influential American circles had supported such efforts since the late nineteenth century.[2]

In the Middle East, reminders of history are ever present and affect the daily thoughts and actions of millions from all walks of life. Thus, to this day, both the negative and the positive consequences of this European expansion permeate these lands and peoples. It is not surprising, then, that those now living in the region generally abhor current American imperial expansion into the Mesopotamian Basin.[3] Past historical experience with foreign imperial powers remains vivid in the collective memory.

Palestine and Emperor Julian the Apostate

Through the centuries, the Middle East has served as a strategic crossroad. Periods of invasion and settlement with the concomitant intermingling of race and culture mark the area no less today than in ancient times. Commercial opportunity prompted early development, by land and by sea, of long-distance trade routes from ancient Egypt through the Middle East to the Indian subcontinent, to Central Asia, and to China. Geography conditions military strategy, but also, more significantly, geography conditions both long-distance trade and human interaction across a wide spectrum of activity, including religion and the spread of technical and scientific knowledge.

Western imperial projects designed to restore the Holy Land to the Jews began with the Roman Emperor Julian the Apostate, but reappeared in the modern era as French and British imperial policies of the eighteenth and nineteenth centuries, as promulgated by Napoleon and Palmerston. Although what inspired Napoleon to attempt the restoration of Palestine to the Jews remains unclear, during the same period the assiduous British historian Edward Gibbon (1737–94) retold the story of Emperor Julian the Apostate in his monumental six-volume compilation, *The History of the Decline and Fall of the Roman Empire*.[4] Would French intellectual circles have failed to notice this?

The Roman emperor Julian the Apostate (emperor 361–3 CE) devised a project to strengthen and consolidate Jews in the Holy Land and to rebuild their temple at Jerusalem. In line with this policy, as a committed pagan and initiate of various Eastern mystery cults, he undertook the systematic persecution of Christians. Gibbon says in volume two of his epic that Julian's policy was 'the restoration and encouragement of Paganism' while 'he embraced the extraordinary design of rebuilding the temple of Jerusalem.'[5] Julian commissioned Alypius of Antioch, who served as the imperial deputy in charge of the four Roman provinces in Britain from 355 to 360 CE, to carry out the rebuilding of the temple. Gibbon tells us: 'The restoration of the Jewish temple was secretly connected with the ruin of the Christian church.'[6]

Gibbon explains the emperor's propaganda campaign in support of his doomed plan:

> In a public epistle to the nation or community of the Jews, dispersed throughout the province, he pities their misfortunes, condemns their oppressors, praises their constancy, declares himself their gracious protector, and expresses a pious hope, that after his return from the Persian war, he may be permitted to pay his grateful vows to the Almighty in his holy city of Jerusalem.[7]

The project was not realized because Julian died six months after its inception, and the new emperor restored Christianity. Gibbon adds 'An earthquake, a whirlwind, and a fiery eruption, which overturned, and scattered the new foundations of the temple, are attested, with some variations, by contemporary and respectable evidence.'[8]

Though the attempt to rebuild the temple failed, it lingered in the minds of men for centuries, engendering similar plans, superstitions, and myths along the way. Today, Emperor Julian's project to rebuild the temple in Jerusalem is a central theme for Christian Zionists, who see the rebuilding of the temple as required by their apocalyptic End Times scenario. Their politically explosive plan for rebuilding would require the demolition of the present Dome of the Rock, the third holiest site in Islam. Issues concerning the Holy Places have triggered wars in the past, such as the Crimean War, and thus are closely linked to the Eastern Question.

The Eastern Question

The slow decline of the rambling Ottoman Empire during the eighteenth century gave rise to the 'Eastern Question': the question of who would snatch the various lands under the control of the Ottoman ruler, the Sultan, as his grip over them weakened. The answer depended upon the alignment and alliances of the European powers seeking to expand into Ottoman territories. In the nineteenth century, the Eastern Question provoked two more: the Syrian Question and the Jewish Question. Who would control Syria, the area that would today comprise roughly Syria, Lebanon, and Israel/Palestine? The ruler of Egypt contested the Ottoman Sultan's control of this area during the first half of the nineteenth century but without success. The Jewish Question arose in the context of this issue owing to the creation of settler colonies of Jews transported from Europe to Palestine.

Any European power could see the weakness of the Ottoman Empire. When and how to dismember it – how to divide the spoils – would depend upon the outcome of rivalries among the European powers. The 1781 treaty of alliance between Russia and Austria looked toward a partition of the Sultan's possessions.[9] In the nineteenth century, however, Britain would defend the integrity of the Ottoman Empire against challenges from Russia, France, and Egypt.

In the twentieth century, after the First World War, Britain and France finally carved the Ottoman Empire into a number of Arab states. The League of Nations obligingly allowed the creation of a 'mandate' system, which placed some of these states under European tutelage and control as semi-colonies. Thus through its mandate for Syria, the French obtained influence over Syria, and later Lebanon when it split off from Syria. The British controlled the Palestine mandate and also had influence over Iraq and Transjordan. The modern states of Saudi Arabia, Syria, Lebanon, Iraq, Jordan, and Israel emerged from this carving up of the Ottoman lands.

The strategic location of the Middle East with its land, sea, and air communication links, together with its newly discovered vast hydrocarbon wealth, ensured that the Eastern Question would continue to grow.[10] The Second World War and the Cold War posed new versions of the Question, and today the war in Iraq, the crisis in Lebanon, the tensions with Iran and Syria, and the unresolved Arab–Israeli conflict represent the latest attempts to rephrase it. Today, just as in the past, major world powers have important interests in the region, including the USA, Britain, France, Germany, Russia, China, and Japan.

Russia and the Eastern Question

Russia has long been a primary actor in the Middle East, owing to traditional Russo-Turkish rivalry and Russia's desire to move into the Black Sea region for commercial and strategic reasons.[11] The Russo-Turkish Wars, therefore, mark the systematic eastward expansion of Russia and the consequent weakening of the Ottoman Empire. Russia's expansionist policy sought to gain control of the Black Sea region, notably the Crimea, to conquer the Caucasus, and to dominate the Balkans so as to gain control of the Dardanelles (which connect the Aegean Sea in the Eastern Mediterranean to the Sea of Marmara) and the Bosporus strait (which connects the Sea of Marmara to the Black Sea). British policy was to resist Russian and French designs on the region, by resisting the partition of the Ottoman Empire.

The Great Northern War (1700–21) set into motion Russia's drive toward the Black Sea.[12] During the reign of Peter the Great, Russia was significantly Europeanized and became part of the European *grande république*, the system of European states. At the beginning of the seventeenth century, two European systems were in play, one in what was then considered the west of Europe, and one in the north of Europe – the major actors in the northern states were Sweden and Poland–Lithuania, a dynastic union. During the Thirty Years' War, France aligned with Sweden and Poland in order to outflank the Hapsburgs, thereby merging the operations of the northern and western systems.

The Great Northern War saw a coalition of Russia, Denmark–Norway, Saxony, and Poland–Lithuania aligned against a combination of Sweden and the Ottoman Empire. The coalition defeated the Swedish Empire and concluded the Treaty of Nystad and the Stockholm treaties in 1721. As a result of this war, Peter the Great's Russia became the dominant factor in the Baltic and a major player on the European scene. But encouraged by France, the Ottomans under Sultan Ahmed III entered the war in 1710 and regained Azov in the Crimea through a crushing military victory over Russia, marked by the Peace of Pruth in 1711.

Russia then reconsidered and revised its overall strategy, not losing its interest in eastern expansion.[13] In order to strengthen its military power and reach, Russia had to strengthen its economy by obtaining new trade outlets via access to the Black Sea. To achieve this, it needed an alliance with Austria. Under such an alliance, Azov was regained by the Russo-Turkish War of 1736–9. But then Austria became alarmed over Russian designs in the Balkans owing to the Russian success in Moldavia.

Russia pressed on with its eastern drive in the Russo-Turkish War of 1768–74, provoked by Sultan Mustafa III who, encouraged by France, declared war on Catherine II of Russia. Russia gained the Crimea and swept through Moldavia and Wallachia, parts of today's Romania. The Treaty of Kuchuk Kainarji (1774) ended the war and contained several crucial clauses: the Crimea was made independent of the Sultan; Russia gained large territorial concessions; Russia took on the role of protector of Greek Orthodox subjects of the Sultan; and Russian shipping could navigate the Black Sea and pass through the Straits.

Thus the interests and rivalries of Russia, Austria, Turkey and France impacted greatly on the Eastern Question during this phase. However a separate, though parallel, rivalry was also set into motion at this time: the rivalry between Britain and France.

Britain and France and the Eastern Question

Given its strategic location, the Middle East inevitably became one of the fields of competition between Britain and France and the scene of a series of Russo-Turkish wars. In order to better understand how the present situation in the Middle East resulted from past Great Power machinations, we should consider relevant military and diplomatic events in the region, beginning with Napoleon. When Napoleon Bonaparte emerged from the turmoil of the French Revolution contemplating a broad imperial design, a new cycle of European imperial rivalry began. His ill-fated Egyptian campaign inaugurated a grandiose imperial scheme that would shatter Europe and overturn the European states system that had prevailed since 1648 and the Peace of Westphalia.[14]

Rivalry between France and Britain dated from the medieval period, when the Hundred Years' War, a series of dynastic wars between 1337 and 1453, resulted in the British being expelled from the Continent. The Peace of Westphalia in 1648, which ended the Thirty Years' War, created a new Europe-wide states system, but challenges to the European balance of power quickly arose. The main challenge to European stability was the hegemonic drive of Louis XIV in the latter part of the seventeenth century for domination over Europe. In due course, this necessarily sparked continued Franco-British rivalry.

From the late seventeenth century into the nineteenth century, the European states system consisted of five great powers: France, Austria, Russia, Prussia, and Britain.[15] The Ottoman Empire, while not an integral part of the European states system, interacted with it in significant ways. The great powers eyed each other warily and entered into defensive and offensive combinations, when doing so seemed to suit their interests and desire for self-preservation. Foreign possessions and profitable long-distance trade, by land and by sea, were much sought after.

These global commercial and colonial interests impacted directly on the European balance of power and calculations of war and peace. Maritime interests, and naval capability, loomed ever larger in the minds of European statesmen. France, under the great Renaissance statesman Francis I (1494–1547), formed a bold alliance with the Ottoman ruler Suleiman the Magnificent (1494–1566) in 1536 against their mutual rival the Habsburg Empire – the strategic concept being that the Austrian Hapsburgs would be flanked on two sides by great powers. This expedient understanding between a Christian power and a Muslim power is notable with regard to present-day tensions between western and Muslim countries. The understanding brought mutual military and diplomatic benefit at the time, just as did the inclusion of Turkey in the North Atlantic Treaty Organization (NATO) alliance during the Cold War.

Napoleon's war to conquer Ottoman-held Egypt and Palestine in 1799 took place as Ottoman power was in decline, and European powers jostled for advantage.[16] The Egyptian Campaign (1798–1801) was rooted in the strategic considerations, calculations, and emotions bound up in centuries-old Franco-British rivalry. The strategic design, however, was not at all original to Napoleon. It had, in fact, emerged on the heels of the Seven Years' War (1756–63) in the mind of the brilliant French diplomat Etienne François, Duc de Choiseul (1719–85). It was a natural strategy for a revanchist France just stripped of valuable colonial possessions in the New World and in India. Such a move on the chessboard would deny the British Empire its land routes to its colonial possessions in India, while, at the same time, challenging the Austrian empire on its Eastern flank.

The USA and the Eastern Question

Though geographically remote from Europe, North America was inextricably linked to European rivalry in the Eastern Question and general imperial competition. Events in North America, in the Ohio Valley, sparked the Seven Years' War, which pitted the British Empire against the French Empire in a global conflict. Known as the 'French and Indian War' in colonial British North America, this world war had immense and long-term strategic consequences for Europe, North America, and the Indian subcontinent.

Britain's victory over France also had significant near-term consequences. France was humiliated; and it lost valuable possessions in North America, principally Canada, and in the subcontinent. Paris plotted revenge and its duel with the British extended over many centuries. Britain, having removed the French threat to its North American colonies, could now tighten the economic screws on the colonials and their commerce and industry. At the same time, removal of the French threat from Canada and the Ohio Valley emboldened the North American colonies to resist Britain's tightening grip.

The interests of France and the North American colonies aligned against Britain, eventually producing the formal Franco-American alliance that proved so beneficial to Americans during the War of Independence. For the wary French, however, such an alliance required that the American rhetorical Declaration of Independence be upheld by at least some military successes. According to French and continental calculations, the Battle of Saratoga in 1777 indicated a decisive turn of events in favor of the USA, making alliance feasible, if not prudent.

The historic rivalry between Russia and the Ottoman Empire played a decisive role in French calculations. The Russo-Turkish War of 1768, in particular, caught the attention of Parisian statesmen, notably the redoubtable Choiseul, who was looking for a way to deal the British Empire a severe blow in due course. The Ottoman Porte controlled a vast, though creaky, empire and dominated Egypt and the Levant. Defeated by Russian arms in this war, it could no longer conceal its inherent weakness, making the control of strategically located Egypt, and the Levant, an open question. For Choiseul a successful French move, in due course, against Egypt in the eastern Mediterranean would cut the British imperial link to India and make the Mediterranean a French preserve. In Choiseul's calculations, Britain's escalating problems with its North American colonies after 1763 enabled the French to contemplate detaching Egypt from a troubled British imperial system – thereby breaking its key maritime and land link through the eastern Mediterranean to India.

Napoleon, the Jews, and Palestine

Napoleon's intentions for Jews in the Levant have been a subject of discussion and debate among scholars for over a century.[17] Debate continues over the extent of Napoleon's commitment to the restoration of Palestine to the Jews, but his complex program for the organization and 'regeneration' of Jews in France itself is well known and had implications for Jewish emancipation and acquisition of full civil liberties in Europe generally. Tradition has long held that Napoleon intended a restoration of Jews in the Holy Land which, as he was not able to arrange it, became a forerunner of nineteenth-century political Zionism and later the Balfour Declaration.[18]

Napoleon sought as much local support as possible during his campaign in the Holy Land.[19] 'Napoleon was eager for help from any source,' historian Nathan Schur argues, noting he attempted to obtain support from Druze, Maronite Christians and even Muslim elements. Schur believes it is possible that Napoleon made specific promises, although definitive historical evidence has yet to be found to support the case. 'His most lavish promises he might have given to the Jews,' Schur says. 'Those living in the land of their fathers were not very numerous and mostly did not occupy prominent positions.'[20]

Palestine at that time was under the authority of the Ottoman Empire.[21] Its formidable local ruler, Ahmed Djezzar (d. 1804), served the Ottomans as governor of the province of Saida and had his seat at Acre. Schur believes that Napoleon intended to rally the Jewish population of the region: 'It seems impossible that Napoleon's tremendous propaganda effort simply overlooked the Jewish population of Palestine and Syria, and more than it overlooked the Matuwellis or the Christians of Lower Galilee.'[22]

Scholars have sparse evidence from which to build a case suggesting Napoleon as the forerunner of political Zionism. Indeed, such arguments generally have relied on but two brief articles in an official Parisian newspaper of the period, *Moniteur*, one published on 22 May 1799 and one published a few weeks later on 27 July. The 22 May notice, appearing as a message from Constantinople of 17 April, states:

> Bonaparte has had a proclamation published in which he invites all the Jews of Asia and Africa to come and place themselves under his banners to re-establish ancient Jerusalem. He has already armed a great number, and their battalions menace Aleppo.[23]

The 27 July notice states:

> It is not only to render to the Jews their Jerusalem that Bonaparte has conquered Syria; he has the most vast designs ... to march on Constantinople in order to throw Vienna and Petersburg into confusion from there.[24]

Schur points out a third piece of evidence, which some have branded a forgery. It is a German-language version of an alleged declaration from Napoleon's headquarters in Jerusalem dated 20 April 1799. It states that France calls on 'the great nation' of Jews 'to receive what has been conquered already, in order that you will remain there as rulers, and will defend it against all foreigners'.[25] Schur believes that the document might be genuine but that 'the actual effect of the French campaign on the Jewish population was the very opposite of what one would have been led to believe from the contents of this declaration'.[26] As it happened, the French invasion provoked massacres of local Christian populations by Muslims, looting of Jewish communities, the execution of some Jews, and outbreaks of mob violence against Jews and Christians in districts of Galilee:

> And thus there is a vast difference in what was reported in the West about Napoleon's grandiose plans for the restoration of the Jewish nation and the actual situation of the Jewish communities during his campaign and after. What to the French was another glorious campaign of Napoleon's army, was to the Jews of the Holy Land another tribulation in the long chain of their persecutions, harassments and oppressions.[27]

Historian Simon Schwarzfuchs is persuaded that the third document is a forgery:

> One fact remains, nowhere does Napoleon appear as hostile to the Jews. He is accused of, and thanked for, having brought them freedom, and supported their national aspirations. This reputation followed him to Italy, after his return from Egypt.[28]

Schwarzfuchs notes, 'in 1800, after the battle of Marengo, he was still looked upon as the saviour, and all the Jews rejoiced when they heard about his victories in the Italian war'.[29]

It is fair, therefore, to presume that Napoleon did indeed hope for local Jewish support in his campaign in the Holy Land and that he may well have made appeals to the effect that he wished to restore Palestine to Jewish control after wresting it from the Ottomans. On the other hand, local Jewish populations probably prudently supported the Ottomans, recognizing the quixotic nature of Napoleon's grandiose plans for the Holy Land. His supporting naval fleet had already been destroyed by Nelson in the Battle of the Nile in August 1798. Then Ahmed Djezzar crushed French forces at the Battle of Acre. His siege ended on 20 May 1799 and Napoleon left Egypt in August of that year.

Palmerston and British Imperial Policy

Napoleon's lunge into the Eastern Mediterranean, and his policy toward Jews in Egypt and the Levant, could hardly be overlooked by Britain, given the high stakes being played for in the Mediterranean Basin.[30] A British response was inevitable, and it was orchestrated by the redoubtable Henry John Temple, the third Viscount Palmerston (1784–1865).[31]

The Ottoman Empire's holdings at that time included Turkey, all of today's Arab states from Iraq to Libya, present-day Tunisia and Algeria in North Africa, and the European Balkans. The Ottomans remained essentially outside the maelstrom of the Napoleonic War era in Europe that ended in 1815; and, in deference to Russia – which, like Austria and France, had substantial interests in the Middle East – the Congress of Vienna did not consider the Ottoman question. Although Britain's commercial relations in the region dated to the sixteenth century, it had assumed a secondary position with respect to the other three powers. Napoleon's campaign in the Holy Land, however, heightened London's strategic interest, as a naval power, in the Eastern Mediterranean. Significantly, Britain retained its bases in Malta and the Ionian Islands after 1815.

Rising nationalism in the European Balkans, which reflected Christian grievances, gave rise to a struggle for independence from the Porte that had strategic consequences. Greek subjects of the Ottomans, encouraged by wide European sympathy for their cause, revolted and declared their independence in 1822. The Ottoman Porte, in its turn, was backed up by its Egyptian titular vassal, Muhammad Ali.[32] The competing interests of Russia, Austria, France, and Britain in the situation led to various diplomatic initiatives, as well as to military conflict. Finally, agreement for an independent Greece was reached by the London Protocol of 1830 and it was formally created in 1832. By this time, Ottoman holdings were significantly reduced, to the advantage of Russia. Austria was more concerned about Central Europe, and France, than with North Africa.

The French seizure of Algeria, in 1829, sparked British concern over its own strategic position in the Mediterranean. British policy was to maintain control of the western entrance to the Mediterranean and the Sicilian Strait in the middle. Britain's possession of Gibraltar and Malta, therefore, was essential. French control of Algeria was deemed acceptable – so long as France did not also control neighboring Morocco and Tunisia.

In the Eastern Mediterranean, however, a significant problem arose: Egypt. Its pasha, Muhammad Ali, an Albanian by birth, was the titular vassal of the Ottoman Porte but had a mind and a will of his own. His ambition, reflected in expeditions to the Hejaz in 1815 and to Khartoum in 1822, was to extend his influence over the Arab world and even to supplant Sultan Mahmoud II. An Ottoman Empire consolidated and strengthened under the able Muhammad Ali's rule was not acceptable to Britain or to Russia.

Britain could not accept the creation of a unified Arab state comprising the Fertile Crescent and the Arabian Peninsula and extending from the Mediterranean to the Persian Gulf. Such a development would threaten Britain's lines of communication to India and nurture worrisome Russian designs on Persia and Central Asia. Furthermore, the Ottoman situation affected the balance of power in Europe. Russia's traditional desire for partition of the Ottoman Empire, therefore, was out of the question. Britain and Russia tacitly agreed, for a time, to the status quo with respect to the Ottoman Empire. France, on the other hand, saw opportunity and sought to exploit the situation by developing relations with Muhammad Ali and, thereby, greater influence in Egypt.

The Egyptian ruler then launched a war against the Sultan. This move had the unintended effect of strengthening Russo-Turkish relations. Given his superior military preparations, Muhammad Ali defeated the Ottomans at the battle of Konieh in 1832. Russian intervention on behalf of the Sultan, however, altered the situation. In February 1833, the Tsar dispatched a naval squadron to the Bosporus which, naturally, alarmed the British and the French, who responded by sending their own naval forces to the Eastern Mediterranean. The situation calmed when Russia and the Porte signed the Treaty of Unkiar Skelessi on 8 July 1833 – a defensive alliance in which Russia, the stronger partner, became 'protector' of the Ottoman Empire. Muhammad Ali strengthened his rule in Egypt and held sway over Syria and Crete. Britain was at odds with France, and as Austria had mended relations with Russia, Britain prudently bided its time. In due course, London played two decisive cards: one commercial and the other military.

Historians consider Palmerston's success in the crises of 1839 and 1840 as the greatest of his long career. Palmerston's biographer Jasper Ridley explains:

Britain wished to have a powerful Turkish Empire as a bulwark against Russian expansion into Asia and India. Instead, she now had half this Empire controlled by a rebel at Alexandria, and the other, and the central government, by the Russian Ambassador at Constantinople. Palmerston had no plan for remedying the situation, and for six years did nothing but wait for the situation to develop. In the end, the developments benefited him and Britain more than anyone else.[33]

Palmerston did not want a war with Russia, still less a war against an alliance of Russia and Austria. France posed a potential threat should it expand eastward along the North African coast after seizing Algeria in 1829. Ridley argues that

> Palmerston's chief object in wishing to preserve the Turkish Empire in 1840 was not to stop Russian expansion but because he feared that collapse of Turkey would lead to a scramble for the pieces which would trigger off a major European war.[34]

The regional situation again erupted into crisis in April 1839 when Sultan Mahmoud II, after strengthening his empire economically and militarily for several years, launched hostilities against his Egyptian rival for control of the region then called Syria, giving rise to what would become the Syria Question.[35] Britain's relationship with Constantinople had strengthened, thanks to able diplomacy that included a favorable commercial and political treaty between Britain and Turkey in 1838. With a foot well inside the door, in 1839 Britain concluded an arrangement with the Porte to reorganize the Turkish fleet. Palmerston did not encourage the Porte to initiate a war against Egypt but, nonetheless, the Sultan chose war. With French opinion solidly supporting Muhammad Ali's cause, the Egyptians soundly defeated the Turkish forces. For Britain, a French position in the Mediterranean limited to Algeria was acceptable. Dominant French influence in Egypt and Syria was not.

Palmerston insisted that the Sultan regain Syria, while the French took the opposite position, causing an Anglo-French crisis. As Foreign Secretary he outlined the situation to the Queen in a letter dated 11 November 1840:

> There is no doubt that a large party among the leading politicians in France long contemplated the establishment of a virtually, if not actually, independent State in Egypt and Syria, under the direction of France and that party

feel great disappointment and resentment at finding their schemes in this respect baffled. But that party will not revenge themselves on the four powers by making a revolution in France, and they are enlightened enough to see that France cannot revenge herself by making war against the Four Powers who are much stronger than she is.[36]

As the British Cabinet hesitated over Palmerston's bold policy, he offered his resignation to Melbourne on 5 July 1840. To preserve the government, Melbourne supported Palmerston's policy and the Cabinet fell into line – but not without some dissent. In his letter to Melbourne, Palmerston argued that if his advice were not taken the crisis would result in

> the practical division of the Turkish Empire into two separate and independent states, whereof one will be the dependent of France, and the other a satellite of Russia; and in both of which our political influence will be annulled, and our commercial interests sacrificed; and this dismemberment will inevitably give rise to local struggles and conflicts which will involve the Powers of Europe in more serious disputes.[37]

Palmerston's able statesmanship preserved the Ottoman Empire, strengthened the Sultan, blocked the extension of French influence into the Eastern Mediterranean, rolled back the Russians, and gained important advantage for Britain. By the Treaty of London of July 1840, the great powers, except France, agreed to use force to constrain Egypt to agree to terms. A combination of diplomacy and military action produced a resolution in which Muhammad Ali secured hereditary rule in his pashalik in Egypt and Syria, and the Sultan recovered Crete. With the situation thus calmed, the major powers signed the Convention of the Straits of 13 July 1841, in order to regulate the naval situation in the Eastern Mediterranean. Britain gained clear advantage at the expense of Russia, whose exclusive naval privileges in the Straits, under the Treaty of Unkiar Skelessi, were nullified. Security of the Straits now became a shared European undertaking.

Palmerston, Christian Zionism, and Palestine

Against this background, Palmerston's pioneering use of Christian Zionism as a tool of imperial policy stands out in high relief. As Barbara Tuchman explains succinctly in *Bible and Sword*:

> The origins of Britain's role in the restoration of Israel are to be found in two motives, religious and political. One was a debt of conscience owed to the people of the Bible, the other was the strategy of empire which required possession of their land.[38]

Palmerston himself was not a religious sentimentalist. He was, rather, a cold and calculating realist who saw the political utility of appealing to religion in support of his foreign policy. Tuchman, who regards Napoleon's pronouncements on the restoration of Palestine to Jews as authentic, sums up the perceived value of world Jewry to statesmen with imperial designs on the Middle East:

> After Napoleon, it became axiomatic that whenever the powers fell to fighting in the Middle East someone would propose the restoration of Israel, and equally axiomatic that someone would be indulging himself in a happy dream not only of acquiring thereby a sphere of influence over a vital strategic area, but also of drawing to his own side all the supposed wealth and influence of world Jewry.[39]

A consummate politician, Palmerston understood just how usefully religion could mobilize public opinion in support of policy and legislation. Palmerston's son-in-law, Anthony Ashley Cooper (1801–85), who became the seventh Earl of Shaftesbury, played a significant role in Palmerston's policy as an active and influential political figure and religious enthusiast. When rival European powers played the religious card in their penetration of the Levant, the question for Britain became how to compete effectively in this regard: what religious card could Britain play?

Over the centuries a number of Christian churches evolved in the Levant, with special ties to France and Russia. The French had ties, reaching back to the twelfth century, to the Maronite community in what is today Lebanon.[40] For its part, Russia was concerned with those churches linked to the Orthodox world. Britain's challenge, in the face of such French and Russian penetration in the Holy Land, was how to create inroads using religion as a tool and how to find other allies in the Holy Land.

Between 1839 and 1841, Palmerston, with the assistance of Cooper and his circle, solved the problem to his own satisfaction. The Foreign Secretary implemented a logical policy of cultivating the local Hebrew and Druze communities. Gaining public support for such a policy required mobilizing both elite and mass opinion via the press and various philanthropic organizations and activities. 'The question of the restoration of the Jews to Palestine had meanwhile become a matter of sufficient importance to occupy considerable space in the periodical press,' historian Albert Hyamson points out. '*The Times*, as the leading newspaper of the country, in particular devoted much attention to the subject.'[41] Alexander William Crawford Lindsay (1812–80), Lord Lindsay, a close friend and colleague of Lord Ashley, published a book entitled *Letters on Egypt, Edom, and the Holy Land* in 1838 supporting the idea of the restoration of the Jews to Palestine. The British intellectual journal *Quarterly Review* carried, in January 1839, a review favorable to Lindsay's book and ideas, and *The Times* quickly followed up with an article of endorsement that same month.

The Times pointedly placed the issue squarely within British global imperial interests. 'The subject may be new to many of our readers,' the newspaper said, 'but it is one deserving solemn considerations of a people possessing an oriental empire of such vast extent.'[42] Lord Lindsay, it explained, had turned a spotlight upon the claims the Jewish people still had upon the land of Israel as their rightful inheritance and their consequent role in the political struggle of the region. Ever the astute politician, Palmerston both addressed the developing crisis in the Levant and made sure his political flanks were adequately covered by marshalling public support through the press.

Palmerston wasted no time on the diplomatic front and established the first consulate of any power in Jerusalem. Historian Frederick Stanley Rodkey explains:

> At the opening of the period arrangements were being made to send an Englishman named Young as vice-consul to Jerusalem, and it was stated in his instructions that one of his duties would be to afford protection to the Hebrews of the Holy Land. Also, he was instructed to report to Palmerston at an early date on the state of the Jewish population within the territory of his consular jurisdiction.[43]

Young reported that the Jews of Palestine numbered 9,690.

Palmerston was quick to demonstrate, in highly visible ways, Britain's intention to act as the protector of the region's Jews – the same ploy used by Cyrus the Great in ancient times. In May 1840, Palmerston issued a formal diplomatic protest 'to the Porte and to Muhammad Ali against the persecution of Jews at Damascus and on the island of Rhodes". The religious establishment mobilized and the archbishop of Canterbury and the Church of Scotland pressed the British government to defend these Jewish communities. The London Jewish community, for its part, sent a delegation to the Middle East to investigate the situation and received the special protection of the British government for their mission.[44]

Historians like to recall a dinner on 1 August 1840, when Lord Ashley advanced persuasive political, financial, and commercial arguments suggesting to his father-in-law that the Sultan should be pressed to allow Jews to settle in Palestine, once it had been regained from Muhammad Ali. Ridley explains:

> Ashley was President of the Society for the Propagation of the Gospel among the Jews, and believed that God's chosen people should return to the promised land. Palmerston thought that Jews could play a useful part in modernizing the Turkish Empire, and in developing opportunities for British commerce in the Middle East.[45]

Palmerston promptly communicated significant details of his policy in a historically important dispatch to Ponsonby, dated 11 August 1840:

> There exists at present among the Jews dispersed over Europe, a strong notion that the time is approaching when their nation is to return to Palestine ... Consequently their wish to go thither has become more keen, and their thoughts have been bent more intently than before upon the means of realizing that wish. It is well known that the Jews of Europe possess great wealth; and it is manifest that any country in which a considerable number of them might choose to settle, would derive great benefit from the riches which they would bring into it.
>
> ...it would be of manifest importance to the Sultan to encourage the Jews to return to, and to settle in Palestine, because the wealth which they would bring with them would increase the resources of the Sultan's dominions; and the Jewish people, if returning under the sanction and protection and at the invitation of the Sultan, would be a check upon any future evil designs of Mehemet Ali or his successor...
>
> But even if the encouragement held out by the Sultan to the Jews were not practically to lead to the settlement of any great number of them within the limits of the Ottoman Empire, still the promulgation of some laws in their favour would spread a friendly disposition toward the Sultan among the Jews in Europe; and the Turkish Government must at once see how advantageous it would be to the Sultan's cause thus to create useful friends in many countries by one single edict.[46]

Palmerston sent a follow-up dispatch to Ponsonby, suggesting that British consular authorities and the British embassy at Constantinople allow Jews to transmit any complaints to the Porte concerning local officials through official British channels. The Porte, however, rejected this suggestion, indicating displeasure at British meddling.

Such strategic interests, including commercial considerations, guided British policy in Palestine through the nineteenth century. 'Behind the protection of trade and religious minorities,' Albert Hourani observed, 'there lay the major political and strategic interests of the powers.'[47] British diplomatic representation at Constantinople and Jerusalem ensured due consideration of efforts to strengthen the Jewish position in Palestine that continued down to the First World War era and the famous Balfour Declaration, which called for a 'homeland' for Jews in Palestine.[48]

British policy also worked to create a Protestant presence in the Holy Land by establishing with Prussia a joint Anglo-Prussian Protestant see in 1841 and the building of a Protestant cathedral, Christ Church, dedicated in 1849. The Church Missionary Society (founded in 1799 in Britain) and Palmerston's son-in-law's London Society for Promoting Christianity Amongst the Jews (founded in 1809) played roles in this development. Bishops were chosen alternately by the British and the Prussian authorities, but ordained only by the archbishop of Canterbury.

The first bishop was a converted Jew, Michael Solomon Alexander, and the initial concept of the mission was to convert the local Jewish population to Christianity. When success in this endeavor proved elusive, the second bishop turned his attention to the Orthodox Christian community, then under the 'protection' of Russia.

The Crimean War and the Eastern Question

The Eastern Question flared again with the Crimean War (1853–6) and religion was the pretext. The war saw Russia pitted against a coalition of France, Great Britain, the Kingdom of Sardinia, and the Ottoman Empire. France attempted to have the Porte recognize it as the 'sovereign authority' in the Holy Land – a maneuver that provoked Russia. France used a show of naval force to back up demands that the Porte confirm France and the Roman Catholic Church as the preeminent Christian authority in the Holy Land. The French sought to control all of the Christian holy places, including the

Church of the Holy Nativity, the keys to which were held by the Greek Orthodox Church under Russia's protection.

The underlying issue was strategic. The allies wished to resolve the Eastern Question by ending what they saw as the Russian threat to the Ottoman Empire. Their demands underscored the strategic aspect of the war: Russia was to give up its dominant position in the Danube; Russia was to give up its claim to protect the Greek Orthodox subjects of the Porte; the Straits Convention of 1841 was to be renegotiated; and access to the Danube River was to be granted to all nations.

Throughout their contention over the Ottoman Empire's fate, the great powers of Europe used religion as an instrument of policy. During the eighteenth and nineteenth centuries, the USA developed its own policy for the region, based on profitable commercial relations and constructive cultural engagement. As the young republic ventured forth into the maelstrom of international relations, it laid the foundations of American policy in the Middle East. That policy, then devoid of imperial and colonial aspirations, pragmatically sought to develop mutually beneficial relations with Muslim powers.

2

The Early American Republic and the Muslim World

The Bush administration's Iraq War represents a radical break in American Middle East policy. It parallels nineteenth-century European imperial projects and undermines traditional American anti-imperialism and non-intervention.[1] Today, Middle Easterners who reflect on America's past constructive engagement in North Africa and the Middle East rightly ask what has happened to the traditional American approach to the region, which emphasized mutually beneficial commerce and constructive cultural engagement. They are also shocked by the pro-Israel crusade of American Christian fundamentalists. In the nineteenth century, American missionaries focused on education and medical assistance rather than on converting Muslims and erecting a Zionist entity in the Holy Land. Is it any wonder that current polling data show a sharp decline in the international prestige of the USA? A 2007 public opinion survey of four major Muslim countries found that 'in all of them large majorities believe that undermining Islam is a key goal of US foreign policy'. The same poll found that most 'want US military forces out of the Middle East and many approve of attacks on US troops there'.[2]

In this chapter, I illustrate the Bush administration's radical break with American tradition by reviewing the USA's early relations with Muslim powers in North Africa and in the Middle East. These relations, which were primarily commercial, did not involve religious conflict.³ A quick look at the American War of Independence and the founding of the American Republic shows how traditional US foreign policy came to emphasize mutually beneficial commercial relations and a policy of constructive cultural engagement.

The contrast between the positive policy and image of the USA in the nineteenth century and the negative policy and image of today is startling. Chapter 1 outlined the historical context of great powers contending over the Eastern Question. Into this complex and volatile situation, the USA prudently combined the extension of commercial relations, the development of diplomatic relations, and the projection of naval capabilities. In the Middle East, American commercial and cultural engagement extended from the Ottoman *Porte* to Egypt, to Syria (which then included today's Lebanon, Israel, and Palestine), and to Persia.

The USA and the Eastern Question

American engagement with the Middle East prior to 1850 took place within the context of the Eastern Question and its associated Anglo-Russian rivalry, which came to be called the 'Great Game'.⁴ Relations with the Ottoman Porte were critical for Washington given Ottoman titular suzerainty over the Levant, the Arabian Peninsula, and much of the southern Mediterranean basin. At this time, US interest focused strictly on commerce rather than on imperial expansion and associated geopolitical maneuvers. As discussed in Chapter 1, from the 1830s on, British imperial strategy projected a Jewish entity in the Holy Land. The USA, on the other hand, had no such scheme up its sleeve, and no imperial motives, so it enjoyed a positive image throughout the region. The negative image of the USA in the Arab and Muslim worlds began to form after the creation of the state of Israel in 1948 was assisted by the support of the Truman administration.

The end of the Napoleonic Wars and the Congress of Vienna in 1815 signaled changes in the European states system and in the relations between its great powers. The resulting shift in the European balance of power had implications for regions outside Europe, thanks to the major players' imperial interests and pretensions. Because India remained the keystone of the far-flung British Empire, the Eastern Mediterranean, with its routes to India, remained a matter of concern. At the same time the expanding influence of the Russian Empire, in the Caucasus and in Central Asia, gave rise to the aforementioned Anglo-Russian competition for dominance. Persia, as a zone that could insulate India from rivals such as the Russians or the French, also had London's rapt attention.[5] A dramatic new turn, the Greek war of independence of 1821–32, naturally affected developments in the Near East and beyond.

Meanwhile, the USA had forged its favorable relations with the dominant power in the region, the lumbering Ottoman Empire. American interest was energetic. When problems with the Barbary Pirates raised the issue of American relations with the Ottoman Porte, which theoretically controlled the southern Mediterranean area, Joel Barlow, US consul at Algiers in 1796, wrote to Thomas Jefferson (then Secretary of State). Barlow advised establishing consulates at Smyrna, Alexandria, and Salonika. Though President John Adams did appoint a minister to the Porte in 1798, war between France and England complicated matters: the USA did not want to antagonize either power with such a diplomatic initiative.[6]

American merchants established themselves in the Eastern Mediterranean, principally at the thriving port of Smyrna (today's Izmir, Turkey) from which links developed to Beirut and Alexandria. Europeans were well established at Smyrna: the French consulate dated from 1619 and the British consulate from 1621. American merchants benefited from the establishment, in 1801, of the Mediterranean Squadron of the US Navy, which, in 1865 after the American Civil War, became the European Squadron.[7] The US navy protected American merchants and missionaries operating in the region just as the Sixth Fleet protects American interests today.

As formal relations between the USA and the Ottoman Porte developed, the American public became familiar with Turkish affairs through the writings of a number of prominent American travelers to the region. These include John Lloyd Stephens and George C. De Kay, who traveled to Turkey during the 1830s and 1840s. Stephens, a popular author, traveled widely; De Kay, a medical doctor and naturalist, came to Turkey ostensibly to study cholera and on his return to New York penned his *Sketches of Turkey*, published in 1833.

American Independence and the Mediterranean

When 13 British North American colonies launched their War of Independence against the most powerful global empire of the day, they needed allies and friends. A declaration of independence was necessary so that foreign powers would be encouraged to ally themselves with a group of states no longer under the British Crown. Further, these united American states needed to be able to develop international economic relations freely so as to strengthen their domestic economies and joint war effort. Such an initiative was pressed by Richard Henry Lee (1732–93) of Virginia who, on 2 July 1776, presented a resolution to the Second Continental Congress calling for such a declaration.[8] The outcome, of course, was the Declaration of Independence penned by Thomas Jefferson and signed on 4 July 1776. By adopting this document, the Continental Congress moved toward developing diplomatic and economic relations with foreign powers; significantly, however, it took no real steps to forge actual connections until such time as the 13 states could demonstrate their independence militarily. The American victory over the British at the Battle of Saratoga in October 1777 – the turning point of the War of Independence and a decisive American military success – encouraged the French, Spanish, and Dutch to align with the USA against their common British enemy and opened the path to free development of America's international economic relations.[9]

The USA needed access to the Mediterranean in order to develop commercial relations in Spanish, French, and Italian ports; the new nation also hoped to develop new commercial opportunities in North Africa and beyond in the Levant.[10] To this end, the USA put to use the rich tradition of seafaring, shipbuilding, and merchant activity the American colonies had inherited from Britain.[11] The Ottoman Empire – suzerain over much of this region, including the European Balkans, at the time – gradually lost its grip over its Mediterranean possessions. Development of relations with strategically placed Muslim states along the Mediterranean Basin, such as Morocco, topped the foreign policy agenda of Congress during the confederation period (1781–9) prior to the erection of the Republic under the Constitution of 1789.

Early American diplomatic efforts were successful with Morocco and Tunisia. The Barbary pirates along today's Algerian and Libyan coasts, however, posed challenges that took some years to overcome. During the early and mid-nineteenth century, US relations gradually extended to Muscat on the Arabian Peninsula, to Egypt, to the Ottoman Empire, and to Persia.

Morocco controlled the Atlantic approach to the western Mediterranean, since Britain held Gibraltar, so it was with Morocco that the USA first had to deal.[12] Fortunately for the USA, the ruler of Morocco, Sultan

Sidi Muhammad bin 'Abd Allah, had already shown himself to be friendly. He had been the first foreign head of state to formally recognize American independence, when he granted American ships free entry to his ports on 20 December 1777, ordering his corsairs' ships to let the ships pass unmolested. Morocco, a Muslim power, thus became the first state in the region to extend diplomatic recognition to the USA. For many years a framed copy of correspondence between George Washington and the Sultan, commemorating the event and this early friendship, hung in the US Senate Foreign Relations Committee room in the Capitol building. When I served on that committee in the 1980s, it was always pointed out to visitors and was, in fact, the only historical document displayed in that elegant and important room.

In 1784, Sidi Muhammad indicated a desire for a formal relationship. Accordingly, Congress authorized a commission composed of Benjamin Franklin, John Adams, and Thomas Jefferson to negotiate treaties with the four Barbary States. Spain supported the USA in its negotiations with Morocco, and Morocco agreed in 1786 to a mutually beneficial treaty of friendship and commerce during the time when the USA was organized as a confederation prior to the republic.[13]

As a fledgling republic in the New World, the USA sought prudently to avoid unnecessary and costly foreign conflict in order to develop its economy and strengthen its security.[14] George Washington's 'Farewell Address' said the expansion of international commercial relations was a fundamental national objective.[15] In his day, and into the early nineteenth century, the globe was perceived as divided into four primary regions: Europe, Asia, Africa, and America. Historian James A. Field has described how US foreign policy, supported by a growing navy, served the development of commercial relations in these regions: 'As American shipping circled the globe, the government moved with it in the establishment of pioneering treaty arrangements, in Barbary and Turkey, in Muscat and Siam, and ultimately to the openings of Japan and Korea.'[16] Systematic development of effective consular representation played a key role in advancing American commercial interests.

The American Republic pressed eastward in the Mediterranean, securing favorable treaties with Algiers (1795, 1815, 1816), Tripoli (1796, 1805), and Tunis (1797). The treaty of peace and friendship between the USA and Tunis contains a remarkable clause that clearly indicates American willingness to engage foreign cultures constructively. In a decisive nod to Islam, the first three words of the treaty's preamble read: 'God is infinite.'[17] Such American respect for religious and cultural differences stands in stark contrast to the anti-Islamic hysteria of present day Christian fundamentalists in the USA.

Relations with Morocco remained peaceful, though tensions flared along the Barbary Coast, resulting in the First Barbary War (the 'Tripolitan War' of 1801–5) and the Second Barbary War (the 'Algerine War' of 1815). By 1816 this instability had decreased, American relations along the Barbary Coast had stabilized, and new treaties marked a new beginning. As historian Frank Lambert emphasizes, this conflict was commercial rather than cultural and religious: 'The Barbary Wars were primarily about trade, not theology, and rather than being holy wars, they were an extension of America's War of Independence.'[18]

Yankees and Turks

Although formal diplomatic relations took another three decades to establish, the first official American visit to the Ottoman capital occurred in 1800 when a young naval officer, Captain William Bainbridge, commanding the *George Washington*, sailing from Algiers, made it through the Dardanelles with a cargo that included an ambassador to Algeria, bearing presents for the Sultan. The American visit made quite an impression. An English traveler recounts:

> When the frigate came to anchor, and a message went to the Porte that an American ship was in the harbour, the Turks were altogether unable to comprehend where the country was situate whose flag they were to salute ... a messenger came from the Turkish Government to ask whether America were not otherwise called the New World; and, being answered in the affirmative, assured the captain that he was welcome, and would be treated with the utmost cordiality and respect ... The fine order of his ship, and the healthy state of her crew, became topics of general conversation in Pera; and the different ministers strove who should first receive him in their palaces. We accompanied him in his long-boat to the Black Sea, as he was desirous of hoisting there, for the first time, the American flag.[19]

The issue of formal treaty relations was raised with Captain Bainbridge, but several subsequent secret diplomatic initiatives on the part of Washington failed to produce a treaty. Owing to strong pro-Greek feeling in the USA, diplomatic initiatives from the American side to the Porte were kept discreet. On the Turkish side, endless bureaucratic red tape delayed matters over the years.

The Turkish attitude suddenly changed, however, after the Battle of Navarino on 20 October 1827. In this naval battle, ships of allies Britain, France, and Russia delivered the worst defeat to the Turks since the Battle of Lepanto in 1571. When the Sultan needed foreign assistance to rebuild his fleet, a door opened to the Americans, whose industrial revolution was proceeding apace. High-quality American naval construction was internationally renowned. The Sultan could purchase it comfortably, since, as Finnie points out, the USA 'showed no particular signs of having political ambitions in the Mediterranean'.[20]

Diplomatic negotiations with the Porte were first undertaken during the administration of John Quincy Adams (1825–9) but were delayed owing to technical problems. Further development of diplomatic relations, therefore, fell to the incoming administration of Andrew Jackson (1829–37). The US diplomatic representative to the Porte, Commodore David Porter, held the title of *chargé d'affaire*. A capable linguist, William Brown Hodgson, then based in Algiers, was assigned to the irascible Commodore Porter. Hodgson was posted to Algiers in 1826 as a 'pupil-interpreter' in order to undertake the study of Arabic and Turkish.[21] He was the first appointee in Secretary of State Henry Clay's project to develop language specialists by assigning selected young men to the US consuls in the Barbary States (Tunis, Tripoli, Algiers, and Tangier). Hodgson appears to have been a talented linguist as he prepared the first scholarly study of the Berber language. In 1831, an exchange of ratifications of the Treaty of Amity and Commerce between the USA and Turkey was concluded.

American-led naval construction in Turkey during the 1830s was certainly the centerpiece of economic relations, which in this case involved the services of American technical experts and the acquisition of American naval stores by Turkey, and even Egypt. The well-known American naval architect Henry Eckford traveled to Turkey in 1831 and was appointed by the Sultan to head the shipyard of the Turkish navy. Eckford had a team of 15 American craftsmen and about six hundred Greeks, Turks, and Italians operating at the shipyard. After first building a schooner and launch Eckford turned to a battleship project, and the ship *Mahmud* at 3,934 tons was said to be the largest battleship in the world. When Eckford died suddenly of cholera in November 1832, his foreman Foster Rhodes took charge and the shipyard thereby remained under American management. British travel writer John Murray called Rhodes' ships 'the astonishment of everyone who beholds them'.[22]

Thanks to American work on the Turkish fleet, the 1830s marked the highest ever point of American influence in Turkey. In 1839, Rhodes returned to the USA to become a shipbuilder for the US Navy; and the Turkish fleet's admiral sailed into Alexandria, Egypt, and treacherously handed every one of Eckford and Rhodes' fine ships over to Muhammad Ali. British intervention caused the fleet to be returned to Turkey in 1841. According to Finnie:

> The ships built at Constantinople by Eckford and Rhodes sailed the Mediterranean for many years. Most of them must have been in service during the Crimean War. More than the traders, more than the missionaries, these Yankee shipbuilders brought to the East an awesome vision of America's talent and character at a time when the New World was scarcely more than a myth.[23]

Respect for American scientific and technological achievements, as Finnie points out, engendered a positive perception of the USA. Today, we would call this an aspect of America's 'soft power'.[24] Tragically, the Bush administration's war with Iraq and general Middle East policy has all but erased this element of American prestige and good will in Turkey today. Recent polling data documents the collapse of the American image in Turkey. According to a September 2005 article in the *Middle East Review of International Affairs* (MERIA), 'The Turkish people believed that the US decision on Iraq was taken without regard for Turkey's national interests or bilateral relations'.[25] The Pew Global Attitudes Project in June 2007 reported an 83 per cent unfavorable and 9 per cent favorable perception of the USA in Turkey.[26] And in September 2007 the University of Maryland World Public Opinion polling data indicated Turkey has 'the largest percentage of people naming the United States as the country that poses the greatest threat'.[27]

Yankees in Arabia

While the USA developed relations in the Eastern Mediterranean following the conclusion of peace with Great Britain in 1783, Americans also sought out long-distance trading opportunities in the Indian Ocean region and in

Asia. New York merchants sent the famed *Empress of China* out to Canton, China, in February 1784 and, a month later, Philadelphia merchants sent the *United States* out to Pondicherry, India. A brisk international trade thus opened for the USA, which ran through the Indian Ocean and included the Arabian Peninsula and Persia.[28]

For centuries, Arab merchants sailed out of the Gulf region for engagement in coastal and long-distance trade. The Omani cities of Sur, Sohar, and Muscat were well known and active in this trade, which extended from East African ports, to India, to the East Indies, and even to China. As early as 1790, the American ship *Rambler* visited Muscat while doing business in the Indian Ocean.[29] In 1792, American sailors who had shipwrecked made their way to Muscat and were welcomed by representatives of the Sultan of Oman and found their way home courtesy of a British ship. One sailor stayed on for two years working as a carpenter's mate aboard an Omani-owned ship before returning home to Massachusetts. American ships from time to time then stopped in Muscat, a key port for Arabian Gulf commerce.

The trade treaty of 1833 placed commercial relations between Oman and the USA on a formal basis. A prominent American merchant, Edmund Roberts, first raised the issue with Sultan Sayyid Sa'id (ruled 1804–56) in 1828 during the Adams administration.[30] The Sultan, recognizing commercial and security advantages for the Omani side, suggested a formal treaty. The project developed during the Jackson administration through the influence of the Secretary of the Navy, Levi Woodbury, a former US Senator who envisaged establishing formal treaty relations with all trading partners in the Indian Ocean region. Roberts, a relative of Woodbury's, was given the diplomatic rank of Special Agent and instructed to take the American warship, *Peacock*, out to the East Indies and Arabian ports and to negotiate treaty relationships. Roberts visited Cochin, China (today part of Vietnam), and Siam (now Thailand). He concluded a treaty with the latter and then proceeded to Muscat via Mokha. The Sultan of Oman received Roberts, who presented to him a warm letter from President Andrew Jackson. A treaty was duly drawn up in English, along with a parallel Arabic text, and duly signed on 3 October 1833, going into effect the following year. After departing Muscat for the East Indies, Roberts contracted a fever in Siam, died at Macau, and was buried in the East India Company cemetery there.

The Sultan of Oman, wanting to further relations with the USA, sent his own three-masted ship, *Sultana*, to New York City in 1840. These early diplomatic relations between the USA and the Muslim state of Oman were particularly cordial. The Sultan's representative, Ahmad bin Na'aman, brought a cargo that included Omani dates, Mokha coffee, and Persian carpets as well as several gifts for the White House. Writing on the historic bilateral relationship, US Ambassador Hermann Eilts said, 'The crew, like Ahmad and his officers, created a sensation and were widely entertained by enthusiastic New Yorkers.'[31]

In Oman, the USA maintained a consulate at Muscat through 1845 but the American Civil War, the opening of the Suez Canal in 1869, and the advent of steamships in the Indian Ocean altered international patterns of trade. A second consulate was established by the USA in 1880, which closed in 1914 as a result of the commercial uncertainties posed by the First World War. During this period, American medical missionaries from the Dutch Reformed Church still remained active in the Gulf, establishing clinics and providing medical services. President Franklin Roosevelt renewed relations in 1934 by sending a representative with a letter of invitation to the Omani ruler, His Highness Sayyid Sa'id bin Taimur. The Omani ruler visited the USA in 1938 and this smoothed the way for cooperation during the Second World War.

Mutual desire for a strong relationship has kept the USA and Oman closely connected to the present day.[32] The old 1833 treaty was finally updated in 1959 by the Eisenhower administration. In the last two decades, US–Omani relations have been updated owing to Oman's strategic location on the Strait of Hormuz and the Indian Ocean. In June 1980, the USA and Oman concluded an agreement that gave the USA access to Omani air and naval facilities, effectively making Oman a base for the American military in the Persian Gulf. This agreement was revised and renewed in 2000 and its value was highlighted by the subsequent Iraq War.

Yankees on the Nile

The Bush administration's war against Iraq has grievously damaged America's long-standing relations with Egypt, where recent polling data show a 78 per cent unfavorable and 21 per cent favorable public opinion rating of the USA.[33] These figures are especially shocking because the USA had positive relations with Egypt just after the American Civil War and for the last three decades has relied on Egypt as a partner in the Middle East peace process.

Although American travelers had reached Egypt by the end of the eighteenth century, commercial and diplomatic relations took several decades to establish. In 1832, an English merchant, John Gliddon, was appointed American consular agent at Alexandria, opening the way for developing relations as circumstances permitted. Egypt's ruler, Muhammad Ali, was expanding his regional reach at this time; by conquering Syria, he gained the important port of Beirut. As the changing regional situation looked favorable, Washington assigned State Department linguist William B. Hodgson, who was based at Constantinople, a secret mission: to investigate the commercial and political situation in Egypt. He ascertained that Muhammad Ali was favorable to developing relations and identified some commercial possibilities. Given the way in which the extensive Ottoman Empire was organized, the development of relations with Egypt was complicated by the situation that the Egyptian ruler, a vassal, was technically under the authority of the Ottoman Porte. Gliddon's post was upgraded from consular agent to consul, and his son became vice-consul at Cairo. American industrial technology – including the improved cotton gin – was made available to the Egyptian ruler, who desired to modernize his economy.

President Jackson sought to strengthen American commercial relations in the Eastern Mediterranean through a special mission conducted by Lewis Cass, US Ambassador at Paris and former Secretary of War. Departing in April 1837, Cass undertook his fact-finding mission through Egypt, Syria, Turkey, Greece, and the Aegean Islands. In September he met with Muhammad Ali and his heir, Ibrahim. Formal treaty relations were not undertaken at this time, however, and the intervention of the European powers into the Eastern Question contributed to their delay. By 1848, the post at Alexandria was upgraded to consul general. While the USA regarded Egypt as *de facto* an independent power, commerce remained insignificant.

The American Civil War directly affected relations with Egypt. The Union blockade of the South had the effect of restricting the flow of American cotton to European mills. Egyptian cotton production rose, as supply declined and international prices rose. At the same time, countries whose weaving industries depended on American cotton, notably England, considered intervening on behalf of the Confederacy. In response, the Union actively encouraged Egyptian cotton production to forestall the breaking of the blockade by the British.

After the Civil War, a burst of American tourism and congressional support for Egyptian self-determination further endeared the USA to Egypt, as did Washington's continued interest in mutually advantageous commercial opportunities. Not least of these was a proposal for a railroad line from Alexandria to the Red Sea, comparable at the time to the proposed Pacific railroad. In May 1869 the Pacific railroad was completed and six months later the Suez Canal was officially opened. The Pacific railroad, of course, opened American commercial opportunities in trans-Pacific trade with the Orient. The Suez Canal opened a short route for Europeans to the East by eliminating the long journey via the South Atlantic and Cape route.

The ruler of Egypt at this time was Khedive Ismail (1830–95), grandson of the aforementioned Muhammad Ali. Like his grandfather, Ismail was a modernizer. He moved toward eventual independence from the Ottoman Porte by strengthening his economy and military capabilities. As the USA was a major industrial power, behind Great Britain and France, it was logical that the Khedive, distrusting Europeans fixated on the Eastern Question, would turn to Americans for their know-how. With the completion of the Suez Canal, the time was ripe for the Khedive to recruit experienced American military personnel familiar with engineering, mapping, and operations. Several dozen former Union and Confederate officers thus took key positions in Egypt.

General Charles P. Stone of Massachusetts reached Cairo in March 1870 and became Chief of the General Staff. As Ismail was concerned about conflict with his Turkish overlord, particular attention was given to frontier and coastal defenses. General Stone later modernized Egypt's canals and harbors following the transfer of the Department of Public Works to the General Staff in 1873. The Americans reorganized military education for officers and enlisted men and assisted Ismail in his efforts to expand his influence southward, along the Red Sea and inland to Sudan and the Equatorial Lakes.

In 1876, however, the defeat of Egypt in its Abyssinian war and the collapse of its credit in European markets preceded the eventual establishment of a British protectorate over Egypt. As the locus of the Eastern Question shifted toward the Nile and away from the Bosporus, Egyptian finances came under the sway of Europe. As Elbert Farman, the American Consul General, said at the time, 'it is, today, as if the whole country was owned by a company of Paris and London bankers, and the people were either their slaves or serfs, attached to the soil'.[34] By 1878, European financiers had slashed military budgets and discharged most Americans working for the Egypt government.

Only General Stone remained. In 1879, French and British pressure resulted in the Ottoman Porte deposing Ismail in favor of his pliable son, Tewfik. As General Stone promised Ismail that he would stand by his son, he remained at his post. With the British occupation of Egypt in 1882, however, he resigned and returned to the USA, thus concluding an era of constructive engagement between America and Egypt.

It took almost a century for the USA to renew a positive relationship with Egypt. After the Second World War, the Cold War impaired Washington's relations with Egypt, as did Washington's tilt toward Israel – particularly after the 1967 war.[35] Egyptian President Anwar Sadat, however, altered Egyptian foreign policy and opened the door to cooperation with the USA and Europe. Dissatisfied with Egypt's relations with the Soviet Union, Egypt's costly state of war with Israel, and its bleak economic situation, President Sadat reevaluated Egypt's national interest and foreign alignments and concluded that a bold initiative was required. He therefore sought peace with Israel and a normalization of relations with the USA. This dramatic change in Egyptian policy led to the Camp David meetings and to the beginning of a peace process in the Middle East.

Since the pioneering effort of President Carter and President Sadat at Camp David in 1978, Egypt has been a partner for peace in the Middle East.[36] Today, however, Egyptian official circles and most on the 'Arab street' share a deep sense of disillusionment with the USA. Washington's failure to resolve the Arab–Israeli conflict is at the core of Arab and Muslim frustration and anger. The USA appears to the Arab and Muslim world as unable to perform the role of honest broker owing to the decisive power of the entrenched pro-Israel lobby that dominates the White House and Congress. Thus, despite positive relations at different points in history, residual good will in Egypt toward the USA has now all but evaporated.

Indeed, Cairo may well alter its traditional strategic relationships. Relations between the USA and Egypt could now take a turn for the worse as Egyptian political elites assess the disintegrating situation in the Middle East and the rising potential for internal turbulence at home inspired by political Islam and popular unrest.[37] I visited Egypt in June 2002 and spoke with many Egyptian diplomats and senior officials including His Excellency Ahmed Maher El Sayed, the foreign minister. It was clear to me that there was deep concern in key government circles over the direction that US foreign policy had taken under the George W. Bush administration. Officials I spoke with were quite aware of the policy implications of the ubiquitous neoconservative presence in the Bush administration and the influence of the pro-Israel lobby on foreign policy. While I was in Cairo, I had the opportunity to speak with His Excellency Muhammad Sayyed Tantawi, sheik of Al-Azhar University and a senior figure in Sunni Islam. He expressed deep concern over tensions in the region and the possibility of a war launched by the USA that would further polarize the region and increase tensions.

Returning to Washington, my conclusion from this visit was that the USA could well be displaced by China in Egypt's affections, should Cairo consider shifting its friendships and alliances out of frustration with Washington with its regional policy tilt toward Israel and its perceived dark crusade in the Middle East.[38] Anti-Egypt legislation and political pressure, orchestrated by the pro-Israel lobby in Congress, clearly rankled the Egyptian elite. Egypt is not so dependent on American foreign aid that it cannot revise its foreign policy. Nor is Egypt so dependent on American arms that it cannot turn to other sources in the competitive international arms market.

Christian Zionist pressure and lobbying in Washington reinforces this issue, particularly through the work of Jewish pro-Israel organizations such as the American Israel Public Affairs Committee (AIPAC). This is particularly the case in such a sensitive foreign policy area for Cairo as Sudan. For Egypt, Sudan and the larger Nile Basin is a major strategic consideration given the flow of the life-giving Nile River through it and thence through Egypt. China also has significant interests in Sudan owing to its importation of Sudanese hydrocarbons. One veteran Egyptian official told me that Israel had been active in exerting pressure against Egypt from the Nile River Basin region for half a century.

Christian Zionist action not only impairs the Middle East peace process but also exacerbates regional tensions through its militant stance against Islam. However, contemporary Christian Zionism in the USA is a radical break from the traditions of early American Christian missionaries in the Middle East.

American Missionaries

Because of security created by the US navy's presence, American missionaries and travelers ventured into the region from the 1820s.[39] Malta was a primary base for missionary activity during the 1820s, but by the 1830s activity had shifted to Beirut. The missionaries, mostly Congregationalists from New England, very early on abandoned any focus on converting Muslims and concentrated on good works and on working with Christians from the ancient Eastern communities: Greek Orthodox, Armenian, Maronite Catholic, and Nestorian.[40] Missionaries focused primarily on education and medical assistance, establishing numerous schools and medical clinics during the nineteenth century. Despite tensions between the missions and leaders of regional Christian churches opposed to the attempt to poach from their flocks, there is little evidence of significant religious conflict with Muslim authorities.

The American missionaries of the nineteenth century operated from theology radically different from that of the Christian Zionists of today. Their eschatology – their presumptions about mankind's and the world's ultimate destiny – distinguishes them from today's Christian Zionists in the USA. Ideas such as the return of the Messiah, a messianic age, an End Times period and an end-of-days permeate theological discussion in contemporary fundamentalist subculture. Millions of Christian Zionists in the USA today advocate a blindly pro-Israel foreign policy for the USA based upon their belief in a particular eschatology called 'dispensational premillennialism'.

Today's Christian Zionists, who are militant supporters of the state of Israel, embrace a premillennial world view that perceives the present day as situated in the Last Days or End Times of biblical prophecy. They believe that their idiosyncratic End Times scenario requires the return of Jews to the Holy Land to fulfill biblical prophecy. To make room for this ingathering of Jews from the global diaspora, Christian Zionists insist that further territory in Palestine must be made available to a 'Greater Israel'. Given the spiritual stakes, they say, Israeli settlement must continue despite the massive dispossession and displacement of the native Muslim and Christian Arab Palestinian population that has occurred since the 1948 establishment of the state of Israel.

In the USA in the eighteenth and nineteenth centuries, on the other hand, prevailing Christian Protestant eschatology was 'amillennial' or 'postmillennial'. This is to say, Protestants believed that the Second Advent (or Coming) of Jesus would only take place sometime *after* a golden age period of a thousand years and without a literal or a physical kingdom on earth – a view distinct from the 'premillennial' idea that the Apocalypse and subsequent Second Coming (or Advent) will occur *prior* to Christ's thousand-year reign. Some regard postmillennialism as a form of 'optimistic amillennialism', because there is no Apocalypse. This distinction between premillennial and postmillennial ideas may seem arcane to non-Christians, but it explains both the ideology of Christian Zionism during the nineteenth century in the UK and the USA and how this ideology continues to affect politics today.

The USA has experienced several periods of increased religiosity and revival. The 'First Great Awakening', which took place between 1727 and 1746, boosted *postmillennial* eschatology.[41] The Rev. Jonathan Edwards (1703–58) contributed greatly to popularizing this optimistic perspective, a perspective that many American Protestants associated in due course with the American Revolution. The War of Independence and the American Revolution were seen optimistically, by some, as portending the commencement of the millennium. The documentation of a 1998 Library of Congress exhibit on religion and the American Revolution reads:

> The Revolution strengthened millennialist strains in American theology. At the beginning of the war some ministers were persuaded that, with God's help, America might become 'the principal Seat of the glorious Kingdom which Christ shall erect upon Earth in the latter Days'. Victory over the British was taken as a sign of God's partiality for America and stimulated an outpouring of millennialist expectations – the conviction that Christ would rule on earth for 1,000 years. This attitude combined with a groundswell of secular optimism about the future of America to create the buoyant mood of the new nation that became so evident after Jefferson assumed the presidency in 1801.[42]

American foreign missionary activity grew out of the Great Awakenings influenced by Rev. Edwards. During the 'Second Great Awakening', from 1790 to 1844, another American religious revival took place. Edwards inspired the formation of the Baptist Missionary Society in London in 1792 which led, in turn, to the formation of the London Missionary Society in 1795. The work of these organizations inspired the formation of similar organizations in the USA: the New York Missionary Society was organized in 1796 and was quickly joined by the Northern [New York] Missionary Society (1797), Missionary Society of Connecticut (1798), Massachusetts Missionary Society (1799), Standing Committee on Missions of the Presbyterian Church (1802), Missionary Society of Rhode Island (1803), Western Missionary Society (Pittsburgh Synod) (1803), and Standing Committee on Missions of the Dutch Reformed Church (1806). Missionary work in North America focused on settlers on the American frontier, African-Americans, and Native Americans.

The first overseas missionaries were a group of committed Williams College graduates who entered the Andover Theological Seminary, a graduate theological seminary established in 1807 by traditional New England Calvinists. Students and several professors then worked to found the American Board of Commissioners for Foreign Missions organized in 1810.[43] The American Board was Congregationalist in origin but also supported Presbyterian missions (1812–70) and Dutch Reformed missions (1826–57) as well as other denominations. Staunchly evangelical, because they intended to spread the gospel, the theology embraced by the organization was orthodox and Trinitarian, believing in the triune God: Father, Son, and Holy Ghost. With respect to eschatology, the organization was committed to the optimism and cooperative ethos of postmillennialism.

India, Burma, and Ceylon received the first missionary efforts, but the field of action quickly expanded to the Levant – from Egypt and Palestine to Armenia and Persia. The missionary strategy in the Levant focused upon converting Eastern Christians, not Muslims, on the theory that Christian denominations should first be revived prior to any attempt to proselytize Muslims. 'To hope for the conversion of the Mohammedans without the exemplification of a true Christianity seemed vain,' Field says.[44]

Considering positive elements of American engagement in the Middle East during the eighteenth and nineteenth centuries throws the influence of Christian Zionist ideology on American foreign policy into bold relief. Though itself rooted in the nineteenth century, this ideology has ripened and been supported under the George W. Bush administration. Indeed, Christian Zionist support of Israel facilitated public and congressional support for the administration's preventive war launched against Iraq in 2003.

More ominous today, Christian Zionism is poisoning US relations with the Arab and Muslim worlds. The overt militant rhetoric against Islam and

Muslims by Christian Zionist leaders in the USA demonstrates the hostile intention of what many perceive to be America's dark crusade in the Middle East and against Islam generally. A study produced by WorldPublicOpinion.org at the University of Maryland observes:

> An in-depth poll of four major Muslim countries has found that in all of them large majorities believe that undermining Islam is a key goal of US foreign policy. Most want US military forces out of the Middle East and many approve of attacks on US troops there ... Consistent with this concern, large majorities in all countries (average 74%) support the goal of getting the United States to 'remove its bases and military forces from all Islamic countries', ranging from 64 percent in Indonesia to 92 percent in Egypt.[45]

The conclusion of this University of Maryland study is disturbing. As Steven Kull, editor of WorldPublicOpinion.org, put it, 'While US leaders may frame the conflict as a war on terrorism, people in the Islamic world clearly perceive the US as being at war with Islam.'[46]

3

Christian Zionism: Construction of an Ideology

Christian Zionism, an ideology constructed in nineteenth-century Britain, was an instrument of imperialism in the Middle East for the British and remains so today for the USA. Lord Palmerston used it for imperial purposes, when he adroitly took political advantage of Christian Zionists' support for the 'restoration' of Jews to the Holy Land.[1] Barbara Tuchman explains that, 'As the Foreign Secretary saw it, the Jews, given a landed interest in their ancient homeland, would act as a prop at the center of the sprawling, collapsing structure that was the Turkish Empire.'[2] And, of course, Lord Palmerston's son-in-law, Ashley Cooper, argued for restoration on evangelical grounds: 'To him, as to all the Israel-for-prophecy's sake school, the Jews were simply the instrument through which Biblical prophecy could be fulfilled.'[3]

Today, as political analyst Kevin Phillips argues, the USA has become 'the world's leading Bible-reading crusader state, immersed in an Old Testament of stern prophets and bloody Middle Eastern battlefields.' He contends, 'American foreign policy has its own corollary to the end-times worldview: the preemptive righteousness of a biblical nation become a high-technology, gospel-spreading superpower.'[4]

Has American Christian Zionist political influence over the White House and Congress shaped American foreign policy? President Carter says frankly that 'some top Christian leaders have been in the forefront of promoting the Iraqi war, and make frequent trips to Israel, to support it with funding, and lobby in Washington for the colonization of Palestinian territory'. He also points out that 'strong pressure from the Religious Right has been a major factor in America's quiescent acceptance of the massive building of Israeli settlements and connecting highways on Palestinian territory in the West Bank'.[5]

Religion and Culture in the American Colonies and Early Republic

Christian Zionism, embedded with premillennial dispensationalism, arrived in the USA in the mid-nineteenth century.[6] It was quite unlike the traditional optimistic Christian eschatology expressed and expounded in American churches (Protestant, Roman Catholic, and Orthodox) during the War of Independence and Early Republic, throughout the nineteenth century, and in most mainline churches today. While philo-Semitism existed in the American colonies during the seventeenth and eighteenth centuries, it took an abstract and idealized form used for spiritual and civic purposes. B. Eugene Griessman observes:

> The philo-Semitism so often present among the early colonists, especially in New England, was not so much a love of Jews in the flesh as it was a veneration of an ideal type which the Colonists constructed from reading the Hebrew Scriptures.[7]

Colonists interpreted the Old Testament in light of the New Testament. As Griessman and others point out, the colonists thought metaphorically of their new North American home in New England as a 'New Canaan', with Boston as the 'New Jerusalem'. The Great Puritan Migration to New England of the early seventeenth century was an Exodus with King James I seen as Pharaoh. The Atlantic Ocean was likened to the Red Sea. Today's wealthy Connecticut town, New Canaan, was incorporated in 1801 and named after the preexisting Canaan parish established in 1731. Jacob R. Marcus points out that the New Englanders' New Canaan 'was not intended to attract Jews' – instead it was to be a 'Protestant fortress'.[8] For the New Englander, America was the 'New Zion'. However, as Robert Pfeiffer explains, the significance of the Old Testament in early New England culture 'should not lead to the false assumption – not infrequently defended – that the Pilgrims preferred the Old Testament to the New and that they might be considered "Jews not Christians". Pfeiffer correctly dismisses such 'an absurd notion'.[9]

In the seventeenth and eighteenth centuries, scholarship in Hebrew at such institutions as Harvard, Yale, and Princeton supported biblical interpretation (hermeneutics) and the use of rhetoric in preaching (homiletics). Biblical scholarship using ancient Hebrew was carried over from the English universities where many early colonial leaders had received their own education.[10] The first book printed in the colonies, published in Cambridge, Massachusetts, in 1640, was the *Bay Psalm Book*, a translation of Psalms with a preface by Richard Mather (1596–1669).[11] Mather, pastor of Dorchester, Massachusetts Bay Colony, had attended Brasenose College, Oxford. The book contains five Hebrew words, the first appearance of ancient Hebrew in any work printed in the British North American colonies.

'In general, things Hebrew were idealized in the abstract,' Griessman says, 'but Jews in real life were not esteemed unless, perhaps, they were converts to Christianity.'[12] Some colonial leaders – Jonathan Edwards, Cotton Mather, John Eliot, Roger Williams, and William Penn – thought the American Indians were the Ten Lost Tribes of Israel and so encouraged missionary efforts to convert them. Colonial Puritans also sought to convert Jews present in the colonies.[13]

Contemporary Christian Zionism in the USA does not have roots in colonial New England.[14] In fact, it was nineteenth-century British circles, not earlier New England Puritanism, that constructed premillennial dispensationalism, the fundamentalist ideology embraced today by millions of Christian Zionist Americans. And it is this nineteenth-century set of beliefs that directly affects US foreign policy today. This later export from the UK, some two centuries after the founding of the British North American colonies, has created the dangers that President Carter so astutely fears and warns against.

Professor Nabil I. Matar addresses the issue of the restoration of Jews in the Holy Land and the parallel issue of anti-restorationism within the British Puritan clergy. He points out that there was a considerable body of anti-restorationist thought in the seventeenth, eighteenth, and nineteenth centuries. Anti-restorationist writings, however, are not well known today:

> There were various theologians and poets, lunatics and 'prophets', soldiers and scientists who wrote in support of Restoration, and who were subsequently cited by twentieth-century historians bent on supporting Zionist

claims to Palestine. Although those anti-Restorationists include important Biblical scholars and literary figures like Hugh Broughton, Henry Hammond, Joseph Hall, Richard Baxter, Thomas Fuller, John Milton, John Lightfoot, Henry Danvers, and Peter Alix, they have been ignored by twentieth-century historians of Protestantism and Palestine and their works have been allowed to lie undisturbed in libraries. Meanwhile, Restorationist texts have been reprinted, and Restorationist commentaries and millenarian calculations have been advanced in support of the ideology of Zionism.[15]

Restorationism and British Imperial Policy

When Lord Palmerston's son-in-law, Ashley Cooper (later Lord Shaftsbury), persuaded Palmerston that restoring Jews to the Holy Land would benefit British interests in the Middle East, he had the Eastern Question firmly in mind. Palmerston sought to assist the Ottoman Sultan in order to blunt French inroads in Egypt with its ruler Muhammad Ali, a vassal of the Ottomans. He reasoned that Jewish settlement in Palestine could benefit the Ottoman Empire financially through commercial activity and through loans to the Ottomans from Jewish financiers with a philanthropic interest in the restoration of Jews to the Holy Land.

The able Egyptian ruler wished to be independent of the Turkish Sultan who had given him his position and to expand his influence into Turkish-dominated Syria, which included Palestine. Britain's imperial logic under Palmerston was to bolster Turkey by ensuring the Sultan's continued dominance in Syria and to project British influence into the Holy Land through various commercial and diplomatic means. Since France influenced the region through its traditional Roman Catholic allies, the Maronites, and Russia, via the Orthodox community, Britain sought out, and created, local allies. Britain adopted a three-fold strategy in this regard: to cultivate the local Druze, an Islamic sect; to bring Jews to the Holy Land; and to establish an Anglican bishopric in Palestine.

Ashley Cooper was a religious enthusiast deeply involved with evangelical circles, and knew that spiritual landscape well. He understood the increasing British evangelical interest in Palestine and in the restoration of the Jewish people to it. Tuchman describes the public mood at this time. 'The urgency was felt again in England at the time of the Evangelical Revival,' she says. 'For now the pendulum had swung back again, after the Hellenic interlude of the eighteenth century, to the moral earnestness of another Hebraic period.' The French Revolution, she says, spurred this mood shift because 'the propertied class, who, frightened by what was happening in France, were anxiously mending their fences, spiritual as well as political'.[16] Thus, for Tuchman, the evangelical turn in Britain had a conservative spirit that could be used to fortify British imperial policy in the Middle East.

British official circles had become concerned by French advances in the Middle East. Napoleon hoped to appeal to Middle Eastern and African Jews for support for his imperial project in the region. Instead, Jews in the region prudently supported the long-established Ottoman Empire against the French upstart whose navy had already been crushed by the British. Nevertheless, Napoleon sparked activity in religious circles in Britain. He also departed from Palestine with a scorched earth policy. The Rev. Stephen Sizer, a leading Anglican expert on Christian Zionism, explains that, 'stirred by memories of the Napoleonic expedition, Shaftsbury argued for a greater British presence in Palestine and saw this could be achieved by the sponsorship of a Jewish homeland on both religious and political grounds'. As Sizer points out, Shaftsbury believed that British protection of the Jews 'would give a colonial advantage over France for the control of the Middle East; provide better access to India *vis-à-vis* a direct overland route; and open up new commercial markets for British products'.[17]

Cooper succeeded with Palmerston because Christian Zionism, with its support for the transfer and relocation of Jews to the Holy Land, had penetrated various currents of British religious opinion, including the established Church of England.[18] The population of Jews in the Holy Land, however, was small and seemingly not interested in grandiose projects of restoration. The Jews living in the Holy Land, according to Tuchman, numbered under 10,000 and

> ...consisted of some four thousand Sephardim, descendants of the Spanish Jews expelled in 1492 who had been allowed to settle in Jerusalem by Suleiman the Great, and of some three thousand Ashkenazim, poor stragglers from central Europe who came to lay their bones in Zion.[19]

This community appeared cool to outside designs and, to enlarge it, projects for transferring and settling European Jews in Palestine necessarily had to be devised and justified. Wide ranging attempts to identify Jews from the 'Ten Lost Tribes' scattered about the Middle East and Asia were undertaken by

British restoration enthusiasts. Jews thus identified could be then restored to Palestine under British auspices.

Of course, none of these schemes took into account the Arab Palestinian population residing there. In Europe's imperial enthusiasm, the land and people resident on it were taken to be mere objects, to be handled according to the whim of European powers. The late Sami Farsoun, an authority on Palestinian affairs, wrote extensively on the region in recent years, focusing on social and economic conditions. Farsoun observed that, during the first three centuries of Ottoman rule over Palestine, 'no Turkish colonization or Turkification took place'. Under the Ottoman regime, 'Palestine's Arab character remained intact, and many of the ethnic minorities and remnants of invaders became Arabized over the years'.[20]

Additionally, nineteenth-century Western images of Arabs in travel writing and restorationist literature often appeared to give rise to negative stereotypes. Kathleen Christison, a regional specialist and former US government official, argues that the West assumed 'that the real Orient lay somewhere beneath the surface, that the real Palestine was Christian or Jewish (or both) rather than Arab or Muslim'. This attitude, she says, 'constituted a symbolic dispossession of the Palestinians'.[21]

Cooper the evangelical, and Palmerston the politician, correctly calculated public support for the imperial project to establish Jews in colonies in Palestine. They felt confident that a mandate for such action could be garnered through appeals to religion and humanitarianism because Christian Zionism had been on the rise for several decades in Great Britain. Such Christian Zionism took several forms, however, with various theological interpretations.

Dispensationalism and History

According to Rev. Sizer, the two main forms of Christian Zionism that arose in the nineteenth century were 'one based on covenantal premillennialism emphasizing evangelism, the other on dispensational premillennialism which stressed restorationism'.[22] Evangelism refers to the sharing of the gospel with unbelievers, such as Jews, hoping to convert them to Christianity. Restorationism refers to the physical transfer of the Jewish people to the Holy Land.[23] From this perspective, the Church (Christianity) and the Jews (the Jewish 'nation' or 'Israel') remain separate and distinct. Sizer defines restorationism as the 'conviction that the Bible predicts and mandates a final and complete restoration of the Jewish people to Israel'.[24]

Sizer explains 'premillennialism' as an eschatological perspective that sees a literal 1,000-year kingdom on earth *following* the sudden return of Christ. Immediately prior to Christ's return, however, there will be a seven-year period of suffering on earth called the 'tribulation'. During this tribulation period unbelievers and Jews will suffer and the 'Battle of Armageddon' will occur. Dispensationalists believe that there will be a secret 'rapture' during the seven-year tribulation phase in which true believers will be physically removed from earth but then return bodily with Christ when he appears. Belief in the rapture takes three approaches. So-called 'pre-tribulationists' maintain that believers are secretly raptured to heaven *before* the tribulation; 'mid-tribulationists' believe that the rapture occurs midway through the tribulation; and 'post-tribulationists' suppose that believers will be raptured to heaven *after* they suffer throughout the seven-year tribulation.[25]

How does this premillennial perspective view the span of human history? Dispensationalists see history as being divided into seven periods or 'dispensations' during which humanity has been, or will be, tested. They describe the present era, the sixth period, as the End Times or Last Days. As Sizer and other scholars point out, fundamentalists interpret scripture in a literalist way rather than in the traditional allegorical or typological ways used by Roman Catholics and mainstream Protestants respectively. Dispensationalists believe that biblical prophecies, particularly those relating to Israel, refer to *future* events as they have not yet been fulfilled in a literal sense.[26]

Premillennialism Opposed to the Traditional American Civic Culture

'Postmillennialism' (or 'optimistic amillennialism') – the opposite of the deeply pessimistic premillennial perspective – was a significant eschatology in the USA at the time of the founding of the American Republic and, along with amillennialism, persists in mainline churches today.[27] Postmillennialism holds that there will be long period of peace and prosperity on earth *prior* to Christ's return. During this period, the Christian gospel will be proclaimed to all nations and, as a result, Christian values will be universally embraced. In this framework, as in that of its fellow traveler, amillennialism, Armageddon is understood as a symbolic triumph of good over evil and not a physical apocalyptic occurrence.[28] Amillennialism believes that the kingdom of God is present in the world and that Christ rules the church through his Word and the Spirit. This is the school of thought that stimulated early nineteenth-century American missionary activity in the Middle East and became the traditional American postmillennial, or amillennial, view.

American clergy, for their part, used optimistic language in their sermons during and after the War of Independence though, naturally, emphasizing biblical allusions. The influence of the first Great Awakening (1730–45) on American thought has similar associations.[29] The positive and constructive spirit of this first Great Awakening was well described by Joseph Tracy, an American historian writing in 1842:

> The waking up of mind among men of all classes, the revival of those truths in which the free spirit of Puritanism had its origin, the earnest discussion of the principles of freedom and human rights, and the habit of contending for rights sturdily and with religious zeal, which was nourished among men of all orders, were doubtless useful in preparing many minds for the questions that awaited them.[30]

He underscored the optimism of the first Great Awakening:

> The Great Awakening should teach a lesson of faith, of encouragement, of cheerful hope, even in the darkest times. We are too apt to be thrown into despondency by every departure from our own notions of order and propriety, and to think that when every thing does not move exactly as we would have it, everything is going to destruction.[31]

The optimism of American intellectual leaders of the Independence era, both clerical and secular rationalist, owed much to the earlier Great Awakening and the ongoing Second Great Awakening (1780–1830).[32] Americans readily recognized this debt. Rev. Ezra Stiles (1727–95), the president of Yale, in his sermon entitled 'The United States Elevated to Glory and Honor' (1783)[33] referred to then confederated United States as 'God's American Israel' – the fulfillment of the prophecy of Noah and also the realization of Deuteronomy 26:19: 'to make thee high above all nations which he hath made, in praise, and in name, and in honour; and that thou mayest be an holy people unto the Lord they God' (KJV). Americans, of course, under their new constitution could believe (or disbelieve) according to their own convictions. The US Constitution guaranteed religious freedom and, as historian

Frank Lambert argues, 'rather than designing a church-state framework of their own, endorsed the emerging free marketplace of religion'.[34]

Joel Barlow (1754–1812), a Yale graduate who served in various diplomatic posts and an evident rationalist, expressed the view that 'such a state of peace and happiness as is foretold in the scripture and commonly called the millennial period, may rationally be expected to be introduced without a miracle'. From Barlow's optimistic perspective, world civilization progresses through three stages: population of the various parts of the world, interchange of knowledge among nations, and the establishment of international commerce.[35]

In the early American Republic many believed along the same lines as Barlow, that the development of international commerce, which included cultural exchange, would contribute to peace. American optimism was expressed in its national symbols. One of America's best-loved symbols, the Great Seal of the United States, sums up this optimistic postmillennial perspective in its Virgilian mottos, *Annuit Coeptis* and *Novus Ordo Seclorum*. The first can be understood as 'Providence has favored our Undertakings', and the second as the beginning of a 'New Order of the Ages' (the 'American Aera').[36]

Missionary Activity in a Traditional Framework

Given the optimism of the day, an evangelical desire to spread the gospel abroad was natural. Theologically, American missionaries during this period were untainted by the ideology of Christian Zionism, which only came to the USA during the Civil War period and late nineteenth century. American missionary activity in the Near East in the nineteenth century was supported, in particular, by the Andover Theological Seminary, a bastion of traditionalism. Moses Stuart, one of the leading scholars at the seminary, was a graduate of Yale and was influenced by its president, Rev. Timothy Dwight (1752–1817), who followed Rev. Stiles. Significantly, Stuart and his colleagues at the seminary drew on technical aspects of contemporary German biblical criticism, although they maintained the traditional Congregational belief in the authority of the Bible. Late nineteenth-century proto-fundamentalists and twentieth-century fundamentalists in the USA strenuously objected to modern biblical criticism and unceasingly adhered to biblical literalism and the so-called inerrancy of the biblical text.

One of Stuart's pupils, Edward Robinson (1794–1863), later a noted educator associated with the Union Theological Seminary, spent four years in Palestine on geographic and topological research and became known internationally as the father of biblical geography. His research was the most comprehensive since Eusebius and Jerome in the fourth century and he was awarded a gold medal for his work by the prestigious British Royal Geographic Society. His extraordinary work encouraged the establishment of the American Oriental Society at Boston in 1842, many of whose charter members were associated with the American Board of Commissioners for Foreign Missions.[37]

Despite such a strong socially optimistic evangelical and humanist tradition in American Protestantism, dispensational Christian Zionism, with its profoundly pessimistic apocalyptic perspective, its biblical literalism, and its radical restorationist political program, began to filter into the USA. In 1859, the missionary work in the USA of the British Christian Zionist John Nelson Darby (1800–82) began a process that would lead to the establishment of dispensational premillennialism as the dominant eschatology in American fundamentalism. Today, scholars estimate conservatively that between 25 million and 40 million Americans consider themselves as fundamentalists. Fundamentalist church leaders claim 50 million to 100 million Americans.[38] Whatever the actual number, it is from this tremendous mass base that the pro-Israel lobby in the USA mobilizes support from Christian Zionists.

Christian Zionism: The British Founders

The London Society for Promoting Christianity Amongst the Jews, known as the London Jews' Society (LJS) was founded in May 1809. A philo-Semitic philanthropic organization, it emphasized both relief of the sick and education.[39] Significantly, it combined restorationism with its evangelism which, according to Rev. Sizer, 'gave Christian Zionism its first distinct identity as an embryonic movement, and its earliest location within British evangelicalism'. The LJS was founded 'with the assistance of Prof. Simeon of Cambridge, Dr Marsh of Birmingham, the convert J.F. Fry, and the preacher Leigh Richmond'.[40] Tuchman considers it the most popular gospel society of the era. 'Its list of noble patrons glittered like a court circular,' she says. 'Its cornerstone for chapel and school building was laid in 1813 by the Duke of Kent, brother of the King and the father of Queen Victoria.'[41]

Other such organizations espousing covenantal premillennial restorationism emerged later in the nineteenth century: the British Society for the Propagation of the Gospel Among the Jews (1842), the Mildmay Mission to the Jews (1876), and the Barbican Mission to the Jews (1879). According to Rev. Sizer, they 'were driven by a liberal hermeneutic, a covenantal premillennial eschatology and shared a strong commitment to evangelize the Jewish people'.[42]

These sturdy organizations have had long lives. The British Society for the Propagation of the Gospel Among the Jews, based in London, operated from 1842 until 1976 when it merged into the Barbican Mission. The Barbican Mission to the Jews operated primarily in London, Poland, Czechoslovakia, and Yugoslavia. It lives on today in a successor organization called Christian Witness to Israel. From 1846 to the end of the century, the society's foreign agents were mostly in Germany, Austria, Russia, Poland, and Turkey. During the 1920s the Haifa Mission became the principal foreign operation, with a staff of ten by 1925. The book depot there distributed 25,000 texts in Hebrew, Arabic, Yiddish, Russian, German, and English during 1927–8.[43]

British Covenantal Restorationism

Christian Zionism in Britain emerged during the early nineteenth century and took on several forms before John Nelson Darby established his own idiosyncratic interpretation. Covenantal restorationism was one leading form and experts identify four key leaders of nineteenth-century British covenantal restorationism: Lewis Way, Charles Simeon, Joseph Wolff, and Charles Spurgeon. Covenantal restorationism helped to prepare the public mood for the later, more sharply defined Christian Zionism that was to follow.

Lewis Way (1772–1840) was a graduate of Merton College, Oxford, who is considered the founder of the LJS and the central proponent of restorationism and Christian Zionism in his day. When the Napoleonic Wars ended in 1815, Way traveled the Continent advocating Jewish emancipation as well as the settlement of Palestine. He spoke with many heads of state and even presented his case for restorationist Zionism in 1818 to the diplomatic conference of the Great Powers (Britain, Russia, Austria, France, and Prussia) called the Congress of Aix la Chapelle.[44] In Rev. Sizer's view, 'through Way's efforts restorationism came to be embraced by the evangelical establishment and even enjoyed the support of a significant proportion of the English episcopacy'.[45] Way founded a British chapel on Rue Marboeuf in 1824 while serving as chaplain to the British ambassador at Paris.[46] His activity clearly represented a British effort to respond to Napoleon's policy of Jewish emancipation in France and on the Continent.[47]

Charles Simeon (1759–1836), who worked with Way to promote restorationism, played an important role within Anglican evangelical networks. Simeon was educated at Eton College and Cambridge and became a fellow of King's College, Cambridge, in 1782. He took orders and became vicar of Holy Trinity church, Cambridge, in 1783. An advisor to the British East India Company, Simeon was a postmillennialist who believed Jews would return to Palestine – but as Christians.

Joseph Wolff (1795–1862) was a German Jew who first converted to Roman Catholicism at a young age and then later to Anglicanism, although his father was a rabbi.[48] He pursued Oriental and religious studies at the University of Tübingen and at the Vatican's Collegio di Propaganda in Rome. Expelled from the Collegio for doctrinal deviation, he then moved to England, became an Anglican, and pursued his studies at Cambridge. He was fluent in Arabic, Hebrew, Chaldean, Persian, and Syriac. His overseas missionary work for the LJS began in 1821 with a visit to Egypt.

Later, Wolff played a significant role in the Albury Circle, which laid the intellectual foundation for dispensational Christian Zionism. The Albury Circle was established by Henry Drummond, Jr, a prominent London banker and religious eccentric. He traveled far and wide, reaching India, Armenia, and Abyssinia, ministering in particular to Oriental Jews and searching for the Ten Lost Tribes. His own far-ranging travels, and books about them, certainly contributed to a public interest in foreign lands both in Great Britain and in the USA.[49]

Charles Haddon Spurgeon (1834–92), a Baptist, was a leading nonconformist preacher in England who adopted a covenantal premillennial perspective and so endorsed restorationism. He worked with the British Society for the Propagation of the Gospel Among the Jews, a nonconformist version of the then Anglican LJS. Spurgeon, however, repudiated dispensational premillennialism and rejected its contention that God had separate purposes for the Jews apart from the Christian Church. From his perspective, the Christian church and Israel would be united one day as Israel would be converted and both would have faced the tribulation together.[50] For Spurgeon and other covenantal premillennialists, evangelism was the priority while restorationism was a secondary matter.

Along with covenantal premillennialism, however, came the rise of radical and extremist dispensational premillennialism with its Apocalytic End Times scenario. For the dispensationalists, political restoration of Jews to Palestine, and Palestine to Jews, was the priority. I will show in subsequent chapters how this Christian Zionist eschatology became dominant among proto-fundamentalists and fundamentalists in the USA subsequent to John Nelson Darby's series of visits to there to promote it.

British Dispensationalism

The late Yona Malachy, an assistant director of the Department of Christian Affairs in the Israeli Ministry of Religious Affairs, called dispensationalism 'the most extreme form' of premillennialism because it 'focuses its unique eschatological conception on the future of the Jewish people and its destiny in the Last Days'. His scholarly research included an extensive inquiry into dispensationalist ideology, and he edited *Christian News from Israel*. Malachy explained that dispensationalist leaders put their theological beliefs into action 'by initiating public and political action to implement the Zionist idea and the restoration of Jews to Zion'.[51]

Dispensational premillennialism as an ideology was constructed by a small circle of British zealots led by Edward Irving (1793–1834) and John Nelson Darby and it then spread to North America through Darby's personal missionary effort. Edward Irving, a minister in the Church of Scotland, became a well-known pastor in London who, later in his career, promoted the spiritual manifestation of 'speaking in tongues', which in turn influenced the later development of Pentecostalism. In 1825 he presented a controversial sermon, 'Babylon and infidelity foredoomed', in which he advanced a premillennial view that missionary work was futile because God's judgment was about to fall on the lands of the former Roman Empire that would align with the Antichrist. Missionaries and their supporters who espoused the prevailing optimistic postmillennial perspective were, naturally, incensed.

Irving and others in his circle were millenarians who understood the prophetic scripture in Daniel and Revelation as foretelling the imminent return of Christ, perhaps in the nineteenth century.[52] They interpreted the French Revolution, and the events of May 1793 in particular, as the end of the Christian era. Irving's radical perspective is central to American Christian Zionism today. Such fundamentalists in the USA today condemn as 'apostate' all Christian churches that do not subscribe to the Christian Zionist dispensationalist eschatology and the fundamentalist belief in biblical literalism and the inerrancy of the Bible. They assiduously promote the restoration of Jews to the Holy Land and predict the imminent return of Christ within their Apocalyptic End Times scenario.

The Albury Circle

How was Christian Zionism formalized into the ideology subscribed to by Fundamentalists in the USA today? Significantly, it was formalized through the use of prophetic conferences that gathered together hundreds of influential British clerical and lay activists. The prophetic conference format was to become a major engine for the transfer of the ideology to the USA and Canada.

The Albury Circle was formed in 1826 by the London banker Henry Drummond, Jr, (1786–1860). It was named after Drummond's estate, Albury Park, in Surrey, where he held a series of conferences from 1826 to 1830. Drummond recruited a small group of about 20 persons that included Way and Irving, ostensibly to study prophecy and the question of the restoration of Jews to Palestine. Drummond's own book published in 1828, *Dialogues on Prophecy*, maintained that the Last Days were imminent and that God was about to judge the visible church and return the Jewish people to Palestine.[53] Drummond felt confident that 'during the time that these judgments are falling upon Christendom, the Jews will be restored to the land.'[54]

Drummond and his circle at Albury took the position that God's plans for the Christian church were quite separate from his intention to restore the Jews' lost land. Therefore, there would be two 'dispensations', one for Christians and one for Jews. The Albury group believed that 'present Christian dispensation is not to pass into the millennial state by gradual increase of the preaching of the gospel'. They anticipated that soon, without any evangelical activity whatsoever, the Christian dispensation would be ended 'by judgements, ending in the destruction of this visible Church and polity, in the same manner as the Jewish dispensation has been terminated'. Furthermore, 'during the time that these judgements are falling upon Christendom, the Jews will be restored to their own land.'[55]

The Albury Circle's 'Last Times' or 'End Days' clearly resembled beliefs currently advocated by American fundamentalism.[56] American fundamentalists today are mesmerized by the concept of a countdown to Armageddon and the Second Coming, triggered by the establishment of the state of Israel in 1948. Christian Zionist leaders, however, are careful to not be so specific as to pin down any particular year in the future for the Second Coming. By being vague about the precise timing of their apocalyptic scenario, their interpretations of prophecy can be continually adjusted to suit the world situation of the day. Currently, led by such fundamentalist leaders as John Hagee, Christian Zionists are promoting a preventive war against Iran as part of their End Times scenario.

The theme of two separate dispensations, one for Christians and one for Jews, is also central to the ideology of today's American Christian Zionists. Significantly, using the concept of two separate dispensations, American Christian Zionists condemn what they call 'replacement theology'. This is traditionally referred to as supercessionism in the English church or substitution theology in German (*Substitutionstheologie*) and French (*théologie de la substitution*). Supercessionism, in Christian theology, regards God's relationship with Christians as superceding His prior relationship with the Israelites. Thus, in much of traditional theology, God's new covenant with the universal (Christian) Church replaces God's Mosaic covenant with Israel, and Mosaic law in particular. Hence, the Old Testament can be interpreted in light of the New Testament.

The Powerscourt Prophetic Conferences

The formulation of Christian Zionist ideology took a major step forward at the Powerscourt prophetic conferences. Edward Irving died in 1834 leaving the dispensationalist field open to John Nelson Darby. Darby participated in the Powerscourt conferences, a series of meetings held between 1830 and 1833 near Dublin at the estate of Lady Powerscourt, a widow and an active member of the Albury Circle.

The conferences proved influential, says historian LeRoy Froom (1890–1974): 'At Powerscourt Castle in Ireland (1830 and onward) … a new theory was formulated which laid the foundation for a whole new system of belief.'[57] This involved the concept of the rapture, which had been developed earlier by Edward Irving. The idea was that before the final global Tribulation envisaged in the dispensationalist end times scenario, true Christian believers would be taken bodily upwards into heaven, thereby removing them physically from the apocalyptic scenes of the Tribulation unleashed by the arrival of the Antichrist. The rapture concept, according to Froom, was

> based on the 'rapture' of the church – as referring to the resurrected and living saints being 'caught up' to meet the Lord (1 Thess. 4:17) – placed before the final tribulation leaving the rest of the world's population to go through a literal 3½ years of persecution by a future personal Antichrist, before the destruction of that tyrant by the glorious appearance of Christ.[58]

From this Powerscourt formulation of the rapture, says Froom, 'extreme Literalists expanded, systematized, and gave currency to these prophetic views'. The rapture concept is a core belief of most dispensationalists in the USA today. This concept also implies a two-stage Advent, or Second Coming:

> Thus we find introduced a double second advent completely unknown to the early church, a pretribulation rapture that stems back to Jewish traditions and from Irvingite revelations, and a Futurism traceable to the same revelations, and from the Jesuits Ribera and Lacunza, along with Maitland, the Protestant defender of Rome.[59]

Froom explains the double Second Advent as 'a preliminary coming of Christ, regarded by many as secret, to raise and transform the redeemed before the awakening of Israel', followed by the Tribulation, under the Antichrist, and then the second 'visible advent to destroy Antichrist and his hosts and to establish the millennial kingdom on earth'. Next, the Jews are to 'set up their kingdom at Jerusalem, and the survivors of the nations come up to take part in the restored Temple services', beginning the thousand-year millennium. At the millennium's end, 'Satan is unbound and leads the nations in rebellion. Then comes the destruction of the rebellious hosts by fire, the final judgment, and eternity.'[60]

This scenario, fomented at the Powerscourt conferences, is the very one adopted first by American dispensational premillennialists in the late nineteenth century and then by the American fundamentalist movement in the early twentieth century. Popularized for a mass audience in the USA during the 1970s through best-selling apocalyptic End Times novels, and through fundamentalist religious mass media outlets, it became a core belief in contemporary American fundamentalist ideology. The key vector for the transmission of this ideology to the USA during the nineteenth century was John Nelson Darby.

John Nelson Darby: Dispensationalist Vector

John Nelson Darby was ordained in the Church of Ireland in 1825, but, like Edward Irving before him, left his church denouncing both the Anglican and Dissenting churches as 'apostate'.[61] Darby became a major force within the Powerscourt network that consisted of several hundred influential evangelicals from Britain and Ireland. The Powerscourt conferences, dedicated to prophetic interpretation along the Albury Circle line, took a deeply pessimistic view of the current international situation. Darby synthesized concepts developed in the Albury Circle and Powerscourt conferences into a model that reflected this deep pessimism.

Darby asserted that God's plan as it unfolds in history divides into discrete periods of time ('dispensations') – he saw five, but his later followers detected seven. He was convinced that God has two separate purposes and plans, one for the Christian Church and one for the Jewish people. But historical Christianity – Catholic, Orthodox, and Protestant – teaches that God has one purpose, which is to redeem a people (humanity) who have a spiritual and heavenly destiny and, in this context, the Church hopes for the eventual conversion of Jews to Christianity.

Darby's dispensationalist theopolitical ideology teaches that while God's purpose for the Church is spiritual and heavenly, his purpose for the Jewish people is literal and earthly and involves the establishment of an earthly theocratic state centered physically in Jerusalem. According to Darby's view, Jews achieve salvation by keeping the Law under the Old Testament Mosaic dispensation; Christians, by faith in the New Testament. Darby thus uses the doctrine of the two dispensations developed by the Albury Circle and his formulation is that used by today's fundamentalist leaders in the USA.

Darby ultimately created his own church, The Plymouth Brethren, which established congregations in Germany, Switzerland, France, and the USA. He made seven visits to the USA and Canada during and after the American Civil War. As Sizer points out, during these visits 'he came to have an increasing influence over evangelical leaders such as James H. Brookes, D.L. Moody, William E. Blackstone, and C.I. Scofield'. Darby's missions became institutionalized in 'the emerging evangelical Bible schools and also the prophecy conferences which came to dominate both evangelicalism and fundamentalism in the USA between 1875 and 1920'.[62]

4

Christian Zionism on American Shores

During the early 1980s, during my work at the US Senate, I met the late Grace Halsell. She contacted me, wanting to talk, and we met in my office. A journalist with an unusual career at home and abroad, Grace Halsell had worked for President Lyndon Johnson in the White House. To my surprise, she wanted to discuss US policy in the Middle East and the influence of Christian Zionism on it.

The Reagan administration took office in January 1981, by which time lobbying by the Religious Right had moved full speed ahead. Having started working on Capitol Hill in August 1981, I had a ringside seat. I was already familiar with some of the players – the Jewish pro-Israel lobbyists, and the lobbyists of the Christian Right. Dealing with these groups became part of my professional responsibility. All around me, Capitol Hill offices were awash with new staffers with ties to the Religious Right.

Grace Halsell believed that near-cultic support of Israel was threatening not only the possibility of peace in the Middle East, but also America's security. At our first meeting, she gave me a copy of her new book *Journey to Jerusalem*, which focused on this theme. I was riveted by its claim that dispensationalism had become pervasive.[1] In her next book, *Prophecy and Politics*, she claims that most 'Bible schools across the land – denominational and nondenominational – teach dispensationalism and Armageddon theology'.[2]

She uses the phrase 'Armageddon theology' to describe dispensationalism and explains how dispensationalists welcome an apocalyptic nuclear war as part and parcel of the Tribulation in Darby's scenario because they believe that they will be 'raptured' to heaven at this time.

Halsell points out that stepping up the tempo of the restoration of Jews to Palestine speeds up the prophetic clock, bringing Armageddon that much closer. Modern-day dispensationalists don't regret chaotic conditions in the Middle East, she explains: where others see instability, they see evidence that the Second Advent and secret rapture will soon come.

I was naturally interested in just how this way of apocalyptic thinking arose in the USA. The key, she indicated, was John Nelson Darby, the person who brought the Armageddon theology to America.

Darby Brings Dispensationalism to the USA

John Nelson Darby's missions to North America between 1862 and 1877 firmly established dispensationalism in the USA, and it soon dominated evangelicalism. Darby's visits energized American exponents of Christian Zionism, spawned numerous Bible and prophetic conferences, and inspired an extensive network of influential Bible schools and seminaries. Darby was so effective in the USA and Canada, according to Norman Kraus, that after 1901 'for the next 50 years friend and foe alike largely identified Dispensationalism with Premillennialism'.[3] Today dispensationalism dominates the Southern Baptist Conference and strongly influences America's Pentecostal, charismatic, and Holiness movements. In all, approximately 25 million Americans subscribe to beliefs directly inspired by Darby, although some claim the number is closer to 50 million.

Throughout the late nineteenth century, American dispensationalists confronted and fought the growing influence of modern biblical criticism, the 'liberal' or 'modernist' currents in Protestantism, and the rise of the progressive Social Gospel movement. Late nineteenth-century and early twentieth-century immigration brought increasing numbers of Roman Catholics to American shores, and native proto-fundamentalist and fundamentalists reacted energetically against 'Romanism'. The confrontation led to sharp polemics in the late nineteenth century and to the formation of organized 'fundamentalism' during the first two decades of the twentieth century.

Darby, during his visits to the USA, was able to convert a number of key clergy and lay activists to his ideology of dispensationalism and, thus, to Christian Zionism.

Brookes, Moody, and Scofield

As historian Ernest Sandeen explains in his seminal study, *The Roots of Fundamentalism*, 'Darbyite dispensationalism dominated late nineteenth-century American millenarianism, formed the substance and the structure for the *Scofield Reference Bible*, and constituted one of the most significant elements in the history of Fundamentalism.'[4] Darby lived outside Britain for many years, traveling to Switzerland, Italy, France, Germany, Holland, Canada, the USA, the British West Indies, New Zealand, and Australia.[5]

Darby's North American missions produced several key home-grown promoters of dispensationalism in the USA: James H. Brookes (1830–97); Dwight L. Moody (1837–99); William Eugene Blackstone (1841–1935); and Cyrus Ingerson Scofield (1843–1921). Brookes, minister of a Presbyterian church in St Louis, Missouri, could be called the father of American dispensationalism. As Sizer emphasizes, he was 'pivotal in ensuring that the futurist dispensational views associated with the Albury and Powerscourt conferences in England and Ireland came to take root in Middle America.'[6] Brookes probably met Darby in St Louis, where the visiting dispensationalist preached in Brookes' church. Brookes himself had wide influence, thanks to his Bible study classes, his leadership of the annual Niagara Bible Conferences from 1878 to 1897, and his publications – more than 200 books and pamphlets, as well as a magazine, *The Truth*, which became an official organ of the dispensational movement.

Significantly for Americans, Brookes adopted Darby's distinction between Israel and the Church (Christianity) and argued that God's purpose was not converting Jews. Thus he argued against the traditional theological doctrine of supersession, which held that the Old Testament promises for Israel were fulfilled in the Church (Christianity). Brookes preached that 'the Jews will be literally restored to their land.'[7] Brookes' position that Jews should be physically restored to Palestine had a profound influence among clergy and lay activists and marks the rise of Christian Zionism in the USA. Historian LeRoy Froom summarizes the political implication of theological position adopted by Brookes:

Protestant Futurists [dispensationalists] returned to the chiliasm of a type that contained elements from non-Christian sources ... and they carried the early church idea of the literal kingdom on earth to an extreme, and in a direction different from anything the early church dreamed of – a kingdom of the Jews in the flesh, separate from the Christian church.[8]

Dwight L. Moody (1837–99), also strongly influenced by Darby, is best known for the Bible institute that he established in Chicago and the summer prophetic conferences he held in Northfield, Massachusetts. The latter played a leading role in the spread of Darbyite dispensationalism across the USA.[9] Sandeen sees Moody, who was never ordained, as the most influential clergyman in America during the final 20 years of the nineteenth century.[10] At the Northfield conferences, Moody introduced his followers to many British speakers he had met on his own evangelistic tours of the UK.

Dispensationalist doctrine was given wide circulation to the mass public in the USA by means of a Bible laden with annotations reflecting Darby's views. Cyrus Ingerson Scofield (1843–1921) achieved his powerful influence as a promoter of dispensationalism through the 1909 publication of the *Scofield Reference Bible* by Oxford University Press. The Scofield Bible, with extensive interpretive notes inserted by Scofield, has sold millions of copies over the years, and is used by millions of families today. Scofield was a protégé of Brookes, who introduced him to Darby. Sizer contends that 'Scofield plagiarized Darby's works, never acknowledging his sources or indebtedness to Darby'.[11] Craig Blaising, a professor at the influential dispensationalist Dallas Theological Seminary, says the Scofield Bible 'became the Bible of Fundamentalism, and the theology of the notes approached confessional status in many Bible schools, institutes and seminaries established in the early decades of this century'.[12]

Scofield's critical role in the establishment of Darby's dispensationalism in the USA cannot be underestimated or overemphasized. As Froom points out, there were various contending schools of prophetic interpretation in the USA during the late nineteenth century. It was through Scofield's influence, however, that Darby's system was institutionalized among American fundamentalists. Froom asserts:

> It should also be borne in mind that it was not until the first decade of the twentieth century that Dispensationalism, with its rapture theory, and the

separation of the 70th week from the previous 69 weeks of the years of Daniel 9, became general in the then newly forming Fundamentalist wing of Protestantism. This was largely brought about by the acceptance of Dr C.I. Scofield's bold and revolutionary thesis and the aggressive support given this postulate by the Moody Bible Institute of Chicago.[13]

Blackstone, Zionism, and US Foreign Policy

The man personally responsible for linking the American dispensationalist fundamentalists to the international political Zionist movement was William Eugene Blackstone (1841–1935). Blackstone was not a member of the clergy but rather a Chicago businessman, a friend of Brookes, and a follower of Darby. It was Blackstone who led, in 1891, the first nationally organized dispensationalist intervention into US foreign policy in support of political Zionism.

In 1887, Blackstone published *Jesus is Coming*, a tract promoting dispensationalist ideology, which urged the restoration of the Jewish people to Palestine; it was circulated widely in several editions over several decades.[14] Blackstone treated the emerging political Zionist movement in Europe as a sign that the Second Advent was imminent. In 1888, he traveled to England and then on to Palestine and Egypt to see the Holy Land himself. Returning to Chicago in 1890, he enthusiastically promoted European political Zionism, but without support from the local Jewish community. Rabbi Emil Hirsh, for example, announced that 'we modern Jews do not wish to be restored to Palestine ... the country wherein we live is our Palestine ... we will not go back ... to form a nationality of our own'.[15]

Undeterred, Blackstone entered national politics in 1891 to influence US foreign policy on behalf of international political Zionism. He promoted a petition to President Benjamin Harrison that called for an international conference dedicated to restoring the Jewish people to Palestine. Over four hundred prominent American personalities, including John and William Rockefeller, signed the 'Blackstone Memorial', and newspaper editorials across the USA endorsed it. The petition read:

> Why not give Palestine back to them again? According to God's distribution of nations, it is their home, an inalienable possession from which they were expelled by force ... Why shall not the powers which under the treaty of Berlin, in 1878, gave Bulgaria to the Bulgarians and Servia to the Servians now give Palestine back to the Jews?[16]

Blackstone's effort brought him a close working relationship with Louis Brandeis, the first Jewish Justice of the US Supreme Court and a leading American political Zionist.[17]

It would take more than Blackstone and his group of philanthropically minded American enthusiasts to promote Christian Zionism on a mass basis. First, such a work would require an institutional basis. Second, it would require time and patience so that sufficient numbers of American fundamentalists could be organized and mobilized to form a mass base in support of the foreign policy demands of Christian Zionism. These demands sought official US government support for the restoration of Jews to Palestine, for the creation of a Jewish state in Palestine, and for the support of the Jewish state in Palestine by the USA.

The Prophetic Bible Conference Movement

The required institutional infrastructure to support Christian Zionism involved the founding of nationwide Bible conferences together with Fundamentalist Bible colleges, institutes, and seminaries. The series of Niagara Bible Conferences 'was the mother of them all' and 'virtually everyone of significance in the history of the American millenarian movement during this period attended.'[18] The conferences grew out of the Believers' Meeting for Bible Study, which began in New York City in 1868. The conferences, initiated by dispensationalist James Inglis, a New York City Baptist minister, were later held at Queen's Royal Hotel, Niagara-On-the-Lake, Ontario, and so came to be called the Niagara Bible Conferences. Among those present were key leaders of the movement, including Blackstone, Scofield, Charles Erdman, William Moorehead, Adoniram Judson Gordon, Amzi Dixon, and James Hudson Taylor. Another series of British prophetic conferences, the Mildmay Second Advent Conference (1878, 1879, and 1886), held outside London at Mildmay Park, reinforced the Anglo-American ties and interaction between the parallel interconnected millennial movements.

The Niagara Bible Conferences influenced the spread of an extensive and powerful Bible conference movement and its leaders assisted the establishment of, and gave direction to, such conferences across the USA. The Bible institutes and the Bible college movement were similarly inspired. So powerful was the influence of the Niagara Bible Conferences that almost all such schools established before 1930 received advice and personnel from those associated with them. In addition, the conferences also spawned a vast new literature on prophecy and inspired many Christian businessmen across the USA to support churches, schools, missions, and publications.[19]

As historian Stewart Cole explains, dispensationalists and their allies 'believed that their religion was the only divinely acceptable one'. Their activity to support this belief resulted in the 'prophetic conference movement, professional evangelism, Bible schools, tractarian propaganda, and polemic preaching'. In 1876, the first prophetic Bible conference was held at Swampscott, Massachusetts, followed by an important conference in New York City that promoted extreme Adventism and assailed postmillennial theologians. Cole notes that 'the editor of the proceedings advertised the addresses as "a very encyclopedia of pre-millenarianism by the ablest expositors"'.[20] A follow-on conference in Chicago further galvanized support for the dispensationalists.[21] Regional Bible conferences were established at Winona, Indiana, and Denver, Colorado. Local conferences were also established, especially in the agricultural regions of the Middle West.

The Niagara leaders strengthened the prophetic conference movement through separately held conferences of national importance. The First American Bible and Prophetic Conference took place in New York City in 1878. Its success led to the convening of the Second American Bible and Prophetic Conference, which took place in Chicago in 1886. The third conference in the series took place in Allegheny, Pennsylvania, in 1895. Important associated conferences took place in Philadelphia (1887) and in Baltimore (1890).[22]

From an ideological standpoint, the Niagara Conference of 1895 was particularly significant. Gasper explains:

> The conservatives at that conference declared that traditional Protestant Christianity must be regarded as having five important and indispensable poles: (1) the inerrancy of the Scriptures, (2) the virgin birth, (3) the deity of Jesus Christ, (4) the substitutionary atonement, and (5) the physical resurrection of Jesus Christ and His bodily return.[23]

Gasper points out that these five points anticipated the 1910 formulation that became central to American fundamentalism.

Cole, writing in 1931, puts the political agenda of the Christian Right of his era and the social context in which it operated into clear perspective. Of the Bible conference movement he said that:

[it] represented 50 years of conservatives' effort to maintain their Christian witness in a cultural situation that was slipping from their control ... this fellowship was an 'issue' movement, in which the biblical resources of literalism were constantly being pressed against the new cultural standards of the day.[24]

Indeed, the political utility of a conservative religious movement did not escape the purview of secular business and financial interests in the late nineteenth and early twentieth century era of reform and progressive politics. Cole's analysis of the Christian Right as an 'issue movement' well describes its role in American politics generally and its role in support of pro-Israel foreign policy in particular.

Bible Schools, Institutes, and Seminaries

Christian Zionism was institutionalized by means of educational entities established by dispensationalists. A wide network of institutions helped insulate the fundamentalist movement from the negative publicity of the Scopes Trial and helped perpetuate its ideology through the twentieth century.[25]

The first Bible school in North America was established in Nyack, New York, in 1882 by A.B. Simpson, the Canadian founder of the Christian and Missionary Alliance.[26] The Moody Bible Institute followed in Chicago in 1887. The Toronto Bible Training School, established in 1894 as the first permanent Canadian Bible school and the third in North America, modeled itself on the Moody Institute. Stewart Cole explains in his *History of Fundamentalism*, 'Ultraconservatives founded Bible schools to correct the views of the liberal seminaries.' The Moody Bible Institute, originally the Chicago Evangelist Society, 'typified the intent of this educational movement'.[27]

Many similar prominent Bible schools were founded at the same time. They include Northwestern Bible Training School in Minneapolis, established in 1902, which later had Billy Graham as its president between 1948 and 1952.[28] Graham, a member of the Southern Baptist Convention, was educated at the conservative Wheaton College in Illinois. The Bible Institute of Los Angeles was established in 1908 by Lyman Stewart, then president of the Union Oil company, now UNOCAL.[29] Cyrus Scofield himself, in 1914, founded The Philadelphia School of the Bible, which merged in 1951 with the Bible Institute of Philadelphia and is now the Philadelphia Biblical University.[30] The Dallas Theological Seminary, a major force promoting fundamentalism and dispensationalist ideology, began in 1924 as the Evangelical Theological College.[31] It was an outgrowth of the Southwestern School of the Bible headed by Cyrus Scofield during his years as a Dallas pastor. John F. Walvoord, a graduate of Dallas Theological Seminary and a former president of the school (1952–86), is known for his prominent role in advancing premillennial ideology in the post-Second World War era. Sizer says the school 'became dispensationalism's most influential and academic institution'.[32]

Institutionalizing dispensationalist ideology helped mitigate the negative public relations impact of the Scopes Trial in 1925. Any rumors of the death of dispensationalism were much exaggerated. In fact, the ideology persisted and became fully entrenched within the fundamentalist movement in a consolidation phase during the 1930s – during which it also continued to attack mainstream American Protestantism.

Myriad fundamentalist Bible institutes, Bible schools, and seminaries provided continuity through the 1930s and into the 1940s, when the movement actively engaged in national politics. Fundamentalists focused on domestic as well as on foreign policy issues. The entry into foreign policy issues involved the militant Christian anti-communist crusades of the late 1940s and 1950s. The early Cold War era context, exemplified by the Communist takeover of China, the Korean War, and McCarthyism, heightened fundamentalists' attention to international affairs. During this period Carl McIntire, and his American Council of Christian Churches, were at the forefront of militant fundamentalist political activism in both domestic and foreign affairs.

Part II

Christian Zionism and American Foreign Policy, 1917–48

5

Fundamentalism, the First World War, and Palestine

The First World War era saw the rise of dispensationalist-dominated American fundamentalism. During this period, the movement established itself, became well organized, and developed an institutional infrastructure. Publication of *The Fundamentals* between 1910 and 1915, a series of volumes containing chapters by an array of conservative clergy and theologians, served to formalize doctrine and gave rise to the term 'Fundamentalist'.[1] Specialized conferences such as the Moody Bible Institute conference of 1914 moved the process forward. Two major events in 1917 – the capture of Palestine and Jerusalem by the British and the Bolshevik Revolution – impressed premillennialists as portentous 'signs of the times', and thus indicators of an approaching Second Coming.

War with Germany gave fundamentalists a 'patriotic' opportunity to attack modern German biblical criticism and to include political action in their agenda. Furthermore, as war threatened to dissolve the Ottoman Empire, the perennial Eastern Question came to a head: the future of Palestine and the Holy Places was uncertain, at best.[2]

British war objectives in the Near East focused on military defeat of the Ottoman Empire and on diplomatic disposition of territories such as Palestine and Mesopotamia, to be taken away from the Ottomans.[3] The British leadership considered this region vital to British imperial interests regarding

India, Egypt, and oil. Adequate supply of hydrocarbons rightly worried British wartime planners, since modernization of the British fleet would replace coal-fired ships with oil-fueled ones. Consideration of the hydrocarbon supply was also a significant consideration in the management of the vast oil-consuming railroad system in British India.

Since, at the time, Britain had no known oil deposits, it had to locate and secure foreign sources. Prior to the war, Britain established access to hydrocarbon resources in Persia and the Anglo-Persian Oil Company was, therefore, established to supply the Admiralty.[4] During and after the war, the considerable hydrocarbon potential of Mesopotamia drove British policy in what was to become Iraq.[5] In the First World War Britain was dependent upon the USA for some 80 per cent of its oil requirements. To avoid such dependency in the future, other arrangements were sought in order to establish independent sources under British control. This logic of British-controlled sourcing was strongly endorsed by the Admiralty, which, naturally, was concerned about post-war imperial defence and the global operations of the fleet.[6]

What was to become Iraq under British tutelage had formerly been three *vilayets* of the Ottoman Empire: Basra, Baghdad, and Mosul. Over the centuries, the Ottomans created various *vilayets* as administrative districts under military control but with civilian administration. The Mosul *vilayet* was known prior to the First World War to have hydrocarbon deposits and thus became included in the creation of Iraq. The oil potential in upper Mesopotamia also influenced British planning for the disposition of adjacent Palestine, since railroads and other infrastructure could be extended from the Mediterranean port of Haifa into Mesopotamia.[7] In that event, Palestine would serve as a strategic outpost protecting Egypt and the Suez Canal, the routes to India, and the hydrocarbons of Mesopotamia.[8] The British could not openly annex regions in the post-war international environment; instead, they maintained control behind the façade of the mandate system of the League of Nations and through directly or indirectly controlled local rulers.[9]

The Palestine question was sensitive. Through the centuries, the control over the Holy Places of Palestine has been hard fought.[10] As observed by Sir William Fitzgerald:

> The whole history of the world cannot contain many words such so touch the depths of human emotion. The Temple of Solomon, its western wall existing to this very day; Golgotha, the scene of the Crucifixion; the Mosque al-Aqsa;

the Dome of the Rock; these four places are the revered shrines of three of the world's greatest religions, and all four are situated within the walls of Jerusalem. Hence the complexity of the political issue.[11]

Conveniently premillennialists in North America, and in Britain, heralded the British military victory in Palestine in 1917 and capture of Jerusalem as the prime 'sign of the times' of the era triggering the apocalyptic clock that would herald the arrival of the Second Advent at any moment. In such a perspective, the control of Palestine had been wrested from the Muslim world and was now under Christian control thanks to Sir Edmund Allenby and Great Britain. Thus, dispensationalist ideology reinforced British wartime propaganda and strategic policy.

Fundamentalism and Big Business

By the 1920s, political action by fundamentalist mass movements alarmed many observers. Kirsopp Lake, professor of early Christian history at Harvard University, presciently warned, 'there is the terrible danger of political exploitation, and the creation of a "Christian bloc", whose votes will be obtained by politicians willing to pass laws to enforce summarily good conduct and right opinion on all matters'.[12] The emergence a half-century later of the 'New' Christian Right in American politics confirms Lake's concern. Lake explained his reasoning:

> It is not difficult for any large group, who have set their hearts on some one thing to obtain a Legislature almost unanimous in their favour, if they steadfastly refuse to vote for any candidate who is not pledged to their support. They can even bring it about so that it will be scarcely respectable to differ openly from them; though in private it may appear obvious that a majority is not really on that side.[13]

Lake's concerns reflect his own experience during a decade of academic life in the Netherlands. There he saw a Christian rightist theological and political movement in action. His own observations of the rise of the extremely conservative 'neo-Calvinist' (*Gereformeerd*) religious movement to political power in the Netherlands sparked his concern about a potential similar phenomenon in the USA. Today in the USA, influential circles in the Religious Right have specifically adopted the neo-Calvinist theology of this Dutch movement as well as its theocratic political concepts.

The political party of the Dutch religious movement was called The Anti-Revolutionary Party (ARP – *Anti-Revolutionaire Partij*). It had its roots in Dutch politics of the 1840s among those opposed to the spirit of the French Revolution. The political party itself was founded in 1879 by Abraham Kuyper (1837–1920) who, with other religious leaders, broke from the national Dutch Reformed Church to found their own separatist denomination. This denomination, a union of several splinter groups, in 1892 was called the Reformed Church in the Netherlands (*Gereformeerde Kerken in Nederland*). Lake likened the Dutch neo-Calvinists to the rising fundamentalist movement in the USA.

Lake's concerns extended to the ability of financial and industrial interests to use such a religious movement and political party for their own purposes. That is, he saw these could be used to reinforce unregulated laissez-faire capitalism, if not oligarchic control of an economy:

> There is also a more sinister cause which may enormously help Fundamentalism. It may appear to large financial interests that industrial stability can be safeguarded by Fundamentalists who can be trusted to teach 'anti-revolutionary' doctrine in politics and economics as well as in theology. This consideration gained much support in Holland for the Calvinist party in the first decades of this century.[14]

His observation is apt. For example, financing for *The Fundamentals*, a dispensationalist Bible school, and missionary activity came from Lyman and Milton Stewart, both California oil barons. They also financed the re-publication and mass national distribution of Blackstone's *Jesus is Coming*.[15]

Currently in the USA, a number of fundamentalist organizations, such as the Acton Institute based in Grand Rapids, Michigan, advocate unregulated laissez-faire capitalism as biblically sanctioned.[16] And there is continuity with fundamentalist support of unregulated laissez-faire capitalism a century ago. Lake wrote at a time when the fiery conservative evangelist Billy Sunday (1862–1935) had made a profound impact on the American scene. William Martin in his book *With God on Our Side* says

> His economic views consisted of an unreflective espousal of laissez-faire free enterprise ... he counted among his friends and benefactors such names as Rockefeller, Morgan, Carnegie, Wanamaker, McCormick, Armour, Swift, Edison, and Marshall Field ... his wealthy backers must have

found it comforting – and useful – to have the best-known religious figure in the nation championing economic principles that sanctioned their favored positions in society.[17]

Writing some four decades after Lake, David Moberg raised the same comparative issue in a scholarly article:

Certain forces in American society appear either to be planned intentionally to establish vertical pluralism in America or to have latent consequences that may result in it. The historical events and social forces that led to Dutch vertical pluralism and certain analogous trends in contemporary American society support this conclusion.[18]

Moberg noted that membership in the traditional Dutch Reformed Church fell as the neo-Calvinists rapidly rose. The rise over the past several decades of a well-funded and politically active, if not militant, Religious Right in the USA, and falling membership in mainline churches, lends credibility to Moberg's and Lake's analyses.

The Rise of Organized Fundamentalism

Fundamentalism required a recognized body of doctrine as well as the means to promote it. The annotated *Scofield Reference Bible*, first published in 1909, was a major step forward.[19] Next came *The Fundamentals* (1910–15), and according to Cole, in their publication 'the historian finds the clear emergence of fundamentalism'. Referring to clergy, he says, 'the fundamentalist was opposed to social change, particularly as it threatened the standards of his faith and his status in ecclesiastical circles'.[20] With the publication of *The Fundamentals* 'they delivered their orthodox manifesto as a test of Christian loyalty and as a corrective to the position of liberations'. Significantly, he says, this event 'gave the party an aggressive policy and a consciousness of social solidarity in an urgent cause'.[21] Cole believes that 'The far-reaching influence of *The Fundamentals* can scarcely be measured. *The Fundamentals* having accomplished their leavening work, and the war psychology having concentrated religious militancy, *conservatives* became the fundamentalist movement'. In his assessment, 'they undertook reformative measures beyond the church with a view to checking the standards of secular culture and substituting the principles of their historic faith'.[22]

After a decade-long lull, prophetic conferences were revived as a mechanism to promote dispensationalism across the USA. In February 1914, the Moody Bible Institute convened a singularly important prophetic conference.[23] Sandeen points out, 'unlike its predecessor of 1901, this conference clearly and forcefully advocated the Darbyite pretribulationist position'. Sandeen emphasizes that at 'no previous conference was the emphasis upon the details of the Darbyite dispensationalist doctrines so explicit and dogmatic as at this gathering'.[24] The conference inspired a raft of 22 similar meetings the following summer, to which the Moody Bible Institute gave its moral support.[25] National prophetic conferences were held in Philadelphia and New York during 1918, a critical year of the World War.[26] The Philadelphia conference was held in May at the Philadelphia Academy of Music, in a hall seating over three thousand. In 1919, a World's Bible Conference was held at Philadelphia and the opening conference of the World's Christian Fundamentals Association had a distinctly political orientation.

International events, such as the capture of Jerusalem by the British under Sir Edmund Allenby in December 1917, powerfully affected premillennialists in Britain and North America. Several prophetic conferences were subsequently organized and, following the intense activity of British premillennialists, a group of Philadelphia businessmen organized the Philadelphia conference. Another perceived 'sign of the times' was the Bolshevik Revolution in Russia then underway. The Communist takeover of Russia was interpreted in literalist apocalyptic terms as referring to the power from 'the North' that would threaten the restored Israel in the End Times scenario of the Darbyite dispensationalists. From the very start, Zionism–Israel and Communism–Russia became closely intertwined in the minds of American fundamentalists.[27] These political issues received heightened attention and emphasis after the start of the Cold War confrontation between the West and the Soviet Union following the Second World War, after the foundation of Israel in 1948, and after the Six Day War of 1967 in which Israel dealt the Arabs a devastating blow and reunified the city of Jerusalem.

The disposition of the Ottoman Empire after the First World War was a vital concern of the allied powers, particularly given the hydrocarbon dimension – not to mention the international Zionist movement that was focused on creating Jewish state in Palestine.

Wartime Strategy and Palestine

Since nineteenth-century British policy with respect to the Eastern Question required supporting the Ottoman Empire against Russian and French designs, Britain had tried to ensure the neutrality of Turkey well before the First World War. But when the Ottoman Empire joined the Central Powers in August 1914, the situation changed completely and the issue of the eventual disposition of the Arab territories naturally arose. Thus the shift to belligerency by the Ottoman Empire in 1914 necessarily caused a profound reassessment of British war aims.[28]

In the First World War, the Entente, composed of Britain, France, Russia, and Italy (after 1915), faced the Central Powers composed of the German, Austro-Hungarian, and Ottoman Empires. The USA joined the Entente war effort in 1917 and sent the American Expeditionary Force only to the European theater as a result, but there was no state of belligerency between the USA and the Ottoman Empire.[29] Some American circles had hoped to hasten the end of the war by arranging a separate peace initiative involving Turkey but this concept came to naught.[30] If successful such an initiative would have complicated, or possibly vitiated, the plans of political Zionism, which counted upon the dismemberment of Turkey so as to open Palestine for massive Jewish settlement. Russia withdrew from the Entente following the Bolshevik seizure of power in the 1917 Russian Revolution and renounced the Sykes-Picot arrangements and any claims to Ottoman territories. The Sykes-Picot arrangements called for a division of the spoils of the Ottoman Empire between Britain, France, and Russia.

The defeat of the Ottoman Empire in the First World War potentially opened the door to Russian, French, and Italian influence in the Levant.[31] British policy, therefore, sought ways to manage and minimize this potential problem for access to, and control of, the hydrocarbons in the Mesopotamian basin – not to mention the potential problem for control of Egypt and the strategic routes to India.[32] The solution followed by London for this strategic problem involved British post-war control over Mesopotamia and Palestine, albeit veiled behind the Palestine Mandate and the Iraq Mandate under the League of Nations cover.[33] Even after its emancipation from the Mandate in 1932, Iraq was still controlled indirectly through British influence over King Faisal (1883–1933; ruled 1921–1933), King Ghazi I (1912–39; ruled 1933–9), and King Faisal II (1935–58; ruled 1939–58).

British policy toward the Middle East – Palestine and Mesopotamia in particular – was not unified. Politicians in and out of government as well as among policymakers in various governmental settings debated it bitterly. Not surprisingly, strategic policy, necessarily, had something of an ad hoc character, in the shifting international context and fortunes of wartime. The British Admiralty's overriding consideration was access to, and direct British control of, hydrocarbon resources for the post-war imperial fleet, like that achieved earlier via the Anglo-Persian Oil Company.[34] The Foreign Office and Arab Bureau, for their parts, took a generally 'pro-Arab' view, encouraged pan-Arabism, and made plans to set up various monarchies in the former Ottoman territories.[35] The India Office, considering oil requirements for the Indian railway system and the situation of the Muslim population in India, generally took the position that the British Empire should simply annex Mesopotamia and Palestine.[36]

Post-war planning for the region, however, was complicated for the British because of incompatible political commitments to political Zionists and Arab rulers. The Balfour Declaration on Palestine created a problem for post-war British planning because its promises to the international political Zionist movement appeared to conflict with promises made to Arab leaders.[37] Extensive scholarly literature still debates just what was and what was not promised to each side.[38] The 'declaration' – actually a letter of intent to Lord Rothschild, dated 2 November 1917 and signed by Balfour – avowed that the government supported the establishment in Palestine of a 'national home' for the Jewish people. The promise to establish a 'national home' for the Jewish people in Arab Palestine appeared to imply the potential erection of a full-blown sovereign Jewish state at some point in the future. This is how many Zionist leaders understood it and, of course, such a state was declared in 1948.[39]

The British establishment, meanwhile, split into factions over political Zionism and the Balfour Declaration's implications for British Middle East policy.[40] The Asquith government (1908–16) was somewhat cool to political Zionism, but the Lloyd George government (1916–22) embraced it wholeheartedly.[41] Lloyd George himself was considered a friend of political Zionism. As British historian Philip Guedalla said in 1925 in a London speech to the Jewish Historical Society, he was the 'Christian to whom the Jews of the world are more indebted than to any other living statesman – a man who has always tried to help them by word and deed'.[42]

Lloyd George himself was frank about British support for political Zionism in his remarks at the same meeting. 'We also made an appeal to your great people,' he said. 'Unlike Napoleon – let us be quite frank – our motives were mixed ... Therefore we wanted your help. We thought it would be useful.' At the same time that the former Prime Minister insisted that 'there is no reason why Jews should be kept out of their country', he stopped far short of the maximalist demands of political Zionists. 'It is not our conception,' he said, 'and I am certain it is not the conception of Zionists, that anyone should be driven out of Palestine who does not want to go.' On this point he stated, 'Palestine was never a land exclusively of Jews.'[43] Closing the meeting, the Chief Rabbi of the British Empire, Dr Hertz, praised Lloyd George in the following words:

> Like Cyrus of old, the Prime Minister, who authorized the issuance of the Balfour Declaration, who secured to Great Britain the mandate for Palestine from the League of Nations, who appointed a Jew as the first High Commissioner of Eretz Yisrael, may rightly be said to have opened a new chapter in the world-old story of the latter-day descendants of the exiles who wept by the rivers of Babylon when they remembered Zion.[44]

The controversy over the Balfour Declaration reflected the broader – and wholly changed – situation in the Middle East, brought about by the partition of the former Ottoman Empire. With respect to the territorial issue, Dov Gavish explains that at the time of the Balfour Declaration 'demands were made by the Zionists for a cadastral survey of the country in order to identify state-owned, waste and unoccupied lands to provide for the establishment of the Jewish national home.'[45]

Between 1921 and 1923 strong sentiment in Britain, as represented by Lord Curzon for example, supported nullifying the Balfour Declaration, arguing that it had lost its wartime expediency and had become provocative and destabilizing.[46] In the end, Prime Minister Lloyd George and his Secretary of State for the Colonies, Winston Churchill, resolved to continue the Balfour Declaration's commitments to political Zionism.

The USA, which had not been at war with the Ottoman Empire, had a guarded reaction to the Balfour Declaration, which was subject to considerable debate in official circles.[47] This soon changed. President Wilson became more enthusiastic about political Zionism and began to endorse a Jewish commonwealth. Historian Kathleen Christison points out:

> By 1920 the frame of reference in which the Arabs of Palestine were viewed was already firmly set. Palestine had begun to be considered a Jewish land, the Arabs of Palestine had all along been ignored or disdained, and the United States was committed, in the absence of any pressing interest to the contrary, to supporting Zionism.[48]

American political Zionists made expansive territorial claims indeed. As Christison observes, 'US Zionists began insisting that the Balfour Declaration was committed to making all of Palestine a Jewish national home rather than simply, as the declaration actually stated, to forming a Jewish national home *in* Palestine.'[49] US Supreme Court Justice Louis Brandeis, the leader of the American Zionist movement at the time, even told Balfour in Paris in 1919 that all of Palestine would have to be the Jewish homeland. Christison points out that 'the US Congress, even at this early date, was fairly enthusiastic in its support for Zionism.'[50]

The door was opened to an eventual Jewish state in Palestine as the Ottoman Empire was portioned out between the British and the French. The Allies addressed the partition of the Ottoman Empire at the Conference of London in February 1920 and at the San Remo Conference in April 1920 and incorporated the terms in the Treaty of Sèvres, signed in August 1920. The USA did not participate in these negotiations as it had not been at war with Turkey. The Treaty of Sèvres awarded Britain the mandates for Palestine and Iraq and awarded France the mandate for Syria, which then included Lebanon. The specific boundaries of these territories were not decided upon until four years later. In the meantime, however, Turkey mounted a war of independence and rejected the Treaty of Sèvres. The Council of the League of Nations confirmed the arrangements made by the Treaty of Sèvres in July 1922; and the Treaty of Lausanne in 1923 then finalized the process of partition of the former Ottoman Empire. The text of the League of Nations mandate for Palestine incorporated the Balfour Declaration – and thereby embedded the 'national home' project for the restoration of the Jewish people to Palestine into international law. With respect to the Palestine mandate, separate conventions between Britain and the USA were negotiated and agreed to in 1924–5 because the USA was not a member of the League of Nations system.[51]

With the League of Nations mandate in place, Britain had to adjust to its new responsibilities. The Lloyd George government required an institutional reorganization to streamline and implement its policy in the changed Middle East. Churchill became Secretary of State for the Colonies in 1921. In that year, he was victorious in inter-departmental maneuvering over jurisdiction for the Middle East and so he created the new Middle East Department for the Colonial Office. Prior to its creation, the government shifted the administration of Palestine from military to civilian control.

Lloyd George appointed Herbert Samuel, an ardent and able political Zionist, as High Commissioner, and Samuel arrived in June 1920 to assume his authority over the administration from 1 July.[52] Churchill's Colonial Office Middle East Department was regarded as pro-Zionist and it took over the former responsibilities of the India Office for the region in question. Helmut Mejcher explains that 'its sphere of control covered the Arabian Sea, the Red Sea, and the "outlying properties" of Egypt and the Northern Kurds, and Persia'. Within this geographic area, Churchill, according to Mejcher, 'considered vital the control in the triangle Jerusalem–Basra–Aden which he called the ringfence'.[53]

Churchill favored Zionism from a humanitarian point of view.[54] He stated:

> It has fallen to the British Government, as a result of the conquest of Palestine, to have the opportunity and the responsibility of securing for the Jewish race all over the world a home and a centre of national life.[55]

Churchill also foresaw the possible emergence of a Jewish state and, for strategic reasons, wanted it linked to the British Empire:

> But if, as may well happen, there should be created in our own lifetime by the banks of the Jordan a Jewish State under the protection of the British Crown, which might comprise three or four millions of Jews, an event would have occurred in the history of the world which would, from every point of view, be beneficial, and would be especially in harmony with the truest interests of the British Empire.[56]

He strongly endorsed the Balfour Declaration. 'The statesmanship and historic sense of Mr Balfour were prompt to seize the opportunity,' he said. 'Declarations have been made which have irrevocably decided the policy of Great Britain.' And Churchill pointed to General Allenby, saying the Zionist project in Palestine was 'supported by the full authority of General Allenby'.[57]

Allenby, Jerusalem, and War Propaganda

Like their co-religionists in Britain, dispensationalists in the USA closely followed the Palestine situation looking for 'signs of the times' and fulfillment of what they considered biblical prophecy. For them a twentieth-century Palestine, and Jerusalem, under Christian control was a powerful symbol prefiguring the Last Days and the Second Coming. Just how closely Christian Zionists followed developments in modern Palestine may be gauged by examining the program offered at the 1918 Philadelphia prophetic conference. A.E. Thompson, pastor of the American Church in Jerusalem, delivered an address pointing out the biblical prophetic significance of Allenby's capture of Jerusalem on 9 December and his entry into the city on 11 December, indicating Jerusalem had been liberated from Muslim control. Following Thompson, James M. Gray, an editor of the Scofield Bible and dean of the Moody Bible Institute, delivered an address entitled 'The regathering of Israel in unbelief'. The coded phrase 'in unbelief' meant Jews returned to Palestine without recognizing Jesus as their saviour.[58] As Sandeen explains, the dispensationalists 'almost instinctively, grasped the significance of Allenby's capture of Jerusalem and celebrated the event as the fulfillment of prophecy.'[59]

American Catholics, and American Jews supporting political Zionism, also followed the developments in Palestine, but had rather different visions of the future disposition of Palestine and Jerusalem. The British Ambassador at Washington, Sir Cecil Spring-Rice, reported to Balfour that the Cardinal of New York desired Jerusalem to be under the Franciscans and felt that the British government should proclaim the intention of keeping Jerusalem a Christian city. 'At the same time,' Spring-Rice reported, 'I have received many communications from distinguished Israelites who desire my participation in various meetings concerned with the capture of Jerusalem and the future of the Zionist party.'[60]

But the diplomatic situation was complicated because the USA was not at war with the Ottoman Empire. Spring-Rice explained that

> After consultation with the State Department, we agreed upon the following course of action. American Jews, being American citizens, should not have direct relations as such with the foreign representative on a question affecting American policy. The USG [US government] had not declared war on Turkey, and could not participate in any scheme for the partition of Turkey.

Overt acts of sympathy from the State Department, and consequently from a foreign representative, would not be correct and could not be asked for.[61]

Spring-Rice found considerable complexity in the attitude of American Jews toward the British Empire and toward France:

> How far you can build on re-establishing really good and cordial relations with the large Jewish population in this country by a friendly attitude to the Zionist movement is not very certain. The great mass of the Jews appear to be bitterly opposed to the Zionist leaders, and the rich Jews are divided among themselves.[62]

With respect to France, he reported that 'the Jews seem to have great anxiety lest the French Government should come forward as a violent and uncompromising advocate of the claims of Syrian Catholics'. Perhaps it was after rereading his own report that the ambassador concluded it by telling Balfour that 'you must feel rather like the bear who stole the hornet's nest'.[63]

British propaganda for the Palestine campaign was a matter of intense activity.[64] Lloyd George, well aware of the religious symbolism of the struggle over Palestine and Jerusalem and its propaganda value, ordered Allenby to capture Jerusalem before Christmas. Allenby initiated the battle on 19 September 1918 with the assistance of Arab forces and used airpower and artillery to overcome the Turkish forces. The front broken, Allenby rapidly advanced and took Damascus on 1 October and Aleppo on 26 October, after which a ceasefire came into effect.

While London naturally wanted the glory of military victory in Palestine, it did not want to offend and provoke some one hundred million Muslims within the British Empire. The popular press jumped on the Palestine campaign as a 'new' or 'last' Crusade; a raft of Crusade-themed books appeared and similar propagandistic films were screened. Officially, however, the government's Department of Information issued a notice to the press on 15 November 1917, advising:

> The attention of the Press is again drawn to the undesirability of publishing any article, paragraph or picture suggesting that military operations against Turkey are in any sense a Holy War, a modern Crusade, or have anything whatever to do with religious questions. The British Empire is said to contain a hundred million Mohammedan subjects of the King and it is obviously mischievous to suggest that our quarrel with Turkey is one between Christianity and Islam.[65]

Of the propaganda campaign, Eiton Bar-Yosef concludes:

> Notwithstanding its genuine strategic objectives or its complex historical consequences, the Palestine campaign was consciously staged by the British government as an exercise in propaganda, shaped, filtered and capitalized on in order to enhance the nation's morale. Palestine, after all, was unlike any other imperial catch. It was the Holy Land, steeped in religious and historical memories: few seemed more germane than Richard Coeur de Lion's failure to win Jerusalem.[66]

Bar-Yosef, however, distinguishes between the medieval Crusade myth, which the elites assimilated, and the Old and New Testament associations held by the mass public. 'For the majority of the British people,' he says, 'Jerusalem and the Holy Land evoked first and foremost not memories of medieval conquests and European expansion, but rather the sacred memories of the Old and New Testaments.' This popular sentiment, he says, 'invoked a "Jerusalem" which was associated, somewhat self-reflexively, with vernacular religious traditions, with hymns and sermons, Sunday school classes and the family Bible.'[67] North American premillennialists adopted this perspective, and it was reinforced by the close associations and projects of American, Canadian, and British dispensationalists.

Bar-Yosef suggests that the Holy Land theme 'played a more momentous role in the evolution of modern Britain's imperial ethos than has perhaps been realized.'[68] While scholarly research pointed to Protestant biblical discourse as an element in British imperialism, what was overlooked was 'the way in which this imperial quest was conceived and performed in relations to the *geographical* Holy Land.'[69] British foreign policy intentionally sought to prevent the possibility of a Muslim Holy War against Britain, particularly a Muslim uprising in India.

The British Arab Bureau, therefore, sought to align with, if not spark, the trend toward Arab nationalism in order to bring Arab leaders to the allied side during the war. Bar-Yosef argues that, in order to minimize Muslim hostility, the British engaged in a conscious and concerted effort to counterbalance the Balfour Declaration's impact. The War Office characterized Allenby as a 'restorer of justice and fairness among all creeds rather than the arrogant conqueror that the Kaiser would have been.'[70] To keep him in character, it scripted a ceremonial entry into Jerusalem, ordering Allenby to dismount and proceed on foot into the fallen city. This remarkable piece of theater scrupulously avoided overt Christian symbolism, instead making continuous references to Caliph Omar and his gracious act of protecting the Church of the Holy Sepulchre.

For propaganda outside the Holy Land, Sir Percy Sykes insisted on what Bar-Yosef calls 'a conscious emphasis on the biblical associations of Jerusalem and Palestine'. Lloyd George himself promoted this theme in a speech in the House of Commons on 20 December 1917. Bar-Yosef emphasizes this appeal to popular religious culture, arguing that it 'was centred around biblical language and was characterized by highly literalized, often naively personal, readings of Scripture'.[71] Such a popular religious culture and biblical literalist discourse was, of course, part and parcel of the dispensationalist and fundamentalist world then mesmerized by the prophetic significance of the taking of Jerusalem by Allenby.

British propaganda was careful to emphasize the military action, which the War Office labeled the 'Battle of Megiddo'. The choice of the word Megiddo, the biblical Hebrew name for Armageddon, was a coded way of directly engaging dispensationalists who placed the battle within their End Times scenario.[72] According to Bar-Yosef, 'The fact that the field of battle was quite remote from the actual biblical Megiddo suggests that this was yet another conscious act of mythmaking'. Indeed, later Allenby was known as 'Marshal Viscount Allenby of Megiddo and Felixstowe'. Allenby's campaign in Palestine also became the subject of a 1923 film, entitled *Armageddon*.[73]

6

Christian Zionism from the First World War to the Second World War

During the interwar period, fundamentalists kept a low profile in the wake of the negative publicity fallout from the Scopes case, consolidated their movement, and saw the ominous international situation as a continued fulfillment of prophecy.[1] Dispensationalists saw international communism backed by Stalin's regime and the rise of Hitler and the Nazi regime as portentous 'signs of the times', which reinforced their End Times apocalyptic view. The Nazi regime's evil brutality forced European Jews to seek shelter abroad and increased the flow of refugees to Palestine.[2] From the dispensationalist perspective, this movement of Jewish refugees looked like nothing so much as the fulfillment of prophecy – namely, the restoration of the Jewish people to Palestine.

The consolidation of the American fundamentalist movement during this period is significant as it prepared the way for the high-profile Christian 'anti-communist crusades' of the early Cold War period. These, in turn, resulted in the establishment of the politically active 'New Christian Right' during the 1970s. 'To fully understand the New Christian Right,' Clyde Wilcox points out, 'it is important to understand the political history of evangelical, fundamentalist, and charismatic activity in this century.'[3]

The fundamentalist revolt of the 1920s, in its battle against modernism, focused on a campaign against the teaching of evolution in public schools. The resulting Scopes trial, pitting advocates and critics of the teaching of Darwin's theory of evolution against each other, with its national notoriety, ended in a ruling seen widely as a defeat for the fundamentalist movement. Fundamentalist leaders then shifted to an emphasis on anti-communism as support for their crusade against teaching evolution in public schools waned.[4] Vigorous anticommunism fit neatly with the dispensationalist eschatological perspective. Christ's Second Advent comes prior to or during the final battle of Armageddon, which pits the forces of God against the Antichrist and invaders from 'the North' – a direction traditionally taken by dispensationalists from their interpretation of Ezekiel 38:1–2 as referring to the country of Russia. And, of course, in Darbyite doctrine, the threat from the 'North' or Russia quite conveniently fit into Palmerston's imperial foreign policy in the Middle East and later into the Anglo-Russian 'Great Game' over Central Asia.

Two other factors reinforced this anti-Russian and anti-Soviet perspective. First, dispensationalists interpreted the official ideology of the Soviet Union as the atheism the Antichrist wanted to impose upon mankind. Second, because dispensationalists monitor contemporary international affairs searching for 'signs of the times', they inevitably interpret world events as indicating the state of the battleground between God and those opposed to God, the forces of the Antichrist. During the 1930s, for example, fundamentalists viewed the Great Depression as a portentous sign. 'The Great Depression fit well with the pre-millennialist prediction of a collapse of the social and political order that would precede the second coming,' Wilcox says. 'Many prominent preachers foresaw an immediate end to the world.'[5]

The fundamentalist movement's objectives during this period were twofold. Simply put, according to Stewart Cole, 'conservatives directed their energies to gain control of evangelicalism' and 'undertook reformative measures beyond the church with a view to checking the standards of secular culture'. The First World War played a critical role in promoting fundamentalism because 'the war psychology having concentrated religious militancy, conservatives *became* the fundamentalist movement'.[6] During the interwar period, fundamentalists clashed with moderate and liberal modernists within many US denominations across the country. By its end, mainline, moderate Protestant churches began to splinter, as fundamentalist elements within them seceded, forming separate denominations. Such separatism is a significant feature of fundamentalism.[7]

Mainstream American Protestants Realign Theology

A theological realignment of American Protestantism occurred during the 1930s owing to the ominous international situation and to the brutality of the Nazi, Soviet, and Italian fascist regimes. In the face of such a world situation a reassessment of the earlier modernist and liberal American Social Gospel approach began and new theological inspiration was sought out. In Europe, Karl Barth and other Protestant theologians developed the school of 'neo-orthodoxy' – by no means a return to medieval theology, but a revival of interest in Luther, Calvin, St Augustine, and St Paul. Many moderate conservative and liberal churchmen in the USA adopted this approach.

Gasper points out that neo-orthodoxy became 'the dominant theological school of thought in Europe and the United States'.[8] While it appeared conservative in some respects, it synthesized traditional and modernist elements. Fundamentalists denounced neo-orthodoxy for the same reasons the proto-fundamentalists of the late nineteenth century denounced theological liberalism and the Social Gospel. For them modernism, or theological liberalism, could not be tolerated. Why? Fundamentalists built their theological superstructure on the foundation of their own idiosyncratic literalist interpretation of the Bible. Higher criticism challenged their core belief in the inerrancy of the Bible and their interpretation of prophecy.[9]

The Fundamentalist Movement Consolidates

The struggle rocked even denominations with conservative leanings. The Northern Baptist Convention, many leaders of which had grown up in the conservative South, faced a crisis in 1921 provoked by hard-line fundamentalists.[10] 'Many fundamentalist leaders, born and disciplined in the atmosphere of southern Christian orthodoxy,' as Cole points out, 'moved North and brought their inherited viewpoint.'[11] At the time, the Northern Baptist Convention acted in an administrative capacity only, allowing local churches to take their own perspectives on matters of doctrine. This latitude encouraged a militant faction called the Fundamentalist Fellowship to organize a separatist group called the Baptist Bible Union of America, with the express purpose of propagating fundamentalist doctrine.

The Baptist Bible Union, in turn, felt free to organize its own separate missionary department. In the early 1930s, schisms in the Northern Baptist Convention led to the 1932 formation of the General Association of Regular Baptists, North, which followed the Fundamentalist Bible Baptist Union line. The Northern Baptist Convention changed its name to the American Baptist Convention. Fundamentalists established control of the Western Baptist Theological Seminary (now Western Seminary) in Portland, Oregon, and organized the Conservative Baptist Theological Seminary (now Denver Seminary) in Denver, Colorado.[12] After the Second World War, in 1947, the Fundamentalist Fellowship established the Conservative Baptist Association.

Baptists in the Southern Baptist Convention were already generally conservative but even there militant fundamentalists caused controversy and secession. One important militant, J. Frank Norris, led a movement that formed the separatist World Baptist Fellowship, which created the Bible Baptist Seminary and the weekly newspaper called *The Fundamentalist*. Norris edited the newspaper, which conducted a spirited campaign against the Southern Baptist Convention in the South and Southwest.

The Presbyterian Church also saw factional divisions between fundamentalists and liberals.[13] Church conservatives released a 'Back to the fundamentals' statement in 1915, and during the 1920s controversy arose concerning the orthodoxy, or lack thereof, in several Presbyterian seminaries. At that time, the Princeton, Lane, and Omaha seminaries fell into the orthodox category.[14] Princeton Theological Seminary was the most conservative, although the faculty itself was split into conservative and liberal factions.

Professor J. Gresham Machen at Princeton promoted the hard-line conservative doctrine. He had schismatic tendencies, wishing to break away from mainline Presbyterian Church doctrine. In 1929, Machen left the seminary to found the Westminster Theological Seminary, established to teach the fundamentalist doctrine called 'neo-Calvinism'.[15] Cornelius van Til (1895–1987), an American theologian born in the Netherlands, played a prominent role at Westminster. His connection to the Dutch neo-Calvinist movement is significant because it provided a conduit to the American Presbyterians for the conservative theology and political ideology established in the Netherlands under the leadership of Abraham Kuyper.

The Machen group seceded from the mainline Presbyterian Church. The resulting fundamentalist church, called the Presbyterian Church of America, counted among its leaders the president of Wheaton College (Illinois),

J. Oliver Buswell, and Carl McIntire, pastor of the Collingwood Presbyterian Church (New Jersey). Wheaton College became an important center for preparing politically active fundamentalist church and lay leaders, including star graduate and leading evangelist Billy Graham.[16]

Carl McIntire and the American Council of Christian Churches

In 1937, following Machen's death, a further split and separation by a hardline dispensationalist faction led by McIntire resulted in the establishment of the Bible Presbyterian Church and its Faith Theological Seminary, in Wilmington, Delaware.[17] McIntire later became one of the key leaders of the Christian anti-communist crusades of the early Cold War era and an ally of US Senator Joseph McCarthy (Republican – Wisconsin). A protégé of McIntire, Francis August Schaeffer (1912–84), attended both Westminster Theological Seminary and Faith Theological Seminary. After the Second World War, Schaeffer became a major intellectual force in the fundamentalist movement known for his emphasis on Christian political action. Many leaders of the 'New' Christian Right of the 1970s attribute their political activism to Schaeffer's inspiration.

During the interwar period, fundamentalists made skillful use of mass media, including not only newspapers, books, magazines, and tracts, but also the new medium of radio. As early as 1925, Charles E. Fuller broadcast his *Old Fashioned Revival Hour* over independent stations in southern California. During the 1930s, his broadcasts expanded across a wide network so that most Americans could hear the fundamentalist line. As Louis Gasper points out, 'their efforts helped condition the American people to be receptive to their theological viewpoints'.[18]

Mobilization of the various fundamentalist forces took a decided turn in 1940, when the Bible Protestant Church, a separatist Methodist fundamentalist organization, began to explore the possibility of an alliance with the Bible Presbyterian Church. Successful negotiations led these two organizations to form the American Council of Christian Churches (ACCC) in 1941.[19] No members of the moderate Federal Council of the Churches of Christ in America, a mainline organization founded in 1908, were allowed to join, and separation from it was encouraged. The moderate Federal Council merged with the International Council for Religious Education in 1950 and became known as the National Council of the Churches of Christ in America.

With Carl McIntire as its head, the American Council soon obtained radio time allocations equal to the moderate Federal Council from the US Federal Communications Commission and a guaranteed quota of Protestant chaplains for the US armed forces. These bold moves established precedents for subsequent significant penetration of the American mass electronic media and the US armed forces. McIntire's agenda also included an aggressive campaign to encourage remaining fundamentalist elements to separate from churches in the moderate Federal Council. The dispensationalist emphasis on separatism, aside from similarities to the conservative Dutch theopolitical movement, harkens back to Darby and Irving's campaigns against the 'Apostate Church', which called for separation from it.

McIntire boasted that 'the groups that have been called fundamentalists have been chided because they cannot get along together, but they are now proving to the world that the charge is false and that they can work together.'[20] This claim was not entirely true: another group of fundamentalists formed a separate organization called the National Association of Evangelicals (NAE), seceding not over dispensationalist doctrine but over methods of operation. The NAE objected to the strident and militant tone of the ACCC and McIntire's personal style. As Gasper points out, the separation of the NAE from the ACCC was advantageous. It allowed the fundamentalist movement to proceed on two tracks, thereby increasing its penetration of the national evangelical milieu. 'The inclusivist policy of the National Association of Evangelicals,' Gasper says, 'has enabled it to bore within the major trunk of American Protestantism.' The American Council, on the other hand, 'attacks the liberals from without.'[21]

The significance and power of these organizations can be appreciated by a quick look at their growth and at the penetration of fundamentalism into American Protestantism. Three years after its establishment, the NAE claimed one million members; by 1956, it claimed to be the fastest-growing conservative interdenominational organization in American Protestantism, estimating that in 1956 out of 100 million church-going Americans some 58 million were Protestant. Of the Protestants, the NAE claimed 21 million fundamentalists outside the National Council of Churches (the successor to the Federal Council) and 3 million inside the National Council. By this claim, one-half of American Protestants were fundamentalists.[22]

Biblicism and Zionist Colonization in Palestine

Zionist colonization of Palestine proceeded apace during the interwar period. Biblicism, the fundamentalist belief in the absolute inerrancy and authority of the Bible, played a significant role in both internal and external propaganda. Britain, as the mandatory power, had its hands full, as a continuing inflow of Jews increasingly provoked reaction from the Arab Palestinian population. The differing opinions in the British Cabinet as to the utility of Palestine resulted in varying commitments to the political Zionist movement. Curzon, for instance, had written to Balfour in 1919 that he was 'convinced that Palestine will be a rankling thorn in the flesh of whoever is charged with its mandate'.[23]

As local, regional, and strategic considerations shifted, British policy toward Palestine during the interwar period zigzagged. From the Palestinian perspective, says Walid Khalidi:

> it was under British protection and by force of British arms that during the first phase, from 1918 to 1948, the demographic, economic, military and organizational infrastructure of the future Jewish state was laid, at the expense of the indigenous Palestinian people and in the teeth of their resistance.[24]

Zionist use of biblicism during this phase to encourage and justify ongoing colonization of Palestine was well planned and highly developed.

Biblicism among some Jews and political Zionism are thoroughly entwined. H.S. Haddad points out that while

> modern political Zionism attempted, at times, to purge traditional Jewish Messianic nationalism of its miraculous, mystical and eschatological elements by stressing mostly its political and social aspects, the fact remains that it capitalized on the romantico-religious drive among the Diaspora Jews to achieve its political aims.[25]

Even secular Jews held biblical convictions: 'Zionists who are not religious, in the sense of following the ritual practice of Judaism, are still biblical in their basic convictions in, and practical applications of, the ancient particularism of the Torah and the other books of the Old Testament.'[26]

The issue of where religion and nationalism meet is significant in the context of political Zionism and its territorial ambitions in Palestine. Biblicism is used to justify the project of political Zionism to erect a Jewish state in

Palestine. Haddad says the Old Testament 'is the only record available of the ancient Jewish state, its origin and ideology as well as its prophetic and eschatological destiny'. Thus, he argues, 'That the Bible is at the root of Zionism is recognized by religious, secular, non-observant, and agnostic Zionists'.[27] As an example, he points to Moses Hess (1812–75), an early Zionist writer, saying that for Hess 'Jewish religion was, above all, Jewish nationalism'.[28] Haddad goes on to assert that 'biblicism and archaism are distinguishing marks of Jewish settlement in Palestine, in spite of all the modern trappings of Israeli society, its industry and military establishment'.[29]

Biblical emphasis, as Haddad says, 'becomes a very effective public relations tool to influence the Christian world'.[30] This perspective parallels the dispensationalist mindset of Christian Zionists with respect to the issues of restoration of the Jewish people to Palestine and with respect to the geographical considerations associated with Eretz Israel.[31] Thus political cooperation between Jewish political Zionists and dispensationalist Christians in support of a Jewish state in Palestine is facilitated and strengthened.

Zionism and Geography in Palestine

What about the territorial issue and the definition of the boundaries of a Jewish state in Palestine? How are they to be delimited and demarcated? Dispensationalists in the USA often refer to a map of the Middle East designed by Clarence Larkin (1850–1924), author of a number of books promoting premillennialism in the Darby tradition. A map of his dated 18 January 1919 depicts what he calls 'The Royal Grant to Abraham', which shows a territory extending from the Mediterranean Sea to the Euphrates River.[32] The southern boundary runs in a straight horizontal line extending from the Mediterranean to the location of Ur by the lower Euphrates. The northern boundary runs in a straight line from the Mediterranean and through the city of Hama (biblical Hamath) on the Orontes River in northern Syria to the Euphrates. Thus, according to Larkin and dispensationalists, Greater Israel should include not only the contemporary state of Israel but also substantial parts of contemporary Lebanon, Syria, and Iraq.

Political Zionists have proposed various definitions for the territorial Jewish state. Haddad takes note of differing definitions of the Promised Land but concludes 'the locus of Eretz Israel is constant'. He says, 'whether it is defined as "from Dan to Beersheba" and "from the desert to the sea" or, more often, from the Nile to the Euphrates, Jerusalem is the centre around which these circles of varying size are drawn'. Territoriality, therefore, 'is made a theological imperative'.³³ Jerusalem, the West Bank, and the Golan Heights fall within biblical definitions of the Promised Land while the Sinai was not clearly included.

For political Zionists, the least extensive definition of Eretz Israel is 'from Dan to Beersheba', which corresponds generally to the land carved out of geographical Syria under the British mandate. This territory roughly corresponds to the area settled by the tribes of Israel during the period of the Judges. 'The Deuteronomic ambitions for Israel', Haddad says, 'are more grandiose'.³⁴ On this basis, with reference to Deut. 1:6–8 and Deut. 11:24, the territory would include all Canaan and the Lebanon as far as the Euphrates or, put another way, from the Nile to the Euphrates. This area corresponds roughly with that acquired under David and Solomon, as described in the books of Samuel, Kings, and the Chronicles.³⁵ Thus, political Zionists using the Deuteronomic view would correspond to the dispensationalist view as expressed by Larkin, which is in wide circulation in the USA today among Christian Zionists.

Huff's definition of political Zionism – the authoritative Basle Program (1897) approved under Theodore Herzl's leadership of the political Zionist movement – has relevance here. Haddad points out that 'Herzl's idea of the geographical extent of the Jewish state was derived from the biblical romance of the Davidic Kingdom'.³⁶ Interestingly, a British Christian Zionist minister gave Herzl the technical biblical definitions of the geographic boundaries for a prospective Zionist state in Palestine. Reverend William H. Hechler (1845–1931) was Chaplain of the British Embassy in Vienna. Herzl recalls in his diaries: 'Hechler unfolded his Palestine map in our [train] compartment and instructed me by the hour. The northern frontier is to be the mountains facing Cappadocia, the southern the Suez Canal. Our slogan shall be: "The Palestine of David and Solomon".'³⁷

The relationship between history, geographic places, and theopolitical symbolism is critical in both Jewish political Zionism and Christian Zionism. Hence the emphasis placed on all three in political Zionism. Azaryahu and Kellerman raise the issue of Zionist mythical geography in an interesting paper they prepared at the University of Haifa. They argue that places 'permeated with the notion of "sacred history" and heroic mythology are embedded within the symbolic matrix of modern nationhood, sometimes as "sacred centres". Within the context of political Zionism, they explain, 'the motif of return dominated Zionist mythology and praxis'.[38]

Which era in Jewish history was selected by political Zionists for emphasis and what were the reasons? The Second Commonwealth ('Second Temple') era was chosen.[39] It was the period between the successful revolt of the Maccabees (165 BCE) and the two failed revolts against Roman rule (70 BCE and 135 CE). 'This particular history', Azaryahu and Kellerman explain, 'blended national history and national territory, and celebrated the theme of "return" in (re)invented historical memories.' This history resonated 'with contemporary Zionist concerns such as the quest for independence and the struggle for national liberation'. Furthermore, the historical precedent of the Second Commonwealth 'was of extraordinary symbolic resonance for Zionists engaged in the creation of what they believed to be the "Third Commonwealth"'.[40] Christian Zionists today await the rebuilding of the Third Temple because it falls within their End Times scenario. Thus Christian Zionists support both the political Zionist and the messianic Jewish conception of the building of the Third Commonwealth ('Third Temple').

British Interwar Palestine Policy

During the interwar period, British policy also zigzagged on the question of the flow of refugees into Palestine and on the question of territorial partition. Local, regional, and strategic factors in the Middle East played a role, as did interdepartmental policy differences within the British government. Mussolini's invasion of Abyssinia in October 1935, in particular, shook the British establishment and caused changes in British strategic planning.[41]

With respect to Palestine, Norman Rose believes, British politicians were 'under no illusions as to the future result of the National Home policy'; he maintains that there could be 'little doubt that both the Zionists and their Gentile supporters saw the ultimate development of the National Homes as a Jewish State'.[42] Arthur Koestler's assessment of British policy was blunter: 'In fact, the main characteristic of British policy in Palestine up to 1939 was the absence of any consistent design.' As Koestler saw it, Britain's leaders 'had in 1917 somewhat rashly let themselves in for a romantic adventure and did not know how to get out of it'.[43] Neither Rose nor Koestler sufficiently credits the challenges to imperial defense posed by overt Italian, German, and Japanese aggression and the strategic factors affecting the security of Great Britain itself.

During the 1920s, British Christian or gentile supporters of political Zionism, such as Liberal imperialist Josiah Wedgwood, blended biblical and imperial themes in equal measure. Wedgwood wrote in 1928:

> Those who do settle in Palestine are likely to be of real political and commercial service to the Empire, for Palestine is the Clapham Junction of the Commonwealth … With pipe line and railway debouching at Haifa under Carmel, the British fleet can look after the Near East in comfort and safety.[44]

Wedgwood's sweeping proposal for the incorporation of Palestine into the British Empire as a Dominion received mixed reviews. Nonetheless, the conservative political Zionist leader, Vladimir Jabotinsky, 'seemed fascinated by the proposal'. Indeed, Jabotinsky's biographer is quoted by Rose as stating 'The "Dominion" concept gained his unreserved approval.'[45]

In any event, in 1929 the Palestine situation exploded in Arab riots. Various British Commissions of Enquiry and White Papers, as Rose says, placed Palestine 'in the very forefront of political controversy'.[46] Anglo-Zionist relations 'stumbled from crisis to crisis until finally, with the publication of the Passfield White Paper, they ground to an official halt'.[47] The 1930 Passfield White Paper was the product of Sidney Webb (1859–1947), Lord Passfield, Secretary of State for the Colonies and Secretary of State for Dominion Affairs. The controversial paper took a 'pro-Arab' line, insisting that the Jewish National Home project was not central to the British Mandate – although it did affirm Great Britain's commitment to the project.

The situation in Palestine became increasingly tense during the 1930s, and British policy zigzagged over Palestine generally and over the issue of territorial partition specifically.[48] A new round of Arab riots in Palestine in 1936 sparked a rethink.[49] The Italian move into Abyssinia, however, provided a *strategic context*. Under these circumstances controversy for and against partition naturally raged.

In this context, the concept of Palestine as a Dominion, or Crown Colony, reemerged as a result of the activities of the second Lord Melchett and a circle of sympathizers. The Colonial Secretary, William Ormsby-Gore (1885–1964), indicated the timeliness of such an initiative, given a shift of British Mediterranean policy emphasis toward the Eastern Mediterranean and enhanced relations with Turkey.

Rose notes one line of strategic thought that was expressed by Walter Elliot. 'Haifa was the key to the puzzle', Eliot said. 'The acquisition of Haifa as a naval base made it imperative for Britain to get rid of the mandate.' Britain, from a military point of view, he contended, only needed Haifa and the rest of the mandate lands could be cast off. Notwithstanding a range of strategic concepts, as Rose says, 'Palestine was a prime factor in any future planning.' And the issue was 'how best she could be incorporated into any overall planning scheme'.[50]

The Palestine Royal Commission (Peel Commission) appointed in 1936 was charged with making recommendations for improving management of the British mandate for Palestine, and published its report in 1937. The report recommended abolishing the mandate and imposing a partition. The partition would allocate to Jews a portion of the northwest and north of Palestine that included the strategic port of Haifa and territory along the sea southwards almost to Tel Aviv. Jerusalem, with a corridor to the sea, would remain subject to the mandate. It is hardly surprising that all sides exploded into controversy. From the standpoint of British interests, as Rose says, all 'the vital strategic areas in Palestine were to remain in British hands under an emasculated form of the old Mandate'. Rose adds that '[with] these areas under British control all other solutions could be ignored'. As he concludes, 'it is not difficult to escape the conclusion that the Royal Commission, in drawing up their report, were as concerned with the vulnerable nature of Britain's strategic position as with finding a viable solution to Arab–Jewish relations in Palestine'.[51]

Thanks to marked policy differences that divided the Foreign Office and the Colonial Office, British policy in regard to the Middle East and Palestine in particular was in disarray. The Foreign Office generally was sensitive to Arab concerns – but for a reason, says Koestler:

> The Foreign Office experts wanted to see the Arabs as strong so as to be able to justify, before their own conscience and in the eyes of the world, the abandonment of the Zionist experiment as a hopeless and doomed cause. They believed in Arab strength, and tried to bolster it up to justify their belief.[52]

The Colonial Office was less concerned with Arab unity because it believed that Arab rulers would side with Britain, in any case. Koestler says:

The Arab oil countries are as dependent on Western financial support as the Western powers are on Middle Eastern oil ... Loss of the oil royalties would mean immediate bankruptcy for both Iraq and Saudi Arabia, and no Arab Government is willing to commit suicide for the sake of a cause which does not affect its interests except in a remote and sentimental manner.[53]

The Foreign Office therefore objected to the Peel Commission plan for partition as upsetting to Arab unity and opinion. The Colonial Office was inclined initially to support a partition policy; but, in 1938, it opposed the idea on the strength of advice from the military services.[54]

Both Jews and Arabs rejected the Peel Commission report and partition plan. The British government therefore convened yet another commission to review the failure of the Peel Commission and to make new recommendations. The Woodhead Commission was thus established in 1938 within the local context of an ongoing Arab revolt in Palestine. Sir John Woodhead's instructions were to reject the Peel Commission's findings and, given strategic considerations, to find a formula to placate the Arab side. This commission produced a report with several alternate partition plans; but both Jews and Arabs rejected the Woodhead Commission report and its recommendations after an airing at the St James Conference in London in February and March 1939 (the Round Table Conference of 1939).

Finally, on 17 May 1939, a White Paper proposed the creation of a unitary Palestinian state with borders running from the Mediterranean to the Jordan River.[55] The plan called for a cap on Jewish emigration after a five-year period, during which 75,000 Jewish emigrants would be allowed to enter. Further Jewish emigration could take place only with Arab permission. To appease Arabs, the sale of land to Jews was severely curtailed under subsequent land transfer regulations enacted in 1940. Needless to say, the White Paper was highly controversial. Some critics took the position that it violated provisions of the British mandate itself and was, therefore, illegal. The League of Nations itself expired on 18 April 1946, though, and with it the British mandate for Palestine. The British continued to hold Palestine, however, until they turned it over to the newly created United Nations organization in 1947.

British policy, including the White Paper, must be viewed from a wartime strategic perspective. London focused on the overall Middle Eastern situation and hence on the Arab states such as Iraq with its oil, Egypt and Sudan, and the Arabian Peninsula.[56] 'But it was not the Palestinian Arabs whom the British government were particularly worried about,' says Michael J. Cohen, 'it was the Arab states, whose loyalty would be needed in the event of war.'

As war in Europe approached, London need to strengthen its position in the Eastern Mediterranean and closer relations with Turkey were one element in British strategy. Accordingly, in May 1939, a Joint Declaration of Mutual Assistance was signed between Britain and Turkey. Cohen explains:

> To obtain an alliance with Turkey it was necessary for the French to give the Turks the Sanjak of Alexandretta, which was of course a great blow to the Arab population. Paris and London came to the conclusion that a further blow to Arab and Muslim susceptibilities in the form of a forward Zionist policy in Palestine was totally incompatible with military necessities.[57]

Put succinctly, the reality was that 'global strategic factors outweighed local Palestinian considerations'[58] and 'the strategic nuisance value of the Arab States far outweighed any advantages the Zionists could hope to offer'.[59] The White Paper of 1939, therefore, remained British policy until Britain handed over its responsibilities to the United Nations in 1947.

Interwar Christian Zionism in America

The Second World War necessarily raised issues related to Palestine policy for the USA. As Palestine was a British responsibility under the League of Nations mandate, US policy naturally deferred to Britain, although domestic US political pressure on the issue was increasing. Given the fixed British governmental position based on strategic wartime policy and military necessity, it was logical for international Zionism to shift attention to the USA in order to exploit domestic opinion there and thereby pressure US policymakers. The international Zionist movement, therefore, transferred its main center from London to the USA in the early 1940s because the British government would not accommodate the agenda of political Zionism owing to pragmatic wartime policy considerations.

Although political Zionism, from its inception, had been a minority position within the American Jewish community, the horrors of the European situation had produced a marked shift in support of the plans and objectives of political Zionism by 1942. For a time, additional support for political Zionism came from the liberal mainline Protestant community on a humanitarian basis, while fundamentalists adhered to their ideologically driven dispensationalist restorationism.

During the 1920s, the liberal mainline Protestant community appears to have been little interested in Zionism. On the other hand, Zionism found strong support in the fundamentalist movement. Paul Charles Merkley explains that during this period 'both the political and the cultural elites gave up, apparently forever, on the old Christian Restorationism. Well educated churchmen soon followed suit.'[60] Although some liberal churchmen had embraced the Balfour Declaration, any support for Zionism faded quickly. Zionist leaders then turned to the fundamentalists:

> It did not escape their notice that those whose zeal for the establishment of the Jewish homeland had not abated were those who spoke the language of classic Restorationism – who spoke with embarrassing dogmatism of 'God's Plan', of literal fulfillment of biblical promises: the despised 'Fundamentalists'.[61]

American political Zionists naturally kept a close watch on British policy in Palestine. Thus the British Passfield White Paper of 1930 triggered political Zionist action in the USA. With an eye on the 1932 elections, political Zionist activists in the USA established the American Palestine Council (APC) in January 1932 as a joint effort with leading Gentiles. Brandeis spearheaded the move and President Hoover endorsed it, and several Senators, Cabinet members, and Supreme Court Justices were recruited. One of the organizers, Emanuel Neumann, was impressed by the remarks of William R. Hopkins, former city manager of Cleveland, Ohio. Neumann wrote:

> It is Mr Hopkins's view that we are most likely to gain supporters among a certain type of Christians who have been brought up on the Scriptures, and who have a sentimental and emotional attitude toward the Holy Land, which makes them pre-disposed to favor the Zionist cause. He warns us against depending merely on politicians and liberals, who have no such background and sentimental attachment to Palestine.[62]

The APC worked hard to fashion its message so as to appeal to the fundamentalist Christian grass roots base. It drafted carefully a statement of aims and principles and issued press releases. Of particular interest is the wording of one passage in its program, tailored to appeal specifically to American fundamentalists. The language is coded in such a way as to appeal to dispensationalist eschatology by raising the issue of millennialism, the land of Israel, and biblical prophecy:

> The fulfillment of the millennial hope for the reunion of the Jewish people with the land of its ancient inheritance, a hope that accords with the spirit of biblical prophecy has always commanded the sympathy of the liberal Christian world.[63]

The APC leadership stressed coordination of APC activities with the World Zionist organization and with the influential Jewish Agency for Palestine, and Brandeis played an active role behind the scenes. At the same time, another organization surfaced to support political Zionism, the Pro-Palestine Federation of America (PPF), organized by Christian leaders in Chicago in 1932. Regular political Zionist organizations, however, were cool to the Gentile pro-Zionists. Eventually this organization folded around 1940, after which elements of it attached themselves to other similar organizations.[64]

In 1941, the APC revived and stepped up its activities with the assistance of Brandeis. This time the organization had a better financial footing as a result of generous help from the newly formed Emergency Committee for Zionist Affairs (ECZA), later called the American Zionist Emergency Council (AZEC). The proceedings of its second annual banquet held in Washington, DC, on 25 May 1942 were broadcast nationwide by NBC Radio, which announced that 67 US Senators and 143 Congressmen were members. The occasion also marked the 20th anniversary of the pro-Zionist Congressional resolutions of 1922. The organization brought its policy into line with the Biltmore Program of 1942 at its National Conference on Palestine in 1944, which demanded increased Jewish immigration to Palestine and the establishment of a Jewish Commonwealth there.[65]

The activities of the political Zionists who were in favour of a Jewish state in Palestine were echoed in the gentile community. Two Christian organizations emerged during this period in support of the political Zionist program: the Christian Council on Palestine (CCP) and the American Christian Palestine Committee (ACPC). The CCP was organized by leading churchmen – such as Reinhold Niebuhr – assisted by political Zionist activists, including Emanuel Neumann. It targeted clergymen and active lay leaders of Christian opinion. The organization was 'committed to the establishment of a Jewish commonwealth in Palestine'. Merkley points out that the composition of the organization did not include fundamentalists: 'It is clear that CCP,' he says, 'steered by Voss and Niebuhr, deliberately avoided approach to the Fundamentalist-to-Evangelical side of church world.'[66]

Christian Zionism in the USA between the First World War and the Second World War was almost entirely within the fundamentalist subculture. Mainline Protestants, with few exceptions, were not involved significantly in supporting the agenda of political Zionism. But the fundamentalist subculture was expanding and had a strong institutional support base. Thus Christian Zionism would emerge in the post-Second World War Cold War years to provide a strong mass base for nationwide anti-communist crusades as well as for support for the newly established State of Israel, seen by dispensationalists as a fulfillment of biblical prophecy.

7

Zionism from the Second World War to 1948

As London adhered to the policy put forth in the 1939 White Paper, the international political Zionist movement concentrated its efforts on pressuring Washington to support a Jewish state. This pragmatic shift in focus reflected its leaders' realistic assessment of British wartime, and early Cold War, strategy in the Middle East. With guardians of British imperial interests ranking relations with the Arab states ahead of relations with political Zionism, continued adherence to the White Paper could have resulted in the establishment of an Arab majority state after the war and foreclosed any plans political Zionism put forth for a Jewish state in Palestine. Instead, its adherents found that Washington could be influenced through the domestic political process, via coalition politics and interest groups and their support bases. Opportunities for a single binational one-state solution to the Palestine Question were thus lost. International political Zionism achieved the goal set out long ago by the Basle Program and reasserted by the Biltmore Program: to establish a sovereign Jewish state in Palestine.

Political Zionists began mobilizing the American Jewish community urgently in 1941 and Christian support played a supplemental role. American Christian Zionists were already ideologically supportive of political Zionism and its restorationist program. Consequently, political Zionism sought support from mainstream Christian denominations on humanitarian, rather than doctrinal, grounds. Given early reports from Europe of an ongoing Holocaust, and the pressing European refugee situation, humanitarian concern powerfully influenced American opinion, although opinions about how to respond to the unfolding tragedy varied. As George Kirk explains:

> Seen from a narrow Middle Eastern standpoint, Zionism was but the nationalism of a minority of half a million Jews in Palestine; but the anguish and frustration produced by the Nazi persecution had made it also the most powerful force in that world-Jewry whose financial and political world influence vastly exceeded its numerical strength, and this combination of spiritual tension with material resources gave to Zionism a determination and resolution far firmer than that of diffuse and divided Arab nationalism.[1]

Christian support for political Zionism was humanitarian or ideological. Christian humanitarian support organizations included the Pro-Palestine Federation of America, the Christian Council on Palestine, and the American Christian Palestine Committee. Support based on Christian Zionist ideology, by the era of the Second World War, could be found in several dozen small sects in the USA adhering to dispensational premillennialism as well as residual fundamentalist elements within various mainline denominations.

At this time, historian Elmer T. Clark estimated that several million Protestants believed in dispensationalism:

> At the present time many small sects which have emerged from evangelical Protestantism in the United States adhere to some form of premillenarianism. Forty or more sects, with a combined membership of over a million, report it as one of the central ideas in their doctrinal statements; this group includes the sects bearing the Adventist label and which are the offshoots of the Millerite agitation near the middle of the nineteenth century, most of the Holiness sects, and many others. Including the Fundamentalists who have not left their denominations, there are probably three or four million persons who accept the millenarian scheme.[2]

How were international events interpreted by dispensationalists in the interwar and era? Clark explains prophetic interpretation, pointing out how the Books of Daniel and Revelation were used. For example, with respect to the First World War, he shows the Turks are presented as preventing the physical return of the Jewish people to Palestine.[3] Such a mindset among

Christian Zionists by the time of the Second World War necessarily produced strong sentiment in favor of political Zionism and its program.

The Biltmore Program of 1942

The Biltmore Program called for the establishment a Jewish state in Palestine and to support it there was newly united general support of political Zionism by the American Jewish community, which had formerly been sharply divided. Until the late 1930s, political Zionism had remained a distinctly minority position within the American Jewish community. Reform Judaism, for example, still opposed it outright, as did many socialist and communist Jews. Jewish non-Zionists, while favoring Jewish cultural and spiritual presence in Palestine, did not subscribe to the nationalistic call for a Jewish state.

The European situation forced a re-examination of positions within the US government and the American Jewish community. The brutality and anti-Semitism of the Hitler regime combined with the annexation of Austria in March 1938 had produced a worsening refugee situation in Europe. While about 150,000 of some 500,000 Jews had fled Germany by 1938, many remained in areas conquered by Germany. President Franklin Roosevelt, therefore, proposed an international conference to address the refugee situation. It took place at Évian-les-Bains, France, in July 1938 but little action resulted. Although the conference did establish the International Committee for Refugees, this organization had little practical international support.

In this context, the British White Paper of 1939 produced a shock in the American Jewish community, which united in denouncing it as contrary to the Balfour Declaration and the terms of the British mandate. The White Paper's restrictions on Jewish immigration into Palestine to 75,000 over a five-year-period (1939–44) and the decision to halt further immigration on 31 March 1944 particularly appalled American Jews. In the USA, the political response of the Jewish community was the formation of the United Jewish Appeal, which merged Zionist and non-Zionist fund-raising organizations – an unprecedented step given the traditionally contentious relations between the two. 'There is little exaggeration,' Stuart Knee argues, 'in the assertion that the White Paper of 1939 served as a point of union between Zionists and non-Zionists from whence there would be no retreat.'[4]

The 1897 Basle Program's goal of establishing a Jewish state in Palestine had remained prudently in the public background for several decades. As Kirk explains:

> The main body of Zionism had found it expedient not to overstress its original and consistent aim of 'establishing Palestine as a Jewish Commonwealth' as long as the mandatory Power was permitting the National Home to be built up by immigration and land purchase.[5]

The 1939 White Paper and the European situation, however, necessitated a different public profile. The United Palestine Appeal held a meeting in Washington in January 1941 at which it passed a resolution endorsing the 'establishment of Palestine as a Jewish commonwealth'.[6] This Jewish state would be located in the midst of Arab states, which possibly would be organized as an Arab federation.[7] Chaim Weizman, who was in the USA at this time, said in March 1941 that 'it is possible to have a Jewish Commonwealth side by side with this Arab Federation'.[8] Nahum Goldmann of the World Jewish Congress (WJC) said the territorial extent of the Jewish state or commonwealth should include all of Palestine and extend into Transjordan.[9] The militant Zionist Organization of America (ZOA) resolved on 7 September 1941 to demand 'the reconstruction of Palestine within its historic boundaries' as a Jewish commonwealth.[10]

The path to the Biltmore Conference was further smoothed by an important meeting of Zionists and non-Zionists that took place at the Commodore Hotel in New York City on 21 October 1941. Members of the prestigious, and heretofore non-Zionist, American Jewish Committee (AJC) accepted the plan for a Jewish state in Palestine.[11] With members of the AJC coming around, the American branch of the Jewish Agency gave former non-Zionists a larger political role regarding the proposed Jewish state in Palestine. In its turn, the Jewish Agency Executive took the decisive step of formulating and publicly announcing the aims of political Zionism. Knee explains that

> By the end of 1941 the Jewish Agency Executive, combining the wisdom and energy of former anti-nationalists and non-nationalists with those of Weizman and Wise, felt that it was necessary to formulate the ultimate aims of Zionism before the war ended.[12]

The Biltmore Conference convened all Zionist (and non-Zionist) parties and organizations in May 1942. As Kirk explains,

> At the most critical stage of the whole war, in the Far East, the Middle East, and on the Russian front alike, nearly 600 American and 67 foreign Zionists met in conference at the Biltmore Hotel, New York, from 9 to 11 May 1942.[13]

The conference produced a program calling for unrestricted Jewish immigration to Palestine and for the establishment of a Jewish state, to be called a 'Jewish Commonwealth'. The final point of the Biltmore Program stated unequivocally that 'Palestine be established as a Jewish Commonwealth integrated in the structure of the new democratic world. Then and only then will the age-old wrong to the Jewish people be righted.'[14]

The Biltmore Program thus rejected the binational, or one-state, solution to the Palestine question. Only the Socialist-Zionist Hashomer Hatzair group voted against the program because it explicitly rejected any binational solution, such as that proposed by Rabbi Judah L. Magnes, an American scholar and president of Hebrew University in Jerusalem. The Jewish Agency attacked an organization called *Ihud* (Union) formed to promote the concept, claiming that the Jewish Agency alone had the exclusive prerogative to conduct political negotiations.[15]

War, Palestine, and Politics

Meanwhile, also in 1942 and early 1943, the Second World War took a decisive turn in favor of the Allies, as the USA defeated the Japanese at the Battle of Midway in the Pacific in June 1942 and the Soviet Union defeated the Germans at Stalingrad in February 1943; in the Middle East, the British defeat of the Germans at the Battle of Alamein in November 1943 was decisive. Thus the stage was set for the next phase of the quest by international political Zionists for a Jewish state in Palestine.

Support for political Zionism in domestic US politics was considered critical to the success of the project for a Jewish state in Palestine. It is, therefore, not surprising that the national elections of 1944, 1946, and 1948 were prime targets for international political Zionists and their agents on the ground in the USA. The attitude of the Jewish Agency and that of international political Zionism had hardened and became more inflexible on the issue of a Jewish state in Palestine. The tides of war favored the Allies and, therefore, opened up possibilities for the immediate post-war era. Consequently, political Zionist pressure increased on the ground in Palestine as well as in the USA. At the beginning of 1944, General Sir H. Maitland Wilson, British Commander-in-Chief in the Middle East, reported intensified political Zionist activity in Palestine. The report states:

> By January 1944 the attitude of the Jewish Agency towards the Government had hardened to such an extent that any action conflicting with the policy of the Biltmore Program or for enforcing the White Paper met with opposition and obstruction. The Jewish Agency was in some respects arrogating to itself the powers and status of an independent Jewish Government.[16]

Meanwhile, Washington was, as Kirk summarizes:

> under pressures from the barrage of both Zionist and Revisionist agitation within the country, from the desire of the Service departments to obtain further oil concessions and aircraft-landing rights from Sa'ūdī Arabia, and from their diplomatic representatives in the Middle East who reported that Zionist agitation in the United States was having increasingly serious repercussions in the Arab states.[17]

It was in this overall context that the US national elections of fall 1944 loomed, elections in which the Jewish vote promised to be very important to the Democratic Party, as an article in the *Zionist Review* (1946) by Judge Bernard A. Rosenblatt explains:

> New York is entitled to 47 electoral votes, while only 266 electoral votes are necessary to elect a President. Whether the vote of the State of New York goes to one party or another (and that may be by relatively few votes in a population of over 13 million) will make a difference of 94 votes in the electoral college, so that it may be readily understood why a presidential contest may hinge on the political struggle in the State of New York, and to a lesser extent in the large States of Pennsylvania (36 electoral votes), Illinois (27), or Ohio (23).[18]

Politics in Congress reflected increasing political Zionist pressure on behalf of a Jewish state in Palestine. As we have seen, the 1939 White Paper was due to expire on 31 March 1944, thus reopening the issues of Jewish immigration to Palestine, land sales in Palestine to Jews, and the future of the mandate itself. At the beginning of 1944, Zionist lobbying on Capitol Hill produced Congressional resolutions, sponsored by both Democrats and Republicans, that supported turning Palestine into a Jewish commonwealth. They were defeated as a result of testimony before a secret session in the US Senate Foreign Relations Committee, however. The Committee heard from Army Chief of Staff, General George Marshall, speaking with the approval of the Secretary of War and the State Department. Marshall asked for postponement of the resolutions on military grounds owing to strategic considerations about the stability of the Middle East, and political attitudes of the Arab states.

The War Department closely followed the Middle East situation and special missions were undertaken to examine the Palestine issue. Lieutenant Colonel Harold B. Hoskins, a fluent Arabic speaker, visited the region during 1942 and 1943 and kept his own command, the State Department, and the White House, well briefed. Evan M. Wilson, a US diplomat and Middle East specialist, says Hoskins, also 'played a key role, although the published documents do not reveal it, in obtaining in early 1944 the shelving of the proposed Congressional resolutions on Palestine'.[19] The resolutions were reintroduced later in 1944 but were again withdrawn – this time after the Secretary of State, Edward R. Stettinius, indicated to the US Senate Foreign Relations Committee that passing them would be unwise.

As for America's British ally, policy toward Palestine necessarily came under serious review at Cabinet level during 1943 and 1944.[20] The overall strategic situation in the Middle East had to be considered as well as the question of how to handle the British mandate for Palestine. Consensus on the disposition of the mandate was difficult to obtain, given the multiplicity of strongly held views and proposed solutions. Partition was one option, but various other formulas were proposed for the extent, location, and allocation of Jewish and Arab lands.

Lord Moyne, the deputy minister of state at Cairo, favored the creation of a 'Greater Syria' out of Syria, Transjordan, and the Arab areas of Lebanon and Palestine. Under this plan, there would also be a Christian Lebanon, a Jewish state, and a Jerusalem state protected by Britain. This plan later metamorphosed into a concept for a 'Southern Syria' or Greater Transjordan to be created from the Transjordan and Arab Palestine. Churchill, a strong supporter of Zionism, was adamant on the matter of fulfilling the commitments of the Balfour Declaration. He favored concepts advanced in his own 1922

White Paper on Palestine. But, in the end, the only consensus reached was to withhold any final decisions and announcements until the war was over. Nevertheless, anti-British violence flared in Palestine and Lord Moyne was assassinated in Cairo on 6 November 1944 by the Zionist terrorist organization *Lehi*, also called the Stern Gang.[21]

Churchill, too, had to take into account the 1944 elections in the USA. Cohen points out that

> Churchill himself was convinced of the need to delay any decision on Palestine not only until the successful conclusion of the European war but, more specifically, at least until after the American Presidential elections due to be held in November 1944.[22]

Churchill did not want to upset the US election process with any controversial pronouncements on the Middle East or Palestine. For his part, Franklin Roosevelt proposed the moderate and sensible idea of Palestine as a Permanent Trustee State under a High Commissioner responsible to the United Nations. Under such an arrangement a council of Jews, Muslims, and Christians would have responsibilities, and Jewish immigration could continue but within a fixed relationship to the Arab population. Although the British Government did nothing with this scenario at the time, Anthony Eden would later revive Roosevelt's proposal.

The general principle of the policy of the USA toward Palestine was fixed by President Roosevelt in a letter to King Ibn Saud dated 26 May 1943, in which Roosevelt responded to a letter of concern from the King about the Palestine situation. The President's letter stated, 'it is the view of the Government of the United States that no decision altering the basic situation of Palestine should be reached without full consultation with both Arabs and Jews'.[23] Evan Wilson, who held responsibilities for Palestine at the Department of State, points out the significance of this letter:

> The date in question, May 26, 1943, should be regarded as marking the beginning of a formal policy towards Palestine on the part of our government, which had previously confined its public statements on the subject to vague generalities based on the Atlantic Charter.[24]

President Roosevelt favored a trusteeship arrangement for Palestine in which Muslim, Jewish, and Christian interests would be protected. Wilson points out that

[the] President's idea of a trusteeship was elaborated in a Departmental memorandum in late 1943 and was among the topics broached to the British during the London talks in early 1944. The British Foreign Office reacted with enthusiasm to this proposed solution, but like so many other things it was overtaken by events.[25]

The war in Europe terminated on 8 May 1945, 'V.E. Day'. At the British general election that followed two months later, on 27 July 1945, Clement Attlee won a landslide victory and formed a Labour Cabinet. With Churchill (a staunch supporter of political Zionism) out of power, the fortunes of political Zionism were once again in doubt. William Phillips, an American career diplomat who would serve on the Anglo-American Committee on Palestine tersely explained the situation:

> Having in mind the importance of the Jewish vote in New York, as well as the plight of the Jewish refugees in Europe, President Truman publicly urged that 100,000 refugees be admitted to Palestine at once ... the British Government, taking advantage of this criticism, invited the American Government to participate in an Anglo-American Committee of Inquiry to consider the entire problem of Palestine. In the circumstances, the President could not well refuse.[26]

The refugee situation at this time was complicated. In Europe, refugees were located in displaced persons camps and many of those caught attempting to reach Palestine, illicitly circumventing British controls, were also placed in such camps. A key question was how many of these displaced persons desired to go to Palestine and how many wished to remain in Europe. Some argued that most Jewish displaced persons in Europe would wish to remain in Europe rather than emigrate to Palestine or to other locations. Others held the view that the 1939 White Paper ceiling of 75,000 refugees was calamitous, violated the spirit of the Balfour Declaration and the terms of the mandate, and actually was responsible for the unnecessary deaths of many who did indeed wish to flee the Holocaust and its devastating consequences and go to Palestine.

In the face of sharp criticism, the British government pointed out that the entire 75,000 quota had not been taken up and that Britain would extend the five-year deadline past 31 March 1944, allowing the quota to be taken up at the rate of 1,500 per month. By mid-1945, about 3,000 remained of the original 75,000. Any immigration above the 75,000 ceiling remained subject to Arab veto, and land transfers to Jews were severely restricted.

The Anglo-American Committee of Inquiry

The complexities of the situation in the Middle East, the approaching end of the British mandate in Palestine, and the inevitable conclusion of the European war caused increased concern over the Palestine situation in London and Washington. A decision was taken by both capitals to try to work jointly towards an acceptable settlement of the Palestine question. The Anglo-American Committee of Inquiry resulted from international and domestic political considerations, including increased friction between Great Britain and the USA on the Palestine Question. Created by Prime Minister Clement Attlee on 22 August 1945, the Cabinet Committee on Palestine included the new foreign secretary, Ernest Bevin, the secretary of state for war, and the secretary of state for air. Ambassador Halifax in Washington indicated pressure in the USA was mounting against Britain on the Jewish immigration issue.[27] 'Thus the Jews – who in any case could exert considerable pressure on the administration, in Congress and through the mass media – would also be able to carry with them both liberal humanitarians and many anti-Jews on this issue,' Cohen explains.[28]

The committee's composition was not weighted toward the pro-Zionist position, just as Churchill had ensured in his own committee on the matter. Churchill's departure had removed the significant factor of his great personal influence in support of his conception of the spirit of the Balfour Declaration and of political Zionism. The 1939 White Paper reflected a view that Britain's obligation to the Balfour Declaration had been completed. Churchill himself had hoped to associate the USA with British policy in Palestine:

> I do not think we should take the responsibility upon ourselves of managing this very difficult place, while the Americans sit back and criticize. I am not aware of the slightest advantage which has ever accrued to Great Britain from this painful and thankless task. Somebody else should have their turn now.[29]

The new Cabinet committee sought an interim solution to the Palestine problem. Cohen explains:

Within a few months of his entry into the Foreign Office, Bevin was turning against the Zionist cause. The new Labour Cabinet was immediately overwhelmed by domestic and foreign post-war problems, and the Cabinet – unable to agree upon the principles of a new Palestine policy – tended to rely more and more on Bevin's faculty for improvisation.[30]

At the first committee session in September, Bevin said, 'it should be our aim to associate the United States with our long-term policy in Palestine.'[31]

Bevin considered several plans, including one for a 'Federal Union' of Palestine and Transjordan under an Arab king. He convened a meeting of British Middle East representatives in September 1945 in order to gain some consensus on a way forward. 'Mounting agitation in the United States,' Cohen explains, 'fueled by presidential statements, made it necessary to make some interim official policy statements before mid-October, by which time the last white paper immigration quotas would have been issued.'[32]

The fact of powerful Jewish political influence in the USA could not be ignored by London as it posed significant challenges to British policy planning for the Middle East.[33] Attlee's biographer, Kenneth Harris, explains the domestic US political situation at the time: 'American Jews were a powerful political force which no American politician, especially the leader of the Democratic Party, could ignore,' he says.[34] Harris explains that

> President Truman was at heart a Zionist, and politically was ready to fashion his Palestine policy to provide the Democratic Party with Zionist votes and Zionist funds. Finally, if the many pro-Jewish American congressmen became too critical of British policy in Palestine, Britain might not receive the all-important American loan.[35]

The extent of President Truman's own emotional and sentimental commitment to political Zionism was not understood by the Attlee government.[36] Harris argues, 'Attlee and Bevin did not know of Truman's ardent Zionism when they took over the Palestine problem, and they were inclined to regard it only as a response to political pressure.'[37] The difference between Roosevelt's and Truman's positions was not initially understood in London. Paul Charles Merkley says Truman's attitude toward political Zionism differed substantially from Franklin Roosevelt's cautious position in the face of post-war strategic considerations: 'Truman, by contrast, believed that America's commitment to create the Jewish state was clear and unqualified and that there must be no going back.'[38]

Meanwhile, another significant change in the US government affected its Palestine policy. In June 1945, James F. Byrnes replaced Stettinius as secretary of state and soon after Dean Acheson replaced veteran diplomat Joseph C. Grew as undersecretary of state. Wilson explains that

> During Secretary Byrnes' tenure, the role of the Department of State in Palestinian affairs changed considerably. Byrnes' attitude was one of washing his hands of the problem and leaving it to the White House to handle, though he did not always succeed.[39]

Byrnes' attitude opened the door wide for White House staff interested in the issue:

> The result was naturally to diminish the authority of the Department in decisions respecting Palestine and to enhance that of the White House, where David K. Niles, an administrative assistant to the President, exerted a growing influence in this regard.[40]

The foreign policy process in the US government thus was gravely impacted by the removal of the institutional role of the Department of State and by the substitution in its place of an influential White House staff member who had the ear of the President, owing to the influence of the political Zionist lobby. The secretive David K. Niles was a Polish-born Jew who had worked his way up the ranks in American politics in the Progressive movement and in the Democratic Party. As Joseph Pika observes:

> The most distinguishing feature of Niles's nine years of service on Democratic White House staffs was his close association with Zionist groups in the United States. In many respects, working with Jewish groups was no different from working with unions or other organized interests. But in dealing with Jewish interests Niles went beyond being a facilitating intermediary and became an *advocate* within the White House.[41]

As Acheson tersely states in his memoirs:

> I did not share the President's views on the Palestine solution to the pressing and desperate plight of great numbers of displaced Jews in Eastern Europe, for whom the British and American commanders in Germany were temporarily attempting to provide.[42]

Acheson grasped perfectly the grave strategic implications of a Jewish state carved out of the Palestine mandate:

> The number that could be absorbed by Arab Palestine without creating a grave political problem would be inadequate and to transform the country into a Jewish state capable of receiving a million or more immigrants would vastly exacerbate the political problem and imperil not only Americans but all Western interests in the Near East.[43]

By the time he assumed his duties as undersecretary in September 1945, Acheson ruefully recalled, 'it was clear that the President himself was directing policy on Palestine'.[44]

The Truman Letter Triggers an Anglo-American Crisis

Truman, influenced by domestic political pressures, caused a significant breech in Anglo-American cooperation on Palestine that would not be repaired despite an attempt to seek consensus through a joint commission. A letter of 31 August 1945, which Niles drafted for Truman, was sent to Attlee and precipitated a crisis in Anglo-American relations over Palestine. Based on a report Truman had requested from the Harrison Commission on refugee issues and displaced persons, Truman abruptly called on Attlee to grant an additional 100,000 immigration certificates permitting Jews to go to Palestine. Logically, such a sudden and massive influx of Jews would inflame Arab opinion and lead to increased violence and difficulties for British management of the situation.

Pika emphasizes that Niles was

> the leading White House figure in 1945 on Jewish refugee issues and displaced persons problems, helping to advise Truman on pressuring Britain to raise its restrictions on immigration to Palestine and formulating the Harrison Commission, which called for changes in American administration of displaced persons camps and for admission of 100,000 refugees into Palestine.[45]

Further, Niles 'generated support for this proposal in Congress and among state governors while drafting Truman's messages to British Prime Minister Clement Attlee on the matter'.[46]

This Truman letter, says Harris, 'upset Anglo-American relations, spoiled the chances of a joint Anglo-American policy on Palestine, and put a strain on the personal relationship between himself and Attlee which nearly broke their friendship.'[47] Attlee astutely responded with the proposal for the Anglo-American inquiry discussed earlier, an idea suggested by Bevin.

The Anglo-American Committee on Palestine recommended an undivided Palestine that could evolve into a sovereign state that could protect the rights of all citizens irrespective of religious or ethnic identification. To this end, for an interim period of time, it was recommended by the commission that Palestine become a trusteeship under the United Nations, as President Roosevelt himself had earlier suggested. The commission report said that 'Palestine must ultimately become a state which guards the rights and interests of Moslems, Jews and Christians alike; and accords to the inhabitants, as a whole, the fullest measure of self-government.'[48]

Unfortunately, these Anglo-American Committee recommendations became a dead letter given the political situation in the USA, in which political Zionist influence over Congress and the White House was decisive. London thus had no choice but to then adjust its own policy dramatically to prepare for the expiration of the British mandate for Palestine scheduled for 15 May 1948. London handed the matter over to the United Nations.

A cascade of events followed. The United Nations created the United Nations Special Committee on Palestine (UNSCOP) on 15 May 1947 in order to establish a mechanism to resolve the Palestine situation. On 31 August 1947 UNSCOP issued a plan for the partition of Palestine, although a minority of the committee called for a single unitary binational state. The Partition Plan was adopted by the United Nations General Assembly on 29 November 1947 by a vote of 33 to 13 with 10 abstentions. The USA applied political pressure on countries to favor partition. The date intended for the partition to go into effect was 15 May 1948. The UN Partition Plan for Palestine became UN General Assembly Resolution 181 and on 14 May 1948 a new state of Israel declared independence.[49]

According to James G. McDonald, a fervent Christian Zionist who became the first US ambassador to Israel, there was 'no battle of the "die-hards" in the Department of State to thwart the President's plans regarding Israel' because President Truman, 'against his experts' advice had recognized the State of Israel immediately after its proclamation and there then arose the question of the representation which the United States should have in the new State.'[50]

President Truman's consideration of the politics of the upcoming 1948 elections and the need for Jewish support certainly played a role in his decision. The pro-Israel lobby worked overtime on the president. For example, Gus Russo in his book *Supermob* points out the situation in Illinois politics, wherein key supporters of political Zionism such as Jack Arvey, the boss of the 24th Ward, had powerful control over Chicago machine politics and thus could deliver Illinois to Truman: 'In 1948, Arvey's push was considered critical to Truman's eventual victory, with Truman's campaign chairman saying that they would only declare victory when they won Illinois.'[51]

Christian Zionism and the New State of Israel

The new state of Israel appeared to Christian Zionists as a momentous fulfillment of prophecy and a critical advancement of the apocalyptic End Times clock. They paid little attention to the secular socialist government of Israel. As Paul Charles Merkley writes in his sympathetic *Christian Attitudes towards the State of Israel*, 'Christian Zionists would have preferred, other things being equal, to find believing Jews at the helm of the new state.' Indeed, he says, they 'cringed at the politicians' insensitivity to the transcendent meaning of Israel's history, and their ignorance of the eschatological dimension – the meaning of the rebirth of Israel as a stage in God's Plan for History'. But nonetheless fundamentalists looked to the rebuilding of the Temple as a precondition for Christ's Second Advent. Hence, Merkley says, 'Typically, evangelical Christians see the practice of Judaism as more crucial, for the time being, to this unfolding scenario than the fortunes of the Christian communities.'[52] The Christian communities referred to by Merkley are, of course, the dispossessed Palestinian Arab Christians.[53]

Within the context of the unfolding international Cold War, Washington began to see Israel as a potential ally against the Soviet Union. Israel aligned with the West. 'Sometime during the first phase of the Korean crisis of 1950 Israel moved towards a de facto alignment with the West,' explains Uri Bialer:

> Concrete identification with the West gradually became more articulate during the 1960s and the 1970s. This was not simply a matter of momentum; it was also a result of the clear and unmistakable Soviet hostility made manifest by Russian support for Arab Palestinians' accelerating political and military conflict with Israel.[54]

Part III

Christian Zionism and American Foreign Policy, From the Cold War to Bush

8

The Christian Right in the Fifties and Sixties

After the Second World War, the bipolar confrontation between the USA-led 'West' and the Soviet-led 'East' resembled the geopolitics of the nineteenth-century Eastern Question and the Great Game between the British Empire and the Russian Empire, which we considered in previous chapters. The USA, in its Cold War competition with the Soviet Empire, assumed the mantle of the old British Empire. Powerful business and financial circles in the USA, constituting an imperial faction, took advantage of the tense Cold War environment to promote the rise of a national security state at home and an imperial policy abroad.[1] Distortion and falsification of the communist threat presented an overblown picture of the real military threat from the Soviet Union and Communist China, which facilitated the militarization of American society and its foreign policy.[2]

The Post-War Religious Right

As the Cold War set in after the Second World War, the Christian Right gained strength. Although publicly quiescent since the fallout from the 1925 Scopes Monkey Trial, conservative evangelical Protestants adopted a markedly public profile in the troubled post-war era. In its militant anti-communism, the Christian Right supported the militarization of US foreign policy and the Cold War military build-up. During the 1950s and 1960s it mobilized evangelical Christians via anti-communist crusades, mass revivals, and radio as a precursor to its emergence in the political realm through alignment with the political New Right in the 1970s and 1980s (which had identified energizing and delivering the conservative religious vote as a critical element in its agenda for America).³

The Christian Right in the USA has emerged over the past half-century as a major national subculture and political movement. The foreign policy perspective of this 'Christo-fascist' mass movement (to use Chris Hedges' term) is Christian Zionism. The inflated Cold War tensions of the 1950s allowed its followers to link religion and nationalism in support of anti-communism. From the Suez Crisis of 1956 to the Six Day War of 1967, Washington developed closer relations with Israel within the Cold War context.⁴ The dramatic Suez Crisis saw an Anglo-French expedition against Egypt and a coordinated Israeli invasion of the Sinai Peninsula.⁵ Although President Eisenhower sharply criticized the British, French, and Israeli action, his administration perceived that Israel could be an ally against the Soviet Union in the Cold War.⁶ The American Israel Public Affairs Committee (AIPAC), founded in 1959 as a Jewish pro-Israel lobby, promoted this view along with US–Israeli relations in Congress and in the White House.⁷ Closer relations with Israel were naturally welcomed by the conservative evangelical community.

Religious fundamentalists in the USA were also energized by Israel's defeat of Arab forces in the 1967 Six Day War. For them, Israel's reunification of the divided Jerusalem was a portentous fulfilment of prophecy. After the 1967 war, the Johnson administration welcomed Israel as a 'strategic asset' and bulwark against the perceived threat from the Soviet Union and its Arab friends in the Middle East. When, several years earlier, Israel appeared on the verge of acquiring nuclear weapons, the Kennedy administration had provided Israel with sophisticated conventional weapons and also committed to providing assistance to Israel in the event of Arab aggression.

The post-war Religious Right was supported financially by circles that had been the most opposed to the pre-war New Deal. Indeed, some of these circles on Wall Street and in Big Business had even associated with the most reactionary movements in Europe. Gasper neatly summarizes the post-war situation:

Since the end of World War II, a nationalistic fervor dangerously close to chauvinism had gripped the people in the United States in the face of the threat of Russian attack upon them. Somehow religious orthodoxy has been associated with nationalism and the two have become joint factors in the struggle for existence in the mid-twentieth century.[8]

Two prominent and representative Christian Right leaders, Carl McIntire and Billy Graham, emerged during this post-war era. Both skillfully used radio evangelism and launched nationwide 'crusades' to attract supporters and donors. McIntire, creator of the American Council of Christian Churches (ACCC), used it to weld fundamentalist separatist churches in the USA into a united front for social and political action.[9] He also founded the International Council of Christian Churches to pursue the same end in the wider world. Graham found a base in the less strident and confrontational National Association of Evangelicals (NAE), which had emerged from a meeting at the Moody Bible Institute in 1941.[10] McIntire and Graham differed not so much in theology as in style. McIntire struck a harsh, militant, and aggressive pose, while Graham adopted a smoother, flexible, less confrontational posture.

McIntire and Graham went on to crusade vigorously on behalf of the expanding and increasingly politically powerful Christian Right of the 1970s and 1980s. Indeed, both fundamentalist currents – and both styles – have persisted to the present day and still affect American culture and politics. In the period just after the Second World War, McIntire's current attached itself to the ultra-conservative political Right, beginning with US Senator Joseph McCarthy in the early 1950s. Graham's current, also firmly anti-communist and fundamentalist, attracted a wider conservative-to-moderate political spectrum owing to his flexibility and careful attention to public relations. While McIntire operated within the narrow trenches of militant politics, Graham targeted the White House itself, positioning himself as a useful spiritual and political advisor to presidents and as the leading evangelical spokesman nationally. His influence on the Oval Office was that of a strong leader and skilled operative who could deliver a substantial vote at the polls.

The Post-War Radical Political Right

The American scholar Seymour Martin Lipset's classic article, 'The Radical Right: a problem for American democracy', published in *The British Journal of Sociology* in 1955, presents essential context and insight that illumine this phase of American political history. Lipset noted that 'Americanism is an ideology rather than just a nationalist term'. He pointed out that the period 1930 to 1945 was generally characterized by liberal, or reformist, attitudes in American politics, reinforced by the Great Depression and the struggle against fascism and rightist extremism.[11] After the Second World War, the Cold War set in, and the political pendulum shifted to a struggle against communism and leftist extremism – setting the stage for the emergence of the Radical Right in American politics.

The American Radical Right's political agenda opposed the labor movement and trade unions, the income tax, the welfare state, and government planning.[12] In sum, it sought to reverse Franklin Roosevelt's New Deal. The Radical Right's foreign policy perspective was anti-communist and opposed to the United Nations organization. According to Lipset:

> some of the economic radical rightists such as the new millionaires of Texas, or men who were involved in Liberty League activities in the thirties, have accepted the isolationist ideology applied to the past, even though they were not isolationists before World War II.[13]

As Lipset points out, a rich source of support for the Radical Right 'is the important group of newly wealthy individuals thrown up by great prosperity'. He adds that new wealth

> ...most often tends to have extremist ideologies, to believe in some extreme conservative doctrines in economic matters. The new millionaires, such as those concentrated in Texas, have given extensive financial support to radical right movements, politicians, and propaganda organizations, such as Facts Forum.[14]

Such Texas millionaires included the well-known Hunt family, who made their fortune in the oil industry.

The participation of the Hunt family and other representatives of business interests recalls the support corporate America gave to fundamentalist Billy Sunday in the early 1900s, as well as the support Dutch financiers and business interests gave to the extreme right-wing political party and theological movement of Abraham Kuyper and his circle. Lipset emphasized the extremist, and sometimes pro-fascist, sentiments of American big business:

Extreme conservatism on economic matters is, of course, not new. During the thirties it was represented by the Liberty League and by various organized measures of big business groups to block the development of trade unions. In general, one could probably safely say that most big business was willing to use undemocratic, restrictive measures to prevent the emergence of trade unions in the twenties and thirties.[15]

Carl McIntire, Anti-Communism, and Senator Joseph McCarthy

Carl McIntire's anti-communism arose from the underlying premillennial dispensationalism that permeated the fundamentalist movement. Fundamentalist Armageddon theology anticipated an apostate 'world religion' that would emerge to support the Antichrist during the End Times. Fundamentalists perceived the post-Second World War international ecumenical movement as embodied in the World Council of Churches (WCC; founded in 1948) to be such a 'sign of the times'.[16] The United Nations organization and the ecumenical movement together were understood by fundamentalists as a combined religious and political amalgam that would support the activities of the Antichrist who, in turn, would be supported by the power(s) of the North, the Soviet Union.[17]

McIntire associated the ecumenical movement and the WCC with the End Times, the period of 'apostasy' coming before the Second Advent of Christ. His heated rhetoric and militant stance did not conceal his contempt for the Roman Catholic Church.[18] His hostile attitude toward the Catholic Church persisted within conservative fundamentalist circles, which explains, in part, Billy Graham's coolness toward the Kennedy administration.

Three themes characterized the fundamentalists' foreign policy perspective: opposition to ecumenicalism, opposition to the United Nations organization and opposition to international communism. The NAE joined the ACCC in opposition to the WCC and the ecumenical movement. In time, the European Union also fit neatly into the fundamentalists' End Times scenario. Gasper explains that

> in their premillennial doctrine most fundamentalists taught that a regrouping of nations involving Russia, Germany, the Jews in Palestine, and the peoples of the Orient would occur, marking the end of the age immediately preceding the second coming of Christ.[19]

McIntire's militant anti-communism sparked several parallel movements, and his anti-communist crusade was joined by other leaders from the Christian Right. Reverend Billy James Hargis, for example, established his own organization called Christian Crusade. He joined McIntire and other fundamentalist leaders in working hand-in-glove with the erratic and unstable Roman Catholic US Senator Joseph McCarthy (Republican – Wisconsin) to promote McCarthy's sensational investigations on Capitol Hill, likened by some to witch hunts. Despite the Senator's Roman Catholicism, fundamentalists valued his anti-communism so a tactical alliance was possible. The Protestant fundamentalists supporting Senator McCarthy were joined by conservative Roman Catholics such as William F. Buckley, Jr, and his circle. The senator himself had conservative anti-communist Jews, such as Roy Cohn, as key aides.

William Martin explains that

> Hargis soon offered his services to McCarthy, as did McIntire's followers and the senator publicly credited them with providing him with research and speech writing assistance. McCarthy's ability to destroy reputations with unproved allegations during this period was enormous, and association with such power energized his new associates.[20]

The ACCC–ICCC (International Council of Christian Churches)[21] hired Hargis and Fred C. Schwartz, an Australian doctor who later branched out on his own to establish the Christian Anti-Communist Crusade (CACC),[22] which is today based in Manitou Springs, Colorado, and led by Dr David Noebel, president of Summit ministries.[23]

The fundamentalists who worked with McCarthy targeted their opponents in mainline churches. According to Clyde Wilcox:

> Fundamentalist leaders cooperated closely with McCarthy, and urged investigation of prominent modernist religious leaders as possible communists or fellow travelers. By 1953, all of the future leaders of the anti-communist organizations were associated with the ACCC. Even as McCarthy began to self-destruct, these leaders were forming, with the aid of the ACCC, organizations which would constitute the Christian Right of the 1950s ... The leaders of these organizations used nationwide radio shows to communicate with their followers, who contributed increasing amounts to their cause.[24]

McCarthy's support group of fundamentalist Protestants, conservative Roman Catholics, and conservative Jewish operatives foreshadowed the alignment of the political New Right, Christian Right, and Neoconservatives that would develop in the late 1970s and early 1980s. Francis August Schaeffer, founder of the L'Abri center in Switzerland in 1955, was a protégé of McIntire and a primary intellectual contributor to the formation of the 'New' Christian Right of the 1970s. Schaeffer was involved in assisting McIntire in the European activities of the ICCC and moved his family to Switzerland in 1948. It will be recalled that Schaeffer was deeply involved in neo-Calvinist theological circles in the USA who were, in turn, linked to conservative separatist Reformed church and political circles in the Netherlands. This connection to the Netherlands is significant because influential and wealthy conservative Dutch-American circles linked to separatist Reformed churches in western Michigan play an increasingly powerful role within the American fundamentalist movement during and after the 1970s.

Billy Graham Launched by William Randolph Hearst and Henry Luce

William Franklin Graham, Jr (1918–), was born in Charlotte, North Carolina, and studied at Bob Jones College and Florida Bible Institute before finally graduating from Wheaton College in Illinois. Graham was mentored by evangelist Torrey Johnson. When Johnson founded Youth for Christ International in 1945,[25] Graham became its first field director and traveled throughout the USA and extensively abroad. His work with Youth for Christ (YFC) established Graham as an up-and-coming mass evangelist.

The large youth rallies of Youth for Christ and its conservative patriotic orientation caught the attention of two of the most powerful press moguls in the USA: William Randolph Hearst and Henry Luce. After a huge rally at Soldiers' Field in Chicago on Memorial Day 1945, the much impressed Hearst promoted the YFC movement in all of his 22 newspapers. These features led to further media attention including a major story in Luce's *Time* magazine in February 1946.[26] YFC's success inspired other conservative evangelical organizations to target both high-school and college students. In 1951, Bill Bright, a graduate of Fuller Theological Seminary in Pasadena, California, founded the Campus Crusade for Christ movement, which in time surpassed the YFC as a fundamentalist mass youth organization.

Meanwhile, Graham became president of Northwestern College in Minnesota in 1948 and then moved on to pursue mass evangelism. In 1949, Graham scheduled a revival in Los Angles planned to last three weeks; when

William Randolph Hearst took note and promoted it in his newspapers, the revival continued for seven weeks and made Graham a national figure. As Ben Bagdikian explains in his book *Media Monopoly*, 'In late 1949, Hearst sent a telegram to all Hearst editors: "Puff Graham". The editors did – in Hearst newspapers, magazines, movies, and newsreels. Within two months Graham was preaching to crowds of 350,000.'[27] Luce's father having been a missionary in China may account, in part, for Luce's strong interest in Graham. W.A. Swanberg, in his biography *Luce and His Empire*, describes an interesting meeting between Luce and Graham in 1949. Luce, while on a visit to South Carolina, heard that Graham was preaching in Columbia. Luce asked his editor, William Howland, to fly down from New York and meet him in Charleston and then write the story promoting Graham.[28] Thus Graham's national career and future was firmly established by the two most powerful conservative press barons in the USA.

Hearst, Luce, and Fascism

Press baron William Randolph Hearst made no effort to hide his sympathy for European Fascism and National Socialism:

> The fascist party of Italy was organized to quell the disturbances and disorders of communism. The fascist party of Germany was organized for the same purpose. It was intended to and very likely did prevent Germany from going communist and cooperating with Soviet Russia. This is the great policy, the great achievement that makes the Hitler regime popular with the German people…[29]

Henry Luce and his *Time–Life–Fortune* publishing empire shared Hearst's assessment, but placed particular emphasis on Mussolini.[30]

These two press barons, and others, directly and indirectly supported similar reactionary policies in the USA. Professor Gaetano Salvemini, a famous anti-fascist intellectual and member of the Italian Socialist Party, decades ago warned of a 'new brand of fascism' in the USA. While teaching in exile at Harvard, during the 1930s, he pointed to the 'Fascism of corporate business enterprise in this country.'[31] As one succinct definition of the day had it: 'Fascism is the open terrorist dictatorship of the most reactionary, most chauvinist and most imperialist elements of finance capital.'[32] Fascism's main features include the rise of a demagogic leader sponsored by a plutocratic oligarchy; the curtailment of civil liberties; the elimination of a free press; the emasculation of labor and the labor movement; and the destruction of intellectual and political opposition.[33]

American political leaders warned against fascism abroad and at home. Many felt that reactionary circles on Wall Street and in big business wished to bring fascist policies to the USA. Harold Ickes (1874–1952), a progressive Republican who served in Franklin Roosevelt's Cabinet during the New Deal, forcefully condemned fascism.[34] In a speech to the American Civil Liberties Union, on 8 December 1937, he pointed to 'the ability and willingness to turn the concentrated wealth of America against the welfare of America'. Ickes warned his audience not to take democracy and an open society for granted.

The Anti-FDR 'Business Plot'

Although few remember them today, in the 1930s a cabal of Wall Street financiers and industrialists who were enthusiastic supporters of international fascism in Italy and Germany plotted a bizarre *coup d'état*, dubbed the 'Business Plot'.[35] Through business connections, the group's members had formed close relationships with their counterparts in Europe, prominent and powerful elite supporters of international fascism in Germany, France, Italy, and England.[36]

The cabal resolved to overthrow President Franklin Roosevelt and sabotage his progressive New Deal. As soon as Roosevelt was elected, in 1932, the Wall Street cabal took a decision to use strategies and methods already used successfully by European fascists to gain influence and political power; they hoped to form a network of action committees and mass movements, including violent organizations, and to make both political and religious appeals to the middle and working classes. Ambassador William E. Dodd, Franklin Roosevelt's ambassador to Germany, referred in 1937 to the American section of the transnational fascist oligarchy of the era. 'Fascism is on the march today in America,' he said. 'Certain American industrialists had a great deal to do with bringing fascist regimes into being in both Germany and Italy.'[37]

The Business Plot was exposed by the very US Marine Corps general the Wall Street cabal thought they had recruited to lead the coup. Gerald G. MacGuire, a Wall Street bond salesman, was recruited by a circle of financiers first to collect information about the methods of European fascist organizations and then to be the intermediary between the Wall Street cabal and Major General Smedley Butler of the Marine Corps.[38] Butler immediately revealed the plot to President Roosevelt, whom he greatly admired, and then exposed it publicly in newspaper interviews.

Butler also testified before a special investigative committee in the US House of Representatives, the McCormack-Dickstein Committee, established to investigate the alleged plot.[39] The committee found evidence of an intended coup, but suppressed specific information and testimony as to the Wall Street connection. According to the committee report, 'In the last few weeks of the committee's official life it received evidence showing that certain persons had made an attempt to establish a fascist government in this country.'[40]

The committee's work later led to the formation of the US House Un-American Activities Committee (HUAC), which was authorized to investigate subversive communist and fascist activity in the USA. Congressman McCormack later became Speaker of the House (1961–71).

Grayson Prevost-Mallet Murphy, a director of Morgan-aligned companies and a founder of the American Legion, became the treasurer of the American Liberty League.[41] The American Legion war veterans' organization was established in 1919. The National Commander of the American Legion in 1922–3, Colonel Alvin Owsley (1888–1967), put the matter clearly when he said:

> If ever needed, the American Legion stands ready to protect our country's institutions and ideals as the *Fascisti* dealt with the destructionists who menaced Italy ... Do not forget that the *Fascisti* are to Italy what the American Legion is to the United States.[42]

In 1931, the National Commander of the American Legion, Ralph T. O'Neill, gave the Italian Ambassador to the USA a copy of a resolution of the American Legion Executive Committee praising Mussolini as a great leader. It is no wonder that many Americans, and leaders of the New Deal, believed fascism was on the march in the USA at this time.

The Reactionary American Liberty League

In the planning for their proposed coup, the Business Plot conspirators, with additional supporters, created the American Liberty League, a powerful elite organization founded in 1934 and active until 1940.[43] Its intent was to overturn the New Deal and President Franklin Roosevelt and replace

Roosevelt in the presidential election of 1936.[44] To this end, it got behind a Republican opponent – ironically, Governor Alf Landon of Kansas, a moderate and himself a mild supporter of the New Deal. 'By the summer of 1934,' Arthur Schlesinger, Jr, explains in his book *The Politics of Upheaval* (1960), 'growing discontent in the business community had led to the formation of the American Liberty League, which seemed for a moment the spearhead of conservative opposition to the New Deal.'[45]

The Liberty League was specifically modeled on European fascist organizations such as the French Croix de Feu.[46] The financial and big business interests behind the Liberty League in the USA paralleled the Confederazione dell'Industria, the group effort – including industrialists Adriano Olivetti and Giovanni Agnelli – that put Mussolini into power and the Thyssen–Krupp–Voegeler–Flick network that put Hitler into power.[47] *Time* magazine said of Agnelli in 1936: 'Perhaps nothing is more significant in Italy than that Agnelli of Fiat gives the Fascist salute when he encounters the Dictator.'[48]

The leadership of the organization included prominent members of the Wall Street plutocracy and a number of prominent politicians, Democrat and Republican. Among the key Wall Street and big business interests behind the Liberty League were the House of Morgan, the DuPonts, and the Kuhn Loeb investment banking interests. Representatives of industrial interests such as General Motors (controlled by DuPont interests), United States Steel (linked to the Morgan interests), and Remington Arms (controlled by DuPont) were also deeply involved.[49]

The president of the Liberty League was Jouette Shouse (1879–1968), a former member of the US Congress from Kansas (1915–19); he was President Wilson's Assistant Secretary of the Treasury (1919–20), former chairman of the Democratic Party's National Executive Committee, and married to Catherine Filene Dodd of the Boston merchant Filene family. The League's key members included William Knudson of General Motors; oil baron J. Howard Pew; Nathan L. Miller, counsel of US Steel; Irene, Pierre, and Lammot DuPont;[50] Jacob Raskob of DuPont and General Motors (who was a former chairman of the Democratic Party National Committee); and the Hearst interests.[51] Even former Governor Al Smith of New York, the Democratic presidential candidate of 1928, was allied with the League.

William Randolph Hearst's involvement with the Liberty League brought it many important allegiances. The Hearst interests were linked with the financial interests of West Coast financier A.P. Giannini's TransAmerica company and Bank of America. This bank reportedly handled Mussolini's financial interests in the USA. The Hearst interests controlled an important share of the Remington Arms Corporation, of which the DuPont interests had the controlling share. Remington small arms were reportedly to have been made available to 500,000 paramilitary forces operating in the service of the Business Plot, which planned to seize Washington, DC, the nation's capital, by force.

The Hearst interests were also intertwined with the British imperial interests of Sir Henry Deterding and his Royal Dutch Shell group, and with Lord Rothermere's interests in Canada.[52] In addition to their involvement with Americans sympathetic to fascism, Deterding and Rothermere provided financial support to Sir Oswald Moseley's fascist movement in the UK. Deterding made use of the shipping company operated by Hypolite Worms to move Royal Dutch Shell oil around the world.[53] The Lazard Freres Paris office handled Royal Dutch Shell business in France, and the Lazard group organized the Banque Worms in the late 1920s. The New York office of Lazard Freres was the interface to Wall Street.

The Liberty League and its satellite action organizations, such as the 'Crusaders', were guided by influential members of the board of the American Jewish Committee (AJC).[54] These businessmen included Irving Lehman, of Lehman Brothers; Lessing J. Rosenwald, Chairman of Sears Roebuck; Roger W. Strauss, director of Revere Copper and Brass; Louis Edward Kirstein, vice president of Filene's; Joseph M. Proskauer, who was a director of the American Liberty League; Henry Ittleson, who was president of the Commercial Investment Trust A.G. of Berlin; and Albert D. Lasker, who served on the Crusaders' board. The AJC, founded in 1906 as a foreign policy lobby group that focused on human rights in Russia, published *Commentary* magazine. This magazine, edited from 1960–95 by Norman Podhoretz, has been the leading vector for decades promoting so-called 'neoconservative' foreign policy positions – most recently on the Iraq war launched in 2003.

Despite its anti-New Deal stance, the Liberty League was far too controversial for the Republican Party to embrace. Publicly, Landon – and the Republican Party itself – rejected Liberty League endorsement in the 1936 election, calculating that an endorsement by such a reactionary organization would be detrimental to image and to electoral chances.

Fortunately, foiling the 'Business Plot' kept the Liberty League at bay. But after Roosevelt's death, the Wall Street cabal continued its program for a fascist and imperial America during the Truman administration, through the Cold War era, and down to today's White House and Congress. Mobilizing a theocratic subculture and the Religious Right as a support base for this program was an important objective. Michael W. Miles in his *The Odyssey of the American Right* (1980) has noted the persistent influence of the Liberty League in the post-Second World War era:

> The crisis of the 1930s did leave a significant residue of the national upper class maintaining a commitment to the old order. The American Liberty League represented this sentiment, and many right-wing organizations continued to receive the backing of wealthy corporate capitalists in the post-war period.[55]

Miles notes the American Enterprise Institute was 'founded in 1943 to ensure that peacetime reconversion restored a capitalism uncorrupted by public regulation'. He specifically highlights the DuPont and Pew families as 'examples of the persistence of family capitalism'.[56] Thus, in the post-war era, the objectives of the Liberty League were still being promoted.

Post-War Financing of the Religious Right

One example of the continuity between the pre-war Liberty League and conservative projects is the support of the Pew family for the post-war Religious Right. Oil baron J. Howard Pew served on the Liberty League's Advisory Council and Executive Committee and is just one example of how wealthy individuals provided financial support to post-war conservative organizations at this time. He established two significant conservative religious organizations: the Christian Freedom Foundation (CFF) and the Christian Economic Foundation (CEF). Pew created the tax-exempt CFF in 1950 with a $50,000 grant and later, during the 1960s and 1970s, Pew interests donated at least $2.3 million. Some financing was also channeled into Third Century Publishers to assist the Christian Right movement. By 1976, the CFF's declared objective was to make America a 'Christian Republic' by electing Christian conservatives to Congress. The CEF was formed in the 1950s to counter the moderate National Council of Churches. Its publications such as *Christian Economics* were mass-mailed to clergy nationwide. Pew additionally, with Billy Graham's involvement, backed the Gordon-Conwell Theological Seminary merger in 1969 as a conservative Christian missionary training centre.

Pew funded Graham's *Christianity Today* magazine and also the conservative magazine, *The Presbyterian Layman*, published by the fundamentalist Presbyterian Lay Committee.[57]

Graham's growing national prominence and prudent action in the service of conservative evangelism positioned him to effectively lead national religious crusades. Martin points out that Graham was increasingly accepted as a mainstream figure and that organizations such as Youth for Christ and Campus Crusade for Christ were 'flourishing at the end of the fifties'. While the militant anti-communism of Carl McIntire remained within rather narrow bounds, Graham's 'less hard-line approach would dominate evangelicalism in the decade to come'.[58]

Graham's 1957 New York Crusade took place in Madison Square Garden and brought increased national attention to him as a mass evangelist. Gasper says this crusade was 'one of the most effective and united campaigns in Graham's entire career'. Graham saw the event in a Cold War context. 'There is fear that if Russia ever decided to launch a sneak attack against the United States,' Graham said, 'that New York would be the first on the list of targets. This terrifying thought gives us a sense of urgency and responsibility.' Playing to the nuclear fear factor, and appealing to premillennialist dispensationalists, Graham said, 'this crusade could possibly be God's last call to New York'.[59]

Not surprisingly, the event was financially backed by Wall Street and large corporations. As we have seen, conservative business circles in the USA and Europe had long realized the utility of conservative religious movements to support laissez-faire capitalism and political reaction. Gasper explains Graham's tactics for the 1957 crusade in New York City: 'Following the practices of Billy Sunday a generation ago,' he said, 'Graham adopted modern business methods to promote the New York Crusade ... big business was seriously interested in the principles for which Graham stood.'[60]

Billy Graham as White House 'Spiritual Advisor'

The Religious Right in the USA took advantage of Cold War tensions to assume the mantle of patriotism and spiritual leadership of the nation. Billy Graham's more restrained presentation of the conservative evangelical message facilitated his penetration of national politics at the highest levels in Washington. Graham's entry into the White House was facilitated by the work of another evangelist, Abraham Vereide, who had come to Washington to evangelize its politicians. Graham's long run as White House spiritual advisor got off to a bad start with President Truman, however, but Vereide facilitated Graham's relationship with President Eisenhower.

Vereide, a conservative evangelical, had promoted anti-communist and anti-labor positions among circles of wealthy businessmen across the USA throughout the 1930s. He formed an organization called International Christian Leadership and developed what he called 'prayer breakfast' groups as a method of evangelization and attracting donors. In 1953, Vereide organized the first Presidential Prayer Breakfast, which became an annual affair in Washington. In the 1954 event Eisenhower and several Cabinet members attended and Graham was present, although he was not a featured speaker. Nonetheless, Eisenhower and Graham developed regular, although not frequent, contact, during the course of which Graham came to develop a friendship with Vice President Nixon. Vereide's International Christian Leadership grew in political influence over the years and numbers Senators and Congressmen among its tight 'Fellowship'.[61]

Graham's better relationship with President Eisenhower established his national credentials as the public face of conservative, but presentable, evangelism. Martin explains:

> The decade of the fifties had seen Billy Graham emerge as the unquestioned leader and exemplar of evangelical Christianity, particularly that segment of the movement that identified itself as the New Evangelicalism, as distinguished from the Old Fundamentalism represented by Carl McIntire and men of his ilk. In most respects, the basic theology of these two groups was essentially the same, but the New Evangelicals tended to be rather tolerant of minor theological differences among themselves, whereas fundamentalists felt compelled to withdraw fellowship from any suspected of even the slightest deviation from their version of orthodoxy.[62]

Graham's cultivation of Vice President Nixon was useful to both men. Graham increased his national prominence and influence, while Nixon gained access to religious voters whom Graham could mobilize:

> Prior to the 1956 elections, Graham revealed that he was suggesting to friends in 'high ecclesiastical circles' that Nixon be invited to address various religious assemblies during the following year. Given the likelihood that Nixon would run for president in 1960, Graham felt the vice president needed to pay close attention to his public image.[63]

True to his word, Graham arranged to have Nixon, whom he characterized as a 'splendid churchman', speak at major Methodist, Baptist, and Presbyterian conferences in North Carolina during the summer of the 1956 campaign. Also, to enhance his chances of pushing the right buttons, Graham supplied Nixon, unsolicited, with a speech he thought the Vice President might want to use. He also offered to invite several key religious leaders, including a Methodist and an Episcopal bishop, the president of the Southern Baptist Convention, and the Moderator of the Presbyterian Church in the USA (South), to have lunch with the vice president in the Graham home. Graham felt exposure to these and other religious leaders would help Nixon immensely over the long term.[64]

Graham's anti-Roman Catholic stance behind the scenes – and his backing of Nixon in the 1960 election – effectively closed the door to the Kennedy White House. But when Lyndon Johnson assumed the presidency, Graham had good entry.[65] When Johnson announced he would not seek re-election, Graham felt emboldened to support his old friend Richard Nixon more openly. Graham worked to align the religious vote under his influence with the bloc Republicans, then called the 'Silent Majority'. Martin says of Graham's political activity that 'throughout the primary and election campaigns, he made so many favorable comments about Nixon, his high principles, and his deep religious convictions that a formal endorsement would have been superfluous'. Of Nixon's putative piety, Martin says no president 'ever made such a conscious, calculating use of religion as a political instrument as did Richard Nixon'.[66] The Watergate debacle caused Graham to tone down his highly visible public political role. Deftly stepping aside as the Nixon administration crashed and burned, Graham nonetheless continued rallying the conservative evangelical subculture to action.

The Watergate scandal, however, did not derail evangelical interest in politics. During the mid 1970s, when Jimmy Carter, the Governor of Georgia, emerged as a viable presidential candidate, the broader evangelical community – liberal and conservative – rallied to support him. His moderation and liberalism, however, eventually led the conservative fundamentalist evangelical forces, now organized as the 'New' Christian Right, to look ahead to the 1980 election, for which they shifted their support to the Republican candidate, Ronald Reagan.

9

The Christian Right in the Seventies and Eighties

What came to be called the 'New' Christian Right emerged during the decade of the 1970s under the tutelage of the political New Right. By the end of the following decade, this new movement was an influential force in American politics.[1] Its mentor, the 'New Right', first emerged after the Second World War in obscure intellectual circles.[2] When favorite presidential candidate Barry Goldwater lost the 1964 election, Goldwater supporters, eager for extreme political change – for, in effect, a conservative revolution – began to mobilize and guide a conservative political movement.[3] These 'movement conservatives' entrenched themselves in Washington, DC, in the early 1970s in a network of think tanks and political action organizations financed by wealthy conservative business interests, by conservative tax-exempt charitable foundations, and by various fundraising techniques, particularly direct mail.[4]

Working in the US Senate as a foreign policy staffer, I saw first hand the process by which the Christian Right emerged, during the 1980s. Over a decade, I watched its rigidly pro-Israel stance first challenge and then undermine our foreign policy and national security. The process began when the New Right began taking note of the Christian Right as a potential source of voters and money. It tutored Christian Right leaders and their organizations in the arts of political action.

Then, in the early 1980s, the Neoconservative movement, a Jewish intellectual network, penetrated the Republican Party and the Reagan administration. Neoconservatives began tutoring the Christian Right in foreign policy with a particular emphasis on pro-Israel political action.[5] The Christian Right soon aligned itself politically with the Jewish pro-Israel lobby spearheaded by the American Israel Political Affairs Committee (AIPAC).

By the mid-1980s, an intimate working relationship had developed among the New Right, the Christian Right, the Neoconservative movement, and the Jewish pro-Israel lobby. This alliance tightened its political bonds and intensified its political activity in Washington, DC, and across the nation, during the 1990s. It also prepared the domestic political situation that would enable President George W. Bush's later catastrophic crusade in the Middle East – wars in Afghanistan and Iraq and confrontation with Syria and Iran.

The New Right versus Eisenhower

Veteran journalist and author Theodore White presented valuable insight into the origins of the New Right in his book *The Making of a President 1964*. White carefully distinguished between candidate Goldwater himself and the 'Goldwater movement' run by conservative political activists, nicknamed 'primitives', such as F. Clifton White. These activists exhibited 'a mood entirely different from the mood of the Taft conservatives of the forties and fifties who had wanted, simply, to hold the country still,' White pointed out, and 'the new mood of the primitives insisted that the course of affairs be reversed'.[6] As Theodore White emphasized, Eisenhower's goal had been to broaden the Republican Party base in support of his moderate programs but conservative strategists such as F. Clifton White planned to harness the most reactionary southern elements behind a sharp conservative turn in national politics. The South was thus courted by Richard Nixon in his 1968 campaign in what was known as the 'Southern Strategy', which many saw as a veiled appeal to latent southern racism.[7]

In 1964, mainstream Republicans – including Eisenhower – sensed that Goldwater's nomination would result in both electoral and ideological disaster for the GOP. But their attempts to oppose his candidacy were adroitly out-maneuvered by the Goldwater movement. 'Eisenhower was appalled at the prospect of Goldwater's nomination,' says Theodore White.[8] In the event, Eisenhower and the party mainstream proved entirely correct.

Ideologically the McCarthyite Radical Right and the follow-on New Right differed sharply from the old conservative Taft wing of the Republican Party.[9] Jonathan Martin Kolkey draws a sharp contrast between the two in his book, *The New Right* (1983).[10] If the Radical Right and the New Right rejected Taft, they disliked President Eisenhower for his effort to update postwar Republicanism by creating a 'Modern Republicanism'.[11]

The New Right Comes to Washington

Paul Weyrich and Morton Blackwell, both 'movement conservatives' from the Goldwater campaign days, arrived early in Washington.[12] The late Paul Weyrich (1942–2008), a Roman Catholic from Racine, Wisconsin, moved from his local Young Republicans organization to the Goldwater campaign in 1964. Moving in Colorado political circles, Weyrich met an assistant to the Colorado beer baron Joseph Coors and in 1973, with Coors' financial backing, founded the Heritage Foundation, a conservative think tank in Washington specializing in policy research. Over the coming years, the Heritage Foundation, located in a building not far from the US Capitol, became a major ideological influence, by providing policy analysis and recommendations to conservative members of Congress and their staffs.[13]

The New Right worked assiduously to create an organizational infrastructure with which to launch its conservative revolution. In 1974, Weyrich founded the Committee for the Survival of a Free Congress (CSFC), later renamed Free Congress Foundation, to teach practical campaign techniques, recruit candidates, and raise funds for various conservative causes.[14] Recognizing the vast untapped potential of conservative Christians, he helped Robert Grant found Christian Voice in 1977 and Jerry Falwell found the Moral Majority organization in 1979.[15]

The Christian Freedom Foundation and Theocracy

While the political New Right established itself in Washington, the Christian Right began to undertake similar moves – thereby preparing the way for an eventual alliance. The Christian Freedom Foundation (CFF) that J. Howard Pew had established in 1950 as a conservative action organization promoting the Religious Right was deeply troubled by the 1970s, when it was taken over by key Christian Right elements. Its new leaders were allied with a religious publishing house founded in 1974, called Third Century

Publishers. Third Century counted Arizona Republican Congressman John Conlan and Bill Bright, the head of the Campus Crusade for Christ, among its supporters. Third Century published materials to guide Christian activists in political organization and action.

Its directors soon realized that a non-profit tax exempt foundation would be a useful companion organization and moved to take over Pew's Christian Freedom Foundation. Key backers for this move were Richard DeVos of the Amway Corporation, John Talcott of Ocean Spray Cranberries, and Arthur S. DeMoss of the Liberty National Insurance Company. Ed McAteer was hired as the director of the CFF. He later founded the influential Religious Roundtable organization in 1979 and helped Jerry Falwell organize the Moral Majority.

DeVos, the finance chairman of the Republican National Committee 1981–2, comes from Michigan and belongs to the Christian Reformed Church, a conservative neo-Calvinist offshoot of the Dutch Reformed Church founded in Michigan by Dutch immigrants. Wealthy members of this community such as DeVos endorsed political action by the Christian Right in order to transform the American polity into a theocracy – the principle of the separation of church and state required under the First Amendment of the US Constitution was entirely undesirable to them. Such 'dominionism' grew from the intellectual roots put down by Abraham Kuyper (1837–1920), an ultraconservative neo-Calvinist who became a powerful influence in Dutch politics.

The Arthur S. DeMoss Foundation, a leading financial backer of the Christian Right, strongly supported the late Jerry Falwell and his Liberty College, Bill Bright's Campus Crusade for Christ, and a number of other key organizations such as Charles Colson's Prison Fellowship.[16] The DeMoss Foundation, although associated closely with fundamentalist Southern Baptists, developed programs for outreach to Roman Catholics.

The financial backers of the CFF thus span the range of the conservative evangelical movement in the USA from neo-Calvinists to Southern Baptists. Their goal was to unify the conservative evangelical movement so as to better position it for national political action.

The Neo-Calvinist Connection

The friendly takeover of the CFF was significant because it allied the Michigan-based neo-Calvinists, the Southern-based conservative Baptists, and the Pentecostals it promotes. Charles Colson, a convicted felon from the Watergate dirty tricks of the Nixon era, helped bring together the Michigan neo-Calvinists, the Falwell-oriented fundamentalists, and Pentecostal–Charismatic leader Pat Robertson.[17] Colson has helped consolidate fundamentalist unity, while also reaching out to conservative elements in the Roman Catholic Church in the USA.

Colson's activities follow the nineteenth-century political model of Abraham Kuyper's neo-Calvinist Anti-Revolutionary Party (*Anti-Revolutionaire Partij*, ARP). Separatism among American fundamentalist churches can be seen in the context of Kuyper's separation from the liberal Dutch Reformed Church to found in 1892 his own conservative 'Reformed Church in the Netherlands'. Kuyper, of necessity, broke with the liberal mainstream church in the Netherlands because his extremist theology found no place there. Similarly, fundamentalists in the USA split off and separated from denominations they found to be too liberal.

Kuyper's creation of a reactionary political party is significant because it serves as a model for fundamentalists in the USA devoted to action in the political sphere. Kuyper's own vigorous and militant political engagement is seen as exemplary by leading American fundamentalists, who reject quietism with respect to politics. The ARP had its roots in the early nineteenth-century Dutch parliamentary circles that opposed the liberal politics and philosophy of republicanism and the French Revolution. Its intellectual leader was Guillaume Groen van Prinsterer (1801–76), who as a politician and historian opposed liberal tendencies in the Dutch Reformed Church and in Dutch politics.

Abraham Kuyper, Prinsterer's protégé, helped Prinsterer work toward realizing theocracy in the Netherlands. In Dutch politics, Kuyper's ARP formed coalitions with conservative Roman Catholic parties – coalitions that enabled Kuyper to become Prime Minister from 1901 to 1905. This alliance with conservative Roman Catholics is a model for conservative Protestant fundamentalists who are working to forge a united Religious Right in the USA today.

Jeremy Scahill, in his revealing book *Blackwater*, sheds important light on Charles Colson's relation to these Michigan neo-Calvinists.[18] Erik Prince, who founded Blackwater, is the son of a wealthy Michigan businessman who made millions in the automobile industry.[19] His father, Edgar Prince, helped Christian Right leaders James Dobson and Gary Bauer through generous funding of the Family Research Council. Prince's sister married Dick DeVos, Richard DeVos's son, strengthening family ties to the Religious Right. While Prince was raised in the neo-Calvinist environment, he converted to Roman Catholicism later in life. As a philanthropist, Prince funds both fundamentalist Protestant and conservative Roman Catholic organizations.

Charles Colson, a frequent visitor to Michigan, works closely with Michigan-based neo-Calvinists. Colson put forward his theopolitical perspective in 2002 in a speech presented at Calvin College in Grand Rapids, Michigan, in which, according to Scahill, 'the former Watergate conspirator talked extensively about the historical foundation and current necessity of a political and religious alliance of Catholics and evangelicals'.[20]

Scahill explains that

> Colson talked about his work, beginning in the mid-1980s, with famed conservative evangelical Protestant minister turned Catholic priest Richard Neuhaus and others to build a unified movement. That work ultimately led in 1994 to the controversial document 'Evangelicals and Catholics Together: The Christian Mission in the Third Millennium'. The ECT document articulated the vision that would animate Blackwater's corporate strategy and the politics practiced by Erik Prince. The vision is a marriage of the historical authority of the Catholic Church with the grassroots appeal of the modern conservative evangelical movement, bolstered by the cooperation of largely secular and Jewish neoconservatives.[21] Author Damon Linker, who once edited Neuhaus' journal, *First Things*, termed this phenomenon the rise of the 'Theocons'.[22]

Colson himself says that he has been profoundly influenced by Kuyper. 'My statement that the dominating principle of Christian truth is not soteriological but, rather, cosmological is taken directly from Abraham Kuyper,' Colson said in an interview published by the Christian Right's Michigan-based Acton Institute.[23] Colson emphasizes political action by fundamentalists rather than quietism. In the interview, Colson rejected separation and isolation from political action:

> The fundamentalist movement of the Christian church made a grievous mistake early in the twentieth century by withdrawing from the mainstream of society and building its separate, parallel institutions. That decision, as much as anything else, is responsible for the secularization of modern American life, as Francis Schaeffer argued eloquently in *The Great Evangelical Disaster*.[24]

Colson explained that Kuyper had influenced his interest in a fundamentalist alliance with conservative Roman Catholics:

> Father Richard Neuhaus and I saw that Christians from both the Catholic and Protestant confessions are defending the same worldview; we therefore thought that we should join together to seek common ground wherever we could find it, to engage in dialogue to better understand one another's traditions and points of view, and to work toward a common witness in the world.[25]

Thus Colson specifically endorses the same political alignment Kuyper had used in the Netherlands: conservative Protestants and conservative Roman Catholics.

The New Right Tutors the Christian Right

The New Right saw the Christian Right as a coalition partner in the 'politics of morality' focused on social issues such as abortion and the traditional nuclear family. Together both movements confronted what they saw as moral decline in America by taking political positions against abortion, homosexuality, and other perceived social ills that they claimed resulted from a 'liberal' or 'permissive' secular society.[26] Furthermore, the Christian Right absorbed the anti-regulatory, anti-tax, anti-state, anti-New Deal 'free enterprise' ideology of the New Right. The Christian Right mobilized a mass base of voters by emphasizing emotionally charged domestic social issues, particularly abortion. They used these issues to support a pro-Israel foreign policy, invoking the widely held Christian Zionist ideology of the Christian Right and dispensationalism.

The Carter candidacy of 1976 was an important milestone for coalition politics. Clyde Wilcox explains the political situation resulting from the candidacy of Jimmy Carter at this time:

> The Carter candidacy had two important consequences for the future of the Christian Right. First, the mobilization of previously apolitical evangelical voters by the campaign demonstrated to secular political elites the existence of a new potential voting bloc. Leaders of the secular New Right immediately began to devise strategies to further mobilize these evangelicals and woo them to Republican activism. Second, because Carter argued that Christians had an obligation to participate in politics, his candidacy helped to break down the long-standing feeling among evangelicals and fundamentalists that electoral politics was not the proper realm for Christian activity.[27]

The Christian Right developed an array of national organizations to mobilize the grass roots. These organizations pioneered a number of political action techniques used in election campaigns, notably the distribution of voter guides through church networks. Several highly influential Christian Right organizations were established in the late 1970s and early 1980s. They included James Dobson's Focus on the Family (circa 1977); Beverly LaHaye's Concerned Women for America (1979); Louis Sheldon's American Coalition for Traditional Values (1980) (since renamed The Traditional Values Coalition); James Dobson and Gary Bauer's Family Research Council (1981); and Pat Robertson and Ralph Reed's Christian Coalition (1987). The Christian Voice organization was established in 1978 by Dr Robert Grant and Gary Jarmin and today has over 100,000 members including 37,000 pastors from almost 50 denominations.[28]

The Neoconservatives Enter Stage Right

The Neoconservative movement, on which there is a rapidly growing literature, is rooted in the post-Second World War Democratic Party foreign policy of Harry Truman, which incorporated anti-communism and strong support for political Zionism. This policy perspective, sometimes referred to as 'Cold War liberalism', cloaks a central commitment to political Zionism and the state of Israel. Neoconservative ideology reflects the conservative political Revisionist Zionism of Vladimir Jabotinsky, a follower of the German philosopher Friedrich Nietzsche.[29]

The Neoconservative movement emerged from a circle of New York Jewish intellectuals including Irving Kristol, Norman Podhoretz, Daniel Bell, Nathan Glazer, and Seymour Martin Lipset, most of them associated with *Commentary* magazine in the early Cold War period. *Commentary*, which began publication in 1945, is published by the prestigious and influential American Jewish Committee (AJC), established in 1906 as an organization lobbying for Jewish causes including foreign policy issues.[30] From 1943 to 1949, the president of the AJC was the politically influential Judge Joseph Meyer Proskauer (1877–1971),[31] member of the American Liberty League Advisory Council and its Executive Committee. A 1935 article in *New Masses* contends that Proskauer was linked to the Hearst interests.[32]

While some Gentile fellow travelers have participated in the Neoconservative movement over the years, the movement is a Jewish one. The neoconservatives' most recent chronicler, Jacob Heilbrunn, pointedly emphasizes this in his book *They Knew They Were Right* (2008):

> The neocons claim to be an intellectual movement with no ethnic component to speak of, but neoconservatism is as much a reflection of Jewish immigrant social resentments and status anxiety as a legitimate movement of ideas. Indeed, however much they may deny it, neoconservatism is in a decisive respect a Jewish phenomenon, reflecting a subset of Jewish concerns.[33]

Sara Diamond in her book *Roads to Dominion* (1995) presents a detailed explanation of the neoconservative faction within the Democratic Party. During the late 1940s, Cold War liberals still supported New Deal programs and civil rights concerns:

> Yet the centrality of anticommunism as the foundation of a post-war political consensus positioned liberals as supporters, too, of the United States as military and diplomatic *enforcer* of the 'free world'. Supportive of the state's prerogatives, both as *distributor* and *enforcer*, Cold War liberalism was by no means characteristically 'right wing'.[34]

During the 1970s, however, neoconservatives shifted rightward economically to laissez-faire positions, which facilitated their penetration of the Republican Party. The neoconservatives staged a takeover of the American Enterprise Institute, an influential old-school big business think tank based in Washington, DC. This marked the shift in their economic policy and their rise to prominence in heretofore traditional Republican circles. Kristol's column in the *Wall Street Journal* promoted lassiez-faire views and developed his close collaboration with its editorial page editor Robert J. Bartley.

The neoconservative movement has as its express aim to gain political influence over US foreign and defense policy. The problem from the neoconservative perspective was that traditional support bases for Jewish concerns evaporated as the political left and liberal intelligentsia shifted against Israel after the 1967 war. As concern for the rights of Palestinians strengthened, important African Americans, such as Rev. Jesse Jackson and Andrew Young, grew increasingly critical of Israel. To counter such a pro-Palestine and anti-Israel political trend, the neoconservatives strengthened their political organization.

Diamond explains the consolidation of various neoconservative organizations during the early 1970s:

> In the wake of George McGovern's 1972 presidential defeat, a committee of neoconservative intellectuals, university professors, Democratic politicians, and labor leaders announced the formation of the Coalition for a Democratic Majority (CDM). It was the first organized network of neoconservatives and their allies since the dissolution of the Congress for Cultural Freedom. The Coalition's stated purpose was to counter McGovern supporters in the party's left-leaning 'New Politics' wing. 'New Politics' was a catch phrase for the anti-war activists, women's liberationists, and other New Leftists now averse to working within the Democratic Party.[35]

Neoconservatives were concerned by the Nixon and Ford administration's supposed lack of a strong pro-Israel position. *Commentary* magazine and its editor Norman Podhoretz spoke out against a perceived 'evenhandedness' that resulted from craving access to oil and desiring détente with the Soviet Union. Podhoretz and the neoconservatives worried that these administrations might pressure Israel to make 'concessions' to the PLO and Palestinians. 'Precisely at a time when solid US backing for Israel was not to be taken for granted,' Diamond says, 'neoconservatives were seeking political allies both within, and outside of, the Democratic Party.'[36]

The New Right generally was nationalist in its foreign policy orientation while the neoconservatives were cosmopolitan and internationalist. According to Diamond:

> In general the New Right conceived foreign policy questions in *nationalist* terms: what is in the best interests of the United States? Neoconservatives were more likely to view the struggle between 'freedom' and 'communism' as an *internationalist* problem. Within this framework, the geopolitical circumstances of Israel and other allies could be elevated to an importance on a par with US 'national security'.[37]

The arrival of the Carter administration resolved this divergence of view. 'As opponents of the Carter Administration, however, both nationalist New Rightists and internationalist neoconservatives focused on conflict between the United States and the Soviet Union,' Diamond says.[38] Neoconservatives found Jimmy Carter less offensive than McGovern but most had backed US Senator Henry 'Scoop' Jackson. Collaboration across party lines developed through the creation in 1976 of the Committee for the Present Danger (CPD), in which CDM members joined with various Republican Party and New Right elements in a coalition against an exaggerated perceived threat from the Soviet Union.[39] Given the Carter administration's strong push for peace in the Middle East and the Camp David process, which President Carter had successfully launched, neoconservatives focused on the 1980 elections and on penetrating the incoming Reagan administration.[40]

Given its emphasis on a conservative defense policy and military build-up, the CPD supported Ronald Reagan in the 1980s and thereby became a recruiting ground for the new Republican administration. As a result, many prominent neoconservatives, such as Richard Perle, Elliott Abrams, Paul Wolfowitz, Frank Gaffney, Douglas Feith, and Dov Zakheim, secured key posts in the Reagan administration. A number of them, such as Perle, Abrams, Gaffney, and Feith, had served previously as staffers in the US Senate and were well versed in the ways of Washington.

The neoconservative collaboration with the Republican Party, particularly with its New Right and Christian Right factions, has been neatly explained by Irving Kristol in his revealing essay in *Commentary* magazine, 'The political dilemma of American Jews' (1984).[41] Kristol argued that the Jewish community, despite solidarity with the Civil Rights movement for African Americans, had been betrayed by pro-Arab African American leaders:

> The upshot is that the long alliance between Jewish and black organizations is coming apart. Jesse Jackson has substituted Arab money for Jewish money. In foreign policy he is pro-Third World and anti-American, pro-PLO and anti-Israel – and he is on the way to making this the quasi-official foreign policy of the black community.[42]

The solution, according to Kristol, was to find an ally in the rising Christian Right. 'The rise of the Moral Majority is another new feature of the American landscape that baffles Jews ... the Moral Majority is strongly pro-Israel,' he said. 'And what do such theoretical abstractions matter as against the mundane fact that this same preacher is vigorously pro-Israel?'[43] As Heilbrunn put it, by 1983 the neoconservatives 'were firmly embedded in the GOP'. In addition, 'taking their cue from Kristol, they were cultivating the Christian right.'[44]

Christian Zionism in the Seventies and Eighties

International events served to spark Christian Zionist activity in the 1970s. The 1973 Middle East War reinforced pro-Israel support in the conservative evangelical community in the USA. Dispensationalists took it as a further 'sign of the times', foretelling the Last Days. According to a study by Connie de Boer, polling data

> show an increase in American sympathy for Israel during and immediately after the 1967 and 1973 wars and after the withdrawal of the Israeli forces from the Sinai at the end of April 1982. The percentage of those sympathizing with Israel was fairly constant during the intermediate periods.

However, on the other hand she notes that

> The invasion of Lebanon on June 6, 1982 did not have the favorable effect on public opinion in the United States that earlier wars elicited.[45]

In contrast to unbending fundamentalist support for Israel, the mainline Protestant churches in the USA maintained their traditional concern for Palestinian rights, including sovereignty.[46] Concern abroad about a pro-Israel bias in American Middle East policy was not assuaged by the takeover of the Reagan administration.[47]

The 1982 Israeli invasion of Lebanon which appeared to be approved by Washington sent shockwaves through the region and the world. Merle Thorpe, Jr, President of the Foundation for Middle East Peace, aptly summed up the situation:

> It is now widely acknowledged that, having neutralized Egypt, Israel undertook its invasion of Lebanon in 1982 to destroy the Palestinian national movement and to remove any barrier to its absorption of the occupied West Bank and Gaza strip into a biblical 'Greater Israel' – this despite the fact that 97 per cent of the population of these territories is Palestinian and despite the overwhelming world view that the territories are the logical place for a Palestinian homeland.[48]

As the Christian Right strengthened at the national political level, moves were made to reinforce dispensational premillennialism within the evangelical subculture and among the mass public. Pro-Israel sentiment stimulated by Christian Right mass popular culture activities such as the production of sensational novels, television programming, and movies has had significant impact. According to Stephen Sizer, Hal Lindsay 'is undoubtedly the most influential of all twentieth-century Christian Zionists'. His first novel, *The Late Great Planet Earth* (1970), propelled him into the mass public consciousness and he has written over 20 books, most of which promote dispensationalism and Christian Zionism.[49]

Billy Graham in his book *Hope for the Future* (1970) made similar claims:

> Today Israel is back in the ancient land of Palestine. Her national emblem, the Star of David, flies from ships sailing the seven seas. She has her own government ... The very presence of Israel in her own land is causing a world crisis in the Middle East and throughout the world. This is precisely as the Bible predicted in scores of places ... the present situation has all the indications of being the setting of the stage for some of the last events of human history.[50]

To this end, Religious Right activists Hal Lindsay and Tim LaHaye produced potboiler novels that incorporated premillennial End Times Armageddon scenarios and sold by the millions of copies. Highly profitable to the authors, these novels created a sensation, promoted a pro-Israel foreign policy perspective, and sparked a stream of 'prophecy' novels by various fundamentalists espousing dispensationalism. Prophecy novelist LaHaye founded the influential Council for National Policy (CNP) in 1981, which brought together key Christian Right and New Right leaders as well as wealthy financial backers such as the Hunt family interests and the DeVos family interests.[51] The CNP focuses on promoting politicians and legislation in line with a theocratic agenda, in a mode reminiscent of the American Liberty League of the 1930s and 1940s.

The linkage between the New Right, the Christian Right, and the Jewish component of the Israel lobby tightened during the mid-1980s. Phyllis Bennis and Khaled Mansour explain:

> In the mid-1980s, the American Israel Public Affairs Committee (AIPAC), Israel's major lobbying group on Capitol Hill, started re-aligning itself with the rising right-wing in the US ... Fundamentalist Christians were ready to lend support to Israel even after the breakup of the 'Evil Empire' because their position was rooted in theological rather than strategic considerations.[52]

AIPAC sought increased links to the Religious Right and the Republican Party. Robert Kuttner of the *New Republic* explains how Republican Party candidates attracted Jewish financial backing: 'They have only to demonstrate sufficient loyalty to Israel and they can all but lock out their democratic challengers from a substantial fraction of Jewish support.'[53] The reliance on Jewish campaign finance by many politicians is not likely to diminish, as Bennis and Mansour point out: 'Challenging the power and influence of the Christian right, especially in Congress, is a dubious possibility.'[54] This is especially true as the New Right and Christian Right successfully promote candidates for the US Senate and the House of Representatives. The trend over the past three decades has been a steadily rising presence in Congress of members whose personal religious beliefs are consistent with those of the Christian Right and which include a pro-Israel perspective, whether based on dispensationalist eschatology or not.

The Christian Right, Neoconservatives, and the Israeli Right

In the late 1970s, establishment of a close working relationship between the Christian Right in the USA and the Israeli political and Religious Right instigated a significant new phase of Christian Zionist activity.[55] On the Israeli side, increased understanding of the fundamentalist movement in the USA was important to the effort. In 1978 a key academic study by a brilliant young Israeli scholar, Yona Malachy, emerged as an operational guide for Israeli Likud political strategists targeting the USA.[56]

Pursuant to a desire for increased relations with American fundamentalists, the Israelis rolled out the red carpet for Religious Right leaders. Jerry Falwell opened a key channel, by undertaking a number of trips to Israel in the late 1970s and early 1980s, where he developed close ties with Menachem Begin (1913–92) leader of the right-wing Herut Party and the Likud alliance. The strategy was twofold. First, Falwell sought to develop political ties with conservative politicians in Israel. Second, he wanted to strengthen pro-Israel sentiment in the USA via expansion of tourism to Israel by Christian groups and the development of links to the Israeli Religious Right. As Israel Shahak and Norton Mezvinsky note in their book *Jewish Fundamentalism in Israel*, Jewish fundamentalists in Israel saw the utility of such an alignment:

As Jewish fundamentalists who abominate non-Jews, they forged a spiritual alliance with Christians who believe that supporting Jewish fundamentalism is necessary to support the second coming of Jesus. This alliance has become a significant factor in both US and Middle Eastern politics.[57]

Following Falwell's lead, a phalanx of Christian Right leaders and pastors in the USA developed lucrative tourism projects that encouraged their flocks to visit Israel. Grace Halsell, who traveled with Falwell to Israel in 1983 as he led one of his early visits for Christian groups, provides insight into Falwell's arrangements with Israel in her book *Prophecy and Politics*. She explains, for example, how Falwell in 1982 sent Moral Majority organizers to Israel 'where they collaborated with top Israelis devising package plans for Christian pilgrims'.[58]

New organizations appeared in Washington, which, as part of their pro-Israel activity, specifically promoted US political ties with the Israeli religious and political right. They actively lobbied both Congress and the White House and reinforced the already powerful influence of Israel lobby organizations such as AIPAC and the Conference of Presidents of Major Jewish Organizations. Four organizations were particularly active at this time: the International Christian Embassy Jerusalem (ICEJ), the Jewish Institute for National Security Affairs (JINSA), the Center for Security Policy (CSP), and the National Unity Coalition for Israel (NUCI) (renamed the Unity Coalition for Israel, UCI).

The ICEJ appeared in Jerusalem on 20 September 1980 and subsequently opened an office in Washington, DC. It now has offices in Europe and around the world.[59] Investigative journalist Jason Vest ably explains the role of its fellow organizations, JINSA and the CSP:

> Just as the right-wing defense intellectuals made CPD a cornerstone of a shadow defense establishment during the Carter Administration so, too, did the right during the Clinton years, in part through two organizations: the Jewish Institute for National Security Affairs (JINSA) and the Center for Security Policy (CSP) ... For this crew, 'regime change' by any means necessary in Iraq, Iran, Syria, Saudi Arabia and the Palestinian Authority is an urgent imperative.[60]

The CSP was founded in 1988 and its leading light since is the ever active Frank Gaffney, a protégé of the neoconservative defense policy icon Richard Perle.[61]

During the 1980s and early 1990s, I watched the growing influence of JINSA and CSP on Capitol Hill. Both organizations articulated the neo-conservative foreign policy and defense perspective in great detail through myriad papers and policy briefings. It was particularly interesting to note the relationship between CSP and the Christian Right. The Christian Right, which mainly focused on domestic social issues, had more than enough policy specialists in this area. But when it came to foreign affairs and defense issues, the CSP was more than ready to help the Family Research Council develop its pro-Israel foreign policy positions. CSP worked closely with the Zionist Organization of America to provide policy papers and briefings to Congressional members and staff as part of their joint outreach activity.[62]

NUCI, established in 1991 by Esther Levens, emerged as an influential lobby promoting the Christian Zionist perspective in coalition with Jewish and other organizations. Not surprisingly, it has close links to the ICEJ and the neoconservatives. On Capitol Hill, NUCI works in parallel with the well-established and influential AIPAC to influence Congress on legislation and policy relating to the Middle East.[63]

Senator Jesse Helms: From New Right to Christian Zionist

The New Right was not by any means uniformly pro-Israel in the 1970s and 1980s. William F. Buckley's faction had been pro-Israel since the 1950s and had excoriated President Eisenhower for his handling of the Suez Crisis; but several New Right senators – including arch-conservative Jesse Helms (Republican – North Carolina) – supported President Reagan in the 1981 vote to sell arms to the Kingdom of Saudi Arabia.[64] The pro-Israel lobby aggressively opposed these arms sales, but, in the end, after much contention, Congress approved them. After losing the battle, the pro-Israel lobby redoubled its efforts on Capitol Hill.

The late Senator Helms was a leading figure in the New Right. Before 1992, he consistently supported America's allies in the Middle East, such as Saudi Arabia, on the pragmatic grounds that the Cold War and America's need for hydrocarbon resources required such allegiances.[65] In the 1970s, he expressed his concern for the Palestinians and his opposition to Israeli occupation of the West Bank. Thus, Senator Helms had the reputation of being strongly 'pro-Arab' in the eyes of the pro-Israel lobby. In his Senate speeches, however, Helms consistently condemned international terrorism by Arab and Muslim extremists.[66] He harshly criticized both Syrian occupation of Lebanon and the theocratic regime in Iran.[67] Overall, until staff changes in 1992, Helms' position was a relatively balanced one that supported US national interests in the Middle East.

In 1984, during Helms' re-election bid, the Jewish community took him to task for his allegedly 'anti-Israel' positions. Monitoring of campaign contributions revealed that wealthy Jewish donors from New York and elsewhere were actively supporting the Democratic candidate. Pro-Israel activists in North Carolina began circulating mass mailings accusing Helms of being anti-Israel and voting against Israel and urged voters to support his opponent. The claim that his votes reflected anti-Israeli bias was plain political deception by the Israel lobby, however.

Senator Helms countered such pressure, through both the Jewish community and the Christian Right. His office made use of its relationships with conservative Republican Jews, such as the well-connected New York attorney Roy Cohn (1927–86), who had achieved notoriety as a key staffer for Senator Joseph McCarthy in the 1950s. On Helms' behalf, Cohn arranged meetings and discussions with key players in the pro-Israel lobby in New York to assuage any fears of an anti-Israel bias.[68] Arthur J. Finkelstein, a conservative Jew living in New York and a well-known Republican campaign strategist and pollster, was similarly helpful: he had worked for Helms campaigns and had appropriate contacts. A series of meetings took place in Washington and New York City that successfully averted massive funding of Helms' opponent in North Carolina by the pro-Israel lobby. Because the race was close, limiting the opponent's fundraising capability outside North Carolina was considered a factor in Helms' win.

US Senator Jacob 'Chic' Hecht (Republican – Nevada), (1928–2006), greatly assisted Senator Helms in improving his relations with the American Jewish community.[69] Darryl Nirenberg, later Senator Hecht's son-in-law, helped. Nirenberg worked for Senator Helms first on the Senate Agriculture Committee, later on the Foreign Relations Committee, and finally in Senator Helms' personal Senate office. The Hecht family is well known for its philanthropy in Israel, having donated the Hecht Synagogue to the Hebrew University on Mount Scopus.[70] In the summer of 1984, and after his re-election to a six-year term, Helms travelled to Israel to visit the Hecht synagogue among other sites.

With his relations with Jewish members of the Israel lobby on the mend, Helms reached out to leading Christian Zionists such as Jerry Falwell of the Moral Majority. He solidified the support he already received from influential Christian Right members of the Council for National Policy (CNP), a powerful behind-the-scenes conservative organization founded by the dispensationalist Christian Zionist and End Times novelist Tim LaHaye.[71] With both Jewish and Christian Zionist components of the Israel lobby satisfied as to Senator Helms' foreign policy positions, he was re-elected to the US Senate in 1984, 1990, and 1996.

Senator Helms' dramatic and, I would argue, unnecessary tilt toward pro-Israel neoconservative foreign policy, however, did not occur until the early 1990s.[72] After staff changes beginning in January 1992, the Helms' staff on the Senate Foreign Relations Committee took a sharp turn towards neoconservatism.[73] Notably, journalist Danielle Pletka joined the Senate Foreign Relations Committee staff. Pletka, an Australian national, worked for a magazine published by Sun Myung Moon's organization in Washington, DC.[74] She probably owed her new position to Joseph Churba, a controversial former Air Force intelligence analyst and Revisionist Zionist, who reportedly contacted Helms' old friend Admiral James W. 'Bud' Nance to recommend her.[75] Nance, a boyhood friend of Senator Helms from North Carolina and retiree from the US Navy, was a Christian Zionist who assumed administrative duties for the senator at the Senate Foreign Relations Committee in 1991. Ms Pletka took over Middle East issues on the committee for Senator Helms for several years and then moved off Capitol Hill to work at the American Enterprise Institute, a neoconservative bastion. Pletka's hiring indicated Senator Helms' significant shift to a pro-Israel policy position.

Senator Helms' considerable influence and tight embrace of a pro-Israel policy worked against an option for a balanced Middle East policy on the part of the New Right. The Christian Right, working within its own subculture and also in coalition with the Jewish pro-Israel lobby, became a major player in national politics in the USA during the late 1980s and 1990s. The Christian Right supported the George H.W. Bush election campaign in 1988, energizing a significant conservative evangelical voter turnout. Although Bush was not able to profit from his relationship with the Christian Right in the 1992 re-election effort, his son George W. Bush gained valuable experience and links to the Christian Right as his father's outreach director to the evangelical community. This experience in turn solidified the Christian Right's support for his 2000 campaign and for his 2004 re-election campaign. While President George H.W. Bush, a mainline Episcopalian, did not embrace the Christian Zionist foreign policy perspective, President George W. Bush subscribed to this view.

10

George W. Bush and the Dark Crusade

When George W. Bush was elected in November 2000, my circle of friends and colleagues in Washington knew that the USA had a good chance of going to war in the Middle East – given the president's Christian Right perspective and the neoconservatives' already considerable influence on foreign policy.[1] The political ties to the Christian Right that George W. Bush had developed during his father's 1988 presidential campaign owed much to his father's campaign strategists and their recognition that it represented a significant voting block.

Using fundamentalists suffused with Christian Zionism as a political tool to rally support for an imperial policy in the Middle East was an adroit move. Since a crusade against 'Babylon' appealed powerfully to Christian Zionists, George W. Bush and his advisors could count upon them to provide political support for a war in Iraq – and perhaps later for a war against Iran.

The White House was not disappointed; the Christian Right endorsed President Bush's proposed war against Iraq. The Southern Baptist Convention, which had been slowly taken over by conservative elements espousing Christian Zionism, was at the forefront of the fundamentalist call for war against Iraq. The National Association of Evangelicals (NAE) also endorsed the war. Fundamentalist leader John Hagee, a Pentecostal and dispensationalist, also began in 2006 to demand a similar preventive war against Iran.

Informed observers, including former President Jimmy Carter,[2] recognized the threat to peace posed by an alliance of the Bush administration with Christian Zionists. The Bush administration's notion of preventive war in the Middle East, and sociopolitical transformation of the region, was a radical departure from the traditional norms of American foreign policy. Instead of the traditional American policy of constructive commercial and cultural engagement, the administration had embarked on something akin to an imperial adventure or an ideological crusade. Although mainline American churches had sent missionaries to the Middle East in the nineteenth century and later, they had not espoused or promoted Christian Zionism.

The Bush administration's policy to reshape the Middle East, as devised by neoconservatives such as Paul Wolfowitz, Elliot Abrams, Richard Perle, and Doug Feith, required regime change in Iraq, Syria, and Iran. Some neoconservatives even included Saudi Arabia and Egypt.[3] The use of preventive war and coercive diplomacy to reshape the Middle East politically, socially, and geographically was central to this 'unipolar' imperial policy – and the world has seen its results these last devastating eight years.

The Bush administration's objective was nothing less than US hegemony in the region. Its strategy was nothing higher or more moral than controlling hydrocarbon resources by dominating local regimes and freezing out rival powers.[4] In this scheme, Israel plays the role of a 'marcher state', a state on the periphery used as a base from which to project imperial power – the imperial power of the USA. Such policy concepts circulate in American foreign policy elites, Republican and Democratic.[5] It is no wonder that many in the Arab world and the Islamic world see American policy in the Middle East as a dark crusade.

George W. Bush, Vice President Cheney and their neoconservative advisors have never intended to advance the Middle East peace process and achieve a just solution, as the world now has seen. Eight years of *faux* diplomacy from the Bush administration provided Israel with time and space to tighten its illegal occupation of Palestinian lands, to increase the illegal settlements on the West Bank, to build the West Bank barrier, to cut off the Palestinians in Gaza, to continue its illegal occupation of the Golan Heights, and to stall the peace process for another eight years.

George H.W. Bush, the Christian Right, and the 1988 Election

While President George W. Bush daily and comfortably associates with the Christian Right, his father – who first forged the Bush family political alliance with it for his own 1988 campaign – has sometimes found the relationship awkward. During that campaign, Pat Robertson, a Pentecostal and important leader of the Christian Right, made a bid for the Republican Party nomination. His entry into the race pressurized the George H.W. Bush campaign. Political scientist Clyde Wilcox points out that 'Robertson's political platform was quite similar to that of the fundamentalist Right'.[6] This penetration of the Republican Party at the state level later broadened thanks to work by Robertson's grass-roots Christian Coalition organization, headed by the redoubtable Ralph Reed.

Bush's team recognized the potential for a political alliance between conservative Protestants and conservative Catholics, made visible by Robertson's 1988 presidential bid:

> Exit polls indicated that Robertson drew some support from Catholic voters. Unlike the fundamentalists, the Pentecostals have generally welcomed cooperation from like-minded conservative Protestants. The charismatic movement has welcomed Catholics into its ranks, and sees fundamentalists and evangelicals as kindred spirits. The Pentecostals therefore have the potential to accomplish what Falwell claimed to seek: a coalition of conservative Christians united in common political action.[7]

George H.W. Bush needed an assist with the Christian Right and evangelical votes and got it from one Doug Wead, a Pentecostal activist advising the Bush campaign on outreach to evangelicals, who was well connected in conservative evangelical circles. Craig Unger, in his book *The Fall of the House of Bush*, explains Wead's role:

> Wead, an Assemblies of God evangelist who had been a motivational speaker for Amway, had been writing a series of memos for Vice President Bush on building a relationship with the Christian Right. Unbeknownst to Wead, the vice president had forwarded them to his son.[8]

According to Unger, Wead met with George W. Bush in March 1987 to discuss outreach to the Christian Right.

Wead played a central role in preparing an image for Bush that would attract fundamentalists. William Martin in his book *With God on Our Side* presents a detailed view of Wead's campaign role based on interviews with him: 'He recommended that Bush, a theologically moderate Episcopalian, establish an early and close relationship with evangelicals, then back off a bit as the election approached, to avoid appearing to have been captured by them.'[9] Wead carefully briefed George H.W. Bush, prepared detailed memos, and suggested readings from Christian intellectuals such as Francis Schaeffer. He urged Bush to get a thorough briefing from Billy Graham on such matters as the born-again phenomenon and evangelical eschatology, which could help him understand why conservative evangelicals think it is so important for America to have a strong pro-Israel policy.[10]

George W. Bush's conversion to conservative evangelicalism in 1984 left him well placed to reach out effectively to the evangelical community on his father's behalf. The Bush campaign sought and obtained the endorsement of Jerry Falwell, the well-known Southern Baptist leader of the Christian Right. Together, the younger Bush and Wead made substantial political inroads and 'relentlessly pursued one evangelical leader after another', says Unger:[11]

> As a result of such machinations, Vice President Bush beat Robertson handily in such Southern evangelical strongholds as South Carolina, Georgia, Kentucky, Texas, Virginia, and ten other states. He not only won the nomination, but when the 1988 general election came in November, he won 81 per cent of the evangelical vote. He lost the Jewish vote by a huge margin. He lost the Hispanic vote. He lost the Catholic vote. 'So if you can win in a landslide and the only identifiable constituency is the evangelical Christian – whew, said Wead.'[12]

George W. Bush, the Christian Right, and the 2000 Election

Wead would return to assist the Bush dynasty in gaining the presidency for a second time. In the meantime, as Sarah Posner explains in her book *God's Profits*, he had ghostwritten an End Times conspiracy-theory book for John Hagee, an influential dispensationalist and neo-Pentecostal televangelist based in San Antonio, Texas.[13] Hagee's book, *Day of Deception* (1997), developed the old dispensationalist notion that various satanic groups would help out the Antichrist.[14] As presented in Hagee's book, these servants of the Antichrist included the United Nations organization, the New York based

Council on Foreign Relations, and a shadowy esoteric group called the Illuminati – the same sort of arch fiends evoked in the 1950s McCarthy era by Carl McIntire's Christian Right followers.

Wead's collaboration with the increasingly prominent Hagee soon produced the book *God's Candidate for America* (2000), in which Hagee endorsed Bush.[15] As a leading fundamentalist, Hagee's endorsement of Bush and the Republican Party had political weight as he could deliver grass roots votes from the evangelical subculture.

The younger Bush needed strong intervention from fundamentalist leaders for his 2000 campaign because evangelicals had been put off by his father, feeling that the elder Bush had not delivered for them. George W. Bush and his advisors wanted to ensure that conservative evangelicals would turn out at the polls rather than sit at home. In response, he recruited neoconservative policy advisors whose militant Zionism would naturally win favor with the Christian Right. When the election came, thanks to Wead's advice, evangelicals did indeed deliver for Bush – as they would again in 2004.

Bush's Christian Zionist supporters paid him a visit early on in his presidency to ensure his commitment to Israel.[16] Edward McAteer, President of the Religious Roundtable, working closely with Herbert Zweibon, Chairman of Americans for a Safe Israel (AFSI), arranged a meeting at the White House on 30 July 2001. A number of Christian Zionist leaders from around the country were present to support what they referred to as the 'territorial integrity of the Land of Israel'.[17]

In the run-up to the 2004 election, the Bush campaign counted on Christian Right support, particularly from the fundamentalist 'mega-churches'. Conservative evangelicals responded to George W. Bush as one of their own given his 'born again' conversion.[18] Julian Borger for the *Guardian* (London) explains that 'In President Bush, the evangelicals recognise one of their own. He talks their language … Unlike Reagan's secular White House, the Bush White House starts the day with prayers and Bible meetings.'[19]

The influence of Christian Zionists over US politics and foreign policy continued to grow during the Bush presidency and was strengthened through political alliances with Jewish groups in the USA. 'As a result of Christian Zionists' alliance with Likud governments, they now work actively with Jewish groups in the US, even though historically the two have been on opposing sides of key issues,' wrote Jane Lampman for the *Christian Science Monitor* in 2004:

'Christian Zionist groups play an increasingly important role,' says Morton Klein, head of the Zionist Organization of America and a leader of the Jewish lobby, AIPAC. 'In many districts where there are very few Jews, the members of the House and Senate are Israel's supporters in part because of the strong Christian Zionist lobby on Capitol Hill.'[20]

George W. Bush Brings in the Neoconservatives

Because Bush's foreign policy advisory team was composed primarily of neo-conservatives such as Richard Perle, Paul Wolfowitz, and Elliott Abrams, it was not hard to predict a radical shift in US policy toward the Middle East, and toward the world at large, should they gain the upper hand in the councils of the new administration.[21] Coercive diplomacy, confrontation, and preventive war to cause 'regime change' in Iraq, and elsewhere, would be the new order of the day.[22] Some neoconservatives called their policy 'muscular Wilsonianism' after the foreign policy of President Woodrow Wilson, but the genial term simply cloaked the real Nietzschean philosophical core of their policy.

Several policy papers produced by neoconservatives in the mid-1990s revealed their outlook. These papers were produced for an Israeli think tank called the Institute for Advanced Strategic and Political Studies (IASPS), which had offices in Jerusalem and Washington, DC. The paper that achieved the greatest notoriety was entitled 'A clean break: a new strategy for securing the realm' and was presented to Benjamin Netanyahu, the right-wing Israeli politician, as a policy recommendation for the development of Israeli relations with the USA. It was a road map for terminating the peace process.[23]

In early 1997, William Kristol and Robert Kagan founded the Project for a New American Century (PNAC) as a platform for similar views and as a springboard into the next administration – which turned out to be that of George W. Bush.[24] Neoconservatives, as part of their operational style, use think tanks, publications, and committees to promote their policy concepts. PNAC, which numbered Jeb Bush (the brother of George W. Bush) as an early supporter, churned out a seemingly endless series of policy papers and newspaper commentaries promoting their design for US hegemony in a so-called unipolar world.[25]

Many hoped that Secretary of State Colin Powell would provide a decisive counterbalance to such ideas. Instead Vice President Cheney and his ally Secretary of Defense Donald Rumsfeld, with their neoconservative advisors, dominated policy throughout the Bush presidency. Powell was window dressing.[26] Powell's potential influence was undercut first by bureaucratic moves by Vice President Richard Cheney, an old rival, and second by the rise in status and influence of the Secretary of Defense after the 9/11 event and the follow-on wars in Afghanistan and in Iraq.[27] While some observers branded Cheney and Rumsfeld as 'nationalists', in fact, both had moved in neoconservative circles since the mid-1970s.

Their link to these circles, Robert Allen Goldwin, has been largely overlooked by those curious about why Cheney and Rumsfeld recruit neoconservative advisors. Goldwin, a product of the University of Chicago, is a follower of Leo Strauss, a major influence and icon in the Irving Kristol wing of the Neoconservative movement. For many critics, however, Strauss is at base a Nietzschean and right-wing Zionist trained in Germany by Carl Schmitt, a notorious jurist associated with the National Socialist regime.[28] Goldwin served in the Ford White House, where he worked closely with Cheney and Rumsfeld. From 1973 to 1974, Goldwin served as special advisor to the ambassador of the US mission to the North Atlantic Treaty Organization (NATO), Donald Rumsfeld. From 1974 to 1976, he was a special consultant to President Ford and in 1976 was special assistant to Secretary of Defense Donald Rumsfeld.[29] In these sensitive positions, Goldwin was well placed to promote Straussian and neoconservative perspectives. His mentoring of Rumsfeld and Cheney during the Ford administration explains their receptivity to neoconservative foreign policy positions throughout their subsequent careers, including their time at the George W. Bush White House.

Tilt to Israel and Confrontation with Iraq

In the fall of 2000, I talked with old Republican Party colleagues in Washington about what the Bush election victory might portend and where foreign policy might be headed. Several friends with whom I had worked on Capitol Hill are exceptionally well-informed public affairs consultants specializing in Middle East issues. They told me they had spoken privately with Bush foreign policy advisor Stephen Hadley some months before, and he had indicated plainly that Iraq would be at the top of the Bush agenda – there was little interest in the Middle East peace process. Hadley, a lawyer and neoconservative ally, belonged to a small circle of foreign policy advisors that had coached candidate Bush during his presidential campaign.

Clearly, neoconservatives would have a powerful influence over administration foreign policy and a decidedly pro-Israel tilt was in the offing. Hadley became Condoleezza Rice's deputy at the National Security Council and then became national security advisor after Rice became the secretary of state.

Bush's circle of primarily neoconservative advisors was nicknamed 'The Vulcans' and included neoconservatives Paul Wolfowitz and Elliott Abrams, among others. Condoleezza Rice, a protégé of George Shultz and a neoconservative ally, was a member of the group and served as something of a coordinator interfacing with candidate Bush and putting the foreign policy concepts into simplified language he could digest.[30] The group was first chronicled by James Mann in his book *Rise of the Vulcans* (2004).[31] The neoconservative perspective dominated the Vulcan group and was shared by the co-chairmen of the Bush Campaign: George Shultz and Richard Cheney. It was well known that the neoconservative intellectual network for many years advocated the use of force for regime change purposes in the Middle East, particularly with respect to Iraq, Syria, and Iran.[32]

While many of us with Washington experience and knowledge of matters 'inside the Beltway' believed well before the administration took office that the USA was headed for severe problems with respect to Middle East policy, this was not the view given to the general public by the media. Former Secretary of the Treasury Paul O'Neill, who resigned from the George W. Bush administration, finally set the historical record straight in an unusually frank memoir, *The Price of Loyalty* (2004), written by Ron Suskind. O'Neill revealed that at the very first National Security Council meeting, on 30 January 2001, President Bush made it clear that the peace process was to be set aside in favor of a tilt toward Israel and confrontation with Iraq. 'We're going to correct the imbalances of the previous administration on the Mideast conflict,' O'Neill recalled President Bush saying. 'We're going to tilt it back toward Israel. And we're going to be consistent.'[33]

O'Neill confirmed that the Iraq policy position was indeed part of a larger plan for the Middle East. He noted an exchange between President Bush and Rice, now the National Security Advisor, in which Rice pronounced that 'Iraq is destabilizing the region.' O'Neill said she also 'noted that Iraq might become the key to reshaping the entire region.'[34] For those of us familiar with the neoconservatives, the cast of characters advising Bush, and Washington politics, these were hardly revelations; however, the general public had yet to become aware of the militant neoconservative policy network and its implications for US foreign policy. By the time O'Neill's book was published the country was already at war in Iraq.

US Congress Supports Israeli Spring 2002 Offensive

During the spring of 2002, while the Bush administration secretly moved toward war against Iraq, Israel launched a military offensive against the Palestinians.[35] The administration gave Israel a free hand when Congress strongly endorsed Israel's policy in April and granted Israel increased funding in May. 'As President Bush comes under growing international pressure to rein in Israel's military offensive against Palestinians,' wrote Janet Hook in the *Los Angeles Times* on 10 April, 'he faces countervailing pressures from an overwhelmingly pro-Israel Congress where some members are pushing for new statements of support for the country.' Hook explained the massive support in Congress. Despite concerns about upsetting regional diplomacy,

> the unflagging congressional support for Israel – even as Israeli leaders have been slow to respond to Bush's personal pleas to end the incursion into Palestinian-governed territory – is a strong reminder of the tremendous influence wielded by the Jewish community and the pro-Israel lobby in US politics.[36]

Hook noted the Christian Right's support of Israel as an important factor:

> That power has its roots, in part, in sympathy for a democratic regime with which the United States has deep cultural and religious ties. The support base spans many faiths, notably evangelical Christian groups. But the clout also derives from a more direct, practical political reality: The US Jewish community, though only about 2.2 per cent of the US population, is disproportionately represented in big states such as New York, California, Florida and Illinois.[37]

The pro-Israel sentiment in Congress was meticulously orchestrated, by AIPAC among others. As explained by Matthew E. Berger in Cleveland Jewish News.com:

> The American pro-Israel lobby is mounting a new offensive to equate the US-led war on terrorism with Israel's own battle against terror. Timed to coincide with the annual policy conference of the American Israel Public Affairs

Committee, US lawmakers have introduced several pieces of legislation to display support for Israel in Congress and combat what is viewed as increasing pressure on the Bush administration's Middle East policy from Europe, Arab states and the United Nations.[38]

This atmosphere and legislative climate in Washington in the spring of 2002 provided momentum for the Bush administration's overall Middle East strategy, which included the coming war with Iraq.[39] While the Israeli offensive intensified, the Iraq war clouds also gathered during April and May 2002. The Israeli spring offensive served to spur the congressional mood for the 'global war on terror', into which Iraq would soon be assimilated.

The Christian Right and Middle East Policy

The Christian Right took advantage of the Israeli spring offensive to show its support for Israel. As observed by Abraham McLaughlin and Gail Russell Chaddock in the *Christian Science Monitor* on 16 April:

> The latest round of a long-running policy debate also includes a new group of combatants: Christian conservatives. Many in this pro-Israel camp see Biblical prophecy being played out in current events. They're rallying their members – and lobbying ideological allies inside the White House – to push the US to stand squarely behind Israel. While they're hardly dictating policy, it's clear that these conservatives now have a strong voice in the debate.[40]

McLaughlin and Chaddock correctly summarized the Christian Zionist position and their increasingly influential role in the policy debate:

> The debate's new powerhouses are Christian conservatives ... For years, many Christian groups were lukewarm on Israel – reflecting traditional Christian-Jewish tension. But now many see Biblical prophecy bearing on today's events. Some Christians believe the second coming of Christ will occur only after Israel rebuilds God's temple in Jerusalem. They support Israel having full control over that land – not ceding it to Muslims.[41]

At the same time, Alison Mitchell of the *New York Times*, explained graphically the political alliance between the neoconservatives and the Christian Right:

Gary L. Bauer, the Christian conservative who grew up as a janitor's son in Kentucky, and William Kristol, the scion of New York Jewish intellectuals, long ago forged an unlikely but close friendship as warriors of the right. They have fought together on issues like promoting family values and the Supreme Court nomination of Clarence Thomas. But the cause that now rivets them both is Israel, and their joint, consuming devotion to it illustrates the deep pro-Israel sentiment in the conservative movement.[42]

On the domestic political front, the alliance threatened the Republican Party:

The strongly pro-Israel sentiment marks a profound and telling shift inside the Republican Party, political strategists say. With Jews mostly voting Democratic, Republican presidents for decades had been freer to break with Israel. Dwight D. Eisenhower refused to back a British, French, Israeli attack on Egypt after it nationalized the Suez Canal. Mr Bush's father's administration repeatedly clashed with Israel.[43]

The Reagan administration opened the door for the neoconservative and Christian Right penetration of the Republican Party. As a result, Mitchell said in 2002, 'the trends Mr Reagan set in motion have only escalated, and Mr Bush now has to contend with an even more dramatically altered Republican Party.'[44]

Mitchell correctly explained the internal situation in the party:

Republicans attribute the conservative support for Israel to many factors, including the influence of largely Jewish neoconservatives and the rise of the Christian right, with its belief that the Bible mandates support for Israel. The Likud Party in Israel also built ties to conservatives. After the Sept. 11 attacks, other conservatives who embrace a hawkish foreign policy came to see a stand with Israel as important strategy in the war against terrorism.[45]

The Republican Party thus faces a political dilemma. Will it continue to be taken over by extremist Jewish and Christian Zionist factions? If so, will moderate and liberal Republicans migrate en masse to the Democratic Party or will a substantial number simply become independent voters with no party affiliation?

Congress Votes for War

In June 2002, I traveled to the Middle East and Central Asia with colleagues from the National Conference of Editorial Writers. We visited Saudi Arabia, Egypt, and Uzbekistan, meeting with high officials of the countries as well as with American embassy personnel. As for the possibility of war in the region, His Excellency Amr Mousa, Secretary General of the League of Arab States, was emphatic in his remarks to us at the Arab League headquarters in Cairo. 'It would open the gates of hell,' he pronounced. His Excellency Ahmed Maher Al-Sayeed, Minister of Foreign Affairs of the Arab Republic of Egypt, also indicated concern over growing tensions in the region and the possibility of war, which he hoped would be avoided.[46]

I asked Maher about the state of the Middle East peace process, in light of the discussions between Israeli and Palestinian negotiators at the Taba Conference (21–27 January 2001) held in Egypt in the last days of the Clinton administration. The Taba Conference pursued negotiations begun at the earlier Camp David summit of 11–25 July 2000.[47] 'We were 95 per cent there at Taba,' he said.[48]

The incoming Bush administration could have picked up these negotiations without missing a beat, especially with counsel from President Clinton and from President Carter, and could have advanced the peace process in the interest of world peace and in the national interest of the USA. The administration could also have consulted President Carter as he continued his efforts on behalf of Middle East peace in a private capacity.[49] It did not.

I returned to the USA from this Middle East trip more concerned than ever about the approaching war and its potential consequences. My sense from the many discussions with foreign and US officials was that regional leaders felt Iraq was weak and contained and that a 'preventative' war would be utterly counterproductive. Saddam Hussein attempted to conceal the fundamental weakness of the Iraqi state, and the weakness of his regime, through rhetorical bombast and police state measures not untypical of the region.[50] In fact, Iraq had never recovered from the effects of the 1991 Gulf War, and its military was poorly equipped. The subsequent imposition of 'no-fly' zones and economic sanctions had taken an extremely harsh toll on Iraq and its people. Under these circumstances, and given the powerful US presence in the region, local elites believed Iraq was contained and that a preventive war was both unnecessary and potentially destabilizing to the entire region.

Reshaping the Middle East by preventive war and coercive diplomacy is the hallmark of the Bush administration's catastrophic foreign policy. The catastrophe for the USA, and for the world, is the Bush legacy, and it will be felt for decades to come. As the vote in Congress to authorize the use of force against Iraq approached, some international observers accurately informed their readers about the role of the neoconservative policymakers in the Bush administration. As expressed by Brian Whitaker in the *Guardian* on 3 September 2002:

> For the hawks, disorder and chaos sweeping through the region would not be an unfortunate side-effect of war with Iraq, but a sign that everything is going to plan. In their eyes, Iraq is just the starting point – or as a recent presentation at the Pentagon put it, 'the tactical pivot' – for re-moulding the Middle East on Israeli–American lines. This reverses the usual approach in international relations where stability is seen as the key to peace, and whether or not you like your neighbors, you have to find ways of living with them. No, say the hawks. If you don't like the neighbors, get rid of them.[51]

Of course, the administration did not act alone. The US Congress shamefully failed in its constitutional responsibility to the American people by rubber-stamping the administration's 'preventive war' plan for Iraq. There were no searching committee hearings by relevant committees either in the Senate or in the House of Representatives. There was no aggressive Congressional oversight challenging the lies of the administration about the non-existent weapons of mass destruction in Iraq and all the rest. In the run-up to the vote in Congress, the atmosphere in Washington was charged, thanks to all manner of false propaganda about the Iraqi regime and its non-existent weapons of mass destruction. The hysteria, pumped up by the complicit corporate news media, helped facilitate the vote authorizing the use of military force against Iraq.

The legislation sailed through Congress automatically: three-quarters of the Senate and two-thirds of the House approved, as Public Law 107-243, the October 2002 resolution entitled 'Authorization of Military Force Against Iraq Resolution of 2002'.[52] The House voted on 10 October and the Senate voted on 11 October.[53] President Bush signed the legislation into law on 16 October.

Veteran journalist William Pfaff accurately commented on the quality of the debate and vote on 17 October, writing in the *International Herald Tribune* that

Even before the newspaper reports of a plan for lasting military occupation of Iraq, on the model of the post-World War II occupation of Japan, the debate over war with Iraq was awash with unchecked fantasies about the future. The debate has mostly consisted of unproved assertions about Iraq's weapons or lack of them, about the threat that it does, or does not, pose to its neighborhood or Israel or the United States, and about its connection, or lack of connection, with international terrorism.[54]

He correctly pointed out the significant constitutional issue:

The Senate, constitutional custodian of the power to go to war, has abdicated to George W. Bush, conceding to him greater discretion than to any president in history. This is not the conduct of a serious government or a serious nation.[55]

The delusional nature of the national debate on the crucial issue of war in the Middle East epitomized the condition of the nation. As US Senator Robert Byrd subsequently asked rhetorically in his book *Losing America* (2004), 'How can we be so comatose as a nation when so many damaging and radical changes are at once thrust upon us?'[56]

On the Road to War

Irrespective of constitutional issues, the reality was that the USA was indeed headed to war in Iraq.[57] Some had hoped that war could be prevented through international organizational and legal processes. Some observers had believed war could be avoided if the UN Security Council refused to authorize the USA to use force against Iraq. Others felt that pressure on Saddam Hussein's regime could result in Baghdad taking steps that would avert any use of force sanctioned by the UN. But the simple fact is that the Bush administration had determined on a course of war and had been in the process of implementing it for a number of months, official White House denials notwithstanding.

One noteworthy public signal that war was forthcoming was the formation in November 2002 of the Committee for the Liberation of Iraq (CLI).[58] The godfather of this pressure group, and one might say the Iraq War, was George Shultz, the godfather of the Bush administration as the former co-chairman, with Dick Cheney, of George W. Bush's 2000 electoral campaign. Peter Slevin of the *Washington Post* was on top of the story:

> The Bush administration, anticipating a successful UN Security Council vote on an Iraq resolution, plans to embark soon on a campaign to build public support in the United States to challenge and most likely unseat Iraqi President Saddam Hussein, US officials said.[59]

The new pressure group had support from influential Republicans and Democrats:

> With the administration's blessing, a new group is forming to press the case in the United States and Europe for ejecting Hussein from power. Called the Committee for the Liberation of Iraq, the organization is modeled on a successful lobbying campaign to expand the NATO alliance. Members include former secretary of state George P. Shultz, Sen. John McCain (R–Ariz.) and former senator Bob Kerrey (D–Neb.).[60]

Slevin explained that the organization's format was familiar to administration officials because it replicated the US Committee on NATO (USCN).[61] The president of USCN and chairman of CLI, Bruce P. Jackson, is a long-time Bush family ally dating back to the administration of George H.W. Bush. 'The approach is a familiar one to the Bush administration,' he said. 'Hadley, Bush's deputy national security advisor, co-founded the NATO project. Its board members included Rice, Deputy Defense Secretary Paul Wolfowitz and US Trade Representative Robert B. Zoellick. Cheney and Secretary of State Colin L. Powell advised the group. While the Iraq committee was set up as an independent entity, Jackson said, 'Committee officers said they expect to work closely with the administration. They already have met with Hadley and Bush political advisor Karl Rove.' Neoconservatives Richard Perle, Robert Kagan, and Gary Schmitt were also board members of USCN. The CLI board overlapped and included additional neoconservatives.[62]

An additional overlap bears notice. The influential AJC, publisher of the neoconservative *Commentary* magazine, also endorsed the expansion of NATO. As announced by the AJC press release of 30 July 2002:

> The American Jewish Committee today urged NATO to extend formal invitations for full membership to Bulgaria, Estonia, Latvia, Lithuania, Romania, Slovakia, and Slovenia when the alliance's 19 member countries gather in Prague in November. 'Their succession to NATO will serve the national security interest of the United States,' David A. Harris, executive director

of the American Jewish Committee, told a news conference at the National Press Club.[63]

The AJC and neoconservatives align on the NATO issue because both believe a strong NATO can be used to protect Israel. Indeed, there are those who recommend the inclusion of Israel into NATO.

Bush appointed Elliott Abrams as director of Middle East and North Africa affairs at the National Security Council in the White House. Abrams, an arch neoconservative, was a notorious Iran-Contra scandal figure pardoned by President George H.W. Bush for his perjury before Congress – a history that made his appointment to such a sensitive foreign policy position dramatic, to say the least. As Steven R. Weisman wrote in the *New York Times* on 7 December 2002:

> Abrams' appointment thrilled those who had criticized the administration for being too tough on Israel and too deferential to the Palestinians. But it dismayed those, especially at the State Department, who want Israel to ease its crackdown in the West Bank and Gaza. An administration official said that Abram's ascension has created 'serious consternation' at the State Department. It is seen there, he said, as likely to impede the efforts of Secretary of State Colin Powell to work with European nations to press Israel and the Palestinians to adopt a staged timetable leading to creation of a Palestinian state in three years.[64]

Abrams – the son-in-law of first-generation neoconservative Norman Podhoretz and his neoconservative wife Midge Decter – is a militant anti-assimilationist, ardent Revisionist Zionist, and leader in the maximalist pro-Israel camp. Weisman tells us:

> Five years ago, Abrams wrote a book, '*Faith or Fear: How Jews Can Survive in Christian America*', which argues against the loss of religious faith among Jews and criticizes intermarriage as a danger to their survival in America. He also urged Jews to make greater common cause with evangelical Christians in rallying support for Israel.[65]

At the time of his appointment, it was well known that Abrams was a staunch opponent of the Middle East peace process. 'Abrams was a fierce opponent of the Oslo peace negotiations between Israel and Yasser Arafat, the Palestinian leader, even while they seemed to bear fruit,' Weisman wrote.[66]

Neoconservatives and the Christian Right Concern European Allies

In the fall of 2002, Europeans – like many Americans – were fearful of the war that seemed to be coming and its consequences. For example, in September of that year, Rosemary Hollis, head of the Middle East Program at the prestigious Chatham House organization in London, said forthrightly and accurately in the *Observer* that

> despite Iraq's sudden invitation to renew UN weapons inspections, American hardliners will keep up the pressure for war. Regime change might be achieved under cover of disarming Baghdad. But without a serious debate on the objectives of force, there will be no opportunity to consider what could go wrong or how to handle the competing interests.[67]

Hollis emphasized the role of the neoconservatives and their plans:

> A determined stance in the face of regional criticism of administration policy, whether toward Palestine or Iraq, is intrinsic to the US war agenda. The so-called hawks championing the cause of regime change in Iraq have made it clear that they have more than the government in Baghdad in their sights. The neo-conservative wing of the Bush administration is looking for a new regional order, where liberal-capitalist democratic governments aligned with the USA will replace theocratic, dictatorial and otherwise antithetical regimes. It is claimed that forcing such change in Baghdad will send a message to Tehran, Damascus, Riyadh and Cairo that they will face the censure, if not the intervention, of the US unless they fall into line.[68]

Hollis was also frank on the issues of oil and Israel:

> Even if America has some UN cover for a war in the name of ridding Iraq of weapons of mass destruction it has failed to reveal or give up under sanctions and inspections, this is not the only objective of the US hawks. They want to replace the regime with a government with a democratic face, allied to the United States, ready to do business with US companies – especially on oil – and prepared to make peace with Israel.[69]

European allies worried not only about a war against Iraq but also about the state of the Israel–Palestine situation. Glenn Frankel had the story for the *Washington Post* in November 2002:

> Lurking behind the Iraq issue lies a much deeper conflict between the United States and its European allies: what to do about Israel and the Palestinians. A wide range of European officials and analysts believes the Bush administration's Middle East policy has effectively given Israeli Prime Minister Ariel Sharon permission to crack down on the Palestinians whenever he chooses.[70]

Frankel pointed to a European fear of increased terrorism and frustration with American coddling of Israel under pressure from the Israel lobby and the Christian Right:

> Now Europeans fear that an invasion of Iraq will feed Arab discontent and trigger a new wave of anti-Western terrorism. And they reject the idea, expressed by some members of the US administration, that overthrowing Iraqi President Saddam Hussein is a first step toward reordering the Middle East and compelling Palestinians to come to terms with Israel.[71]

America's new belligerent policy in the Middle East was also damaging its traditional European alliances:

> The conflict over Israel brings out some of the worst stereotypes that Europe and the United States hold of each other. Europeans see the Bush administration as a captive of the Israel lobby and the Christian right and utterly insensitive to the suffering of Palestinians. They complain about President Bush's public praise for Sharon as a 'man of peace' and the administration's perceived slowness in deploring violence against Palestinian civilians.[72]

By late 2002, Europeans had begun to take notice of the widespread and damaging effects of the alliance between the neoconservatives and the Christian Right, which was resulting in alterations to US foreign policy. The French *Nouvel Obervateur* published a long piece on this dark alliance in September 2002. The magazine raised the issue of whether or not politics in the USA were headed toward the 'extreme right'. Jean-Gabriel Fredet discussed at length neoconservatives such as William Kristol, Richard Perle, and Robert Kagan, and then turned to coverage of leaders of the Christian Right such as Gary Bauer and Congressman Tom DeLay (Democrat – Texas). Fredet then turned to French foreign affairs analyst Dominique Moisi of the French Institute of International Relations (Institut Français des Relations Internationales, IFRI). Moisi correctly depicted the players influencing the Bush administration's foreign policy as an alliance of neoconservatives and the

Christian Right. He said the neoconservatives 'believe that the United States should govern the world' and the 'Christian fundamentalists' have a 'Manichean vision' which supports the neoconservative 'hostility to the world, their scorn of Europe, and their systematic defense of Israel'.[73]

On 20 March 2003, George W. Bush's Iraq War officially began. With the war against Iraq in motion, Christian Zionists began to turn their attention to their broader agenda in the region.

11

Christian Zionism and the Next War

Will the Obama administration, and other administrations in the future, continue Washington's dark crusade in the Middle East? Christian Zionists and the pro-Israel lobby do not seem concerned that their undue influence over American foreign policy has mired the USA in costly wars that military, diplomatic, and intelligence professionals say cannot be 'won' through military force. Despite the massive costs, both human and financial, of the present wars in Iraq and in Afghanistan, the Christian Right and the Israeli Right still advocate preventive war against Iran and threaten Syria.

At the forefront of those calling for more war are Christian Zionist leaders like John Hagee, who is based at Cornerstone Church, a mega-church in San Antonio, Texas.[1] Christian Zionists question any peace process in the Middle East designed to solve the Arab–Israeli dispute over Palestine.[2] They oppose the Middle East peace process because they oppose a physical division of Jerusalem or Israel. That is, they denounce the principle of exchanging land for peace, which is at the heart of a negotiated peace process. Fundamentalists oppose the idea of a Palestinian state located on territory which, Christian Zionists argue, the Bible says should be in Israel's possession. Fundamentalists have opposed Israeli withdrawal from Gaza on the same grounds, citing scripture to justify their stand. As a prime example, Hagee declares:

> the Roadmap for Peace is an ill-conceived document, one that has Israel giving up Gaza, then the West Bank, and then Jerusalem. It clearly violates the

Word of God. How so? Joel 3:2 says ... My heritage Israel ... they divided up my land. When America forced Israel to give up Gaza, it was clearly violating Joel 3:2.[3]

Fundamentalist biblical literalism within a dispensationalist framework, as exemplified by Hagee's Christian Zionism, has far-reaching implications for the conduct of American foreign policy. The Christian Zionist lobby, as a major component of the pro-Israel lobby in the USA, lobbies the White House and Congress on foreign policy based upon its idiosyncratic interpretation of the Bible. You will not find separation of church and state, or of church and foreign policy, in these circles. Rather, the Christian Zionist lobby acts in the realm of politics and foreign policy to support its bizarre apocalyptic End Times agenda in which Israel, as we have seen, plays a central role.

Reverend Stephen Sizer concisely identifies the political and foreign policy implications of Christian Zionist doctrine with reference to the Middle East. He singles out six key areas:

1. blessing Israel;
2. facilitating Jewish emigration;
3. supporting the settlement program;
4. lobbying for international recognition of Jerusalem as the capital of Israel;
5. funding the rebuilding of the temple; and
6. opposing the peace process, exacerbating relations in the Arab world and hastening Armageddon.[4]

American Christian Zionists are active in each of these areas and mobilize their national network in the USA to systematically pressure the White House and Congress to these ends. Expanding the war in the Middle East is part and parcel of their current agenda.

Hagee's Armageddon Scenario

John Hagee, one of the most the most virulent Christian Right leaders, wants war with Iran and says so openly. Hagee's roles as dispensationalist preacher, End Times conspiracy theorist, and political backer of George W. Bush have put him at the center of a national network of Christian Zionists who want to block the Arab–Israeli peace process and expand America's imperial wars in the Middle East.[5] In 2006, taking a page from the Christian anti-communist crusades of the 1950s, Hagee founded a nationwide Christian Zionist lobby called Christians United For Israel (CUFI), which advocates preventive war against Iran.[6] The crusade against Iran is part of the larger crusade against so-called 'Islamofascism' espoused by the Christian Right: militant Islamist ideology, which the Christian Right and neoconservatives label Islamofascism, now takes its place alongside Communism as a demonic enemy and tool of the Antichrist.[7]

To launch CUFI, Hagee wrote an End Times book, *Jerusalem Countdown: A Prelude to War*, which interprets the current international situation from a dispensationalist perspective and concludes that war against Iran is necessary. The book is dedicated to Derek Prince, whom Hagee calls 'a lover of Israel, a world-class Bible scholar and teacher, a personal spiritual advisor, and a most cherished friend'.[8] Peter Derek Vaughan Prince (1915–2003) was an influential British Pentecostal preacher with a worldwide radio ministry.[9] A militant Christian Zionist, Prince specialized in research on demons and reportedly claimed to have raised two people from the dead while on a ministry trip to Kenya in the 1950s.

Prince was a powerful force in fundamentalist circles in the USA. Prince and his wife arrived there from Canada in the 1960s and became American citizens. He became deeply involved in the Charismatic movement, which in its penetration of Pentecostalism resulted in the neo-Pentecostal movement. The Charismatic movement has also penetrated other denominations and thus is a powerful factor within the Christian Right in the USA. Prince first associated with the Holy Spirit Teaching Mission of Ft Lauderdale, Florida, and subsequently joined the Christian Growth Ministries that spawned the controversial 'Shepherding Movement', which emphasizes the authoritarian rule of pastors over their flocks.[10] Prince spent his last years in Israel promoting Christian Zionism and working closely with Rabbi Eliyahu Ben-Haim, director of an organization called Intercessors for Israel which opposes the 'division of Israel' to create a Palestinian state.[11]

Hagee resolutely rejects coexistence with Islam. He claims

> Those who say that Christianity and Islam are sister faiths need to get their heads out of the sand.
> President George Bush has given moral clarity to this clash of civilizations saying, 'This nation is at war with Islamic fascists'.[12]

Hagee refers to the controversial 'clash of civilization' thesis of Harvard professor Samuel Huntington.[13] In his book *The Clash of Civilizations* (1996), and in an earlier lectures and articles, Huntington proposed the thesis that the Western world and the Islamic world could be heading for a violent confrontation.[14]

On the other hand, Huntington himself explicitly argued in his book for a broader perspective on international politics:

> The security of the world requires the acceptance of global multiculturalism ... Instead of promoting the supposedly universal features of one civilization, the requisites for cultural coexistence demand a search for what is common to most civilizations. In a multicivilizational world, the constructive course is to renounce universalism, accept diversity, and seek commonalities.[15]

But Hagee is far from seeking any form of coexistence with Iran, let alone Islam. He demands preventive war against Iran so as to disarm it:

> There is a clear and present danger to America and Israel from a nuclear Iran. There will soon be a nuclear blast in the Middle East that will transform the road to Armageddon into a racetrack. American and Israel will either take down Iran, or Iran will become nuclear and take down America and Israel.[16]

Within his dispensationalist framework, Hagee welcomes the current situation in the Middle East as portending the End Times and Second Coming.[17] He cites Matthew 24:8:

> Jesus presented a portrait of the end of the age and the coming of the Messiah. He presents a series of signs, including international wars, famines, and earthquakes. He makes a profound statement: 'All these are the beginning of birth pains.' (Matt. 24:8, NIV)[18]

Hagee explains to his readers what this means using the analogy of a woman giving birth:

> The world and Israel are now having contractions (wars, rumors of wars, acts of terrorism, bloodshed, and violence around the globe) that will produce a new Messianic Era. The increasing rapidity and intensifying of these birth pains can be seen on the newscasts every evening. We are racing toward the end of the age. Messiah is coming much sooner than you think![19]

For Christian Zionists, references to Daniel and Ezekiel – standard operating procedure for dispensationalists since the 1820s – foretell a global conspiracy on behalf of the Antichrist. 'God, through Ezekiel, has made some great power to the north of Israel that will destroy the peace and stability of the world at the end of days,' warns Hagee.[20] A being of supernatural power, the Antichrist will arise, and Hagee, with peculiarly twenty-first-century vision, tells readers how to recognize him: 'This man will come out of the European Union and will try to resolve the Islamic/Israeli dispute now raging in Israel.'[21]

For students of Christian Zionism, this bizarre vision is familiar. Reading Ezekiel, Hagee interprets in standard dispensationalist fashion the identity of the main enemy of Israel as Russia. Once again, Daniel 2:31–5 provides a point of departure; in Hagee's interpretation, the king of the North represents Russia; the kings of the South represent Persia (Iran) and the Arab states; and the king of the East is China.[22] In this latest version of the End scenario, Russia and its coalition partners – the Arab states and Iran – will make war on Israel.[23] The USA and the West will do nothing, Hagee says, because this is also foretold in Ezekiel. The invasion will be devastating to Russia: 'God declares He will exterminate all but one-sixth of the Russian axis of evil that invades Israel,' Hagee writes, reading Ezekiel 39:3–4, 6.[24]

The Russian coalition's invasion of Israel will trigger more events in the End Times scenario, according to Hagee. The Antichrist will appear fully and will be found to be none other than 'the head of the European Union.'[25] He would represent the king of the West. And the Rapture will occur – 'the rapture when the church is caught up to meet the Lord in the air.'[26] After Russia and its coalition partners are destroyed, two kings will remain – the king of the East (China) and the king of the West (the Antichrist) – and a final battle will occur: 'These two kings and their armies will meet to battle it out for world supremacy on a battlefield in Israel called *Armageddon*.'[27] Of this, Hagee has no doubt. He need have none – his scenario sticks to the very old script worked out by John Nelson Darby and his delusional circle.

Hagee's Christians United for Israel and AIPAC

So, given the foregoing scenario, what do Christian Zionists advocate as US foreign policy? Hagee, of course, says the USA and/or Israel must make war on Iran in order to avoid Ezekiel's war being triggered in the present time:

Israel and/or America must confront Iran concerning its nuclear weapons program. If Israel and/or America is required to use military force to guarantee Israel's safety and do not crush all eight nuclear sites at one time, Ezekiel's war will follow shortly thereafter.[28]

Numerous organizations currently pressure the White House and Congress for war against Iran and there is no indication that this pressure will be decreased for the Obama administration.[29] The CUFI complements similar organizations in the USA such as the National Unity Coalition for Israel (NUCI) and the International Fellowship for Christians and Jews (IFCJ), founded in 1983 by Rabbi Yechiel Eckstein. The IFCJ primarily works with Christian Zionists in fundraising activities for pro-Israel projects and to date has raised an estimated $250 million in this way. In 2007, the IFCJ became a funding partner of the Jewish Agency for Israel. According to Eckstein, the IFCJ will be donating some $45 million to the Jewish Agency over the next three years, 'almost all of it raised from Christians in North America'.[30] In 2002, Eckstein teamed with former Christian Coalition director Ralph Reed to found Stand for Israel, an advocacy organization.[31]

The launch of CUFI, on 26 February 2006, initiated a new phase of Christian Zionist organization and advocacy at the national level in the USA. The organization has chapters in all 50 states and in over 90 cities. Its board of directors includes Christian Right leaders Gary Bauer and Jonathan Falwell, son of the late Jerry Falwell. David Brog, a former staffer of US Senator Arlen Specter (Republican – Pennsylvania) and a relative of former Israeli Prime Minister Ehud Barak, is the executive director.[32] Brog says frankly that the organization's purpose is to prevent the USA from pressuring Israel to give up land.[33] The second annual CUFI conference, held in Washington, DC, drew over four thousand participants. 'Lobbying Congress was the *raison d'être* of the conference, and its last day was set aside for that purpose,' says researcher Brian Wood, who has studied the organization.[34]

Aside from Hagee's own vast radio and television ministry, CUFI has powerful and sophisticated machinery with which to mobilize the Christian Zionist political base:

> To educate and mobilize Christian support for Israel, CUFI issues a weekly e-mail update and glossy quarterly magazine (*The Torch*; circulation 200,000) and maintains a regularly updated Web site. It arranges for quarterly teleconferences in Washington, DC, between select CUFI members

and Israeli and US officials. Its public policy and lobbying work, beyond the annual conference in Washington, DC, includes electronic rapid response alerts that generate 'millions of phone calls and e-mails' from CUFI members to the executive and legislative branches of federal and state government.[35]

CUFI has a close strategic political relationship with AIPAC, as indicated by Hagee's participation as a featured speaker at the annual 2007 AIPAC conference in Washington, DC. He focused on two foreign policy themes in the speech: war with Iran and the Middle East peace process:

> As you know, Iran poses a threat to the State of Israel that promises nothing less than a nuclear holocaust. I have been saying on national television, in churches and auditoriums across America it is 1938; Iran is Germany and Ahmadinejad is the new Hitler. Ladies and gentlemen, we must stop Iran's nuclear threat and stop it now and stand boldly with Israel, the only democracy in the Middle East. The only way to win a nuclear war is to make certain it never starts.[36]

Hagee's presence at the AIPAC meeting was designed to reinforce AIPAC's demands for US foreign policy in the Middle East. Hagee, therefore, dutifully excoriated the Middle East peace process, the UN, the US State Department, and the land for peace formula, comparing it to Hitler's conquest of Czechoslovakia:

> I am concerned that in the coming months yet another attempt will be made to parcel out parts of Israel in a futile effort to appease Israel's enemies in the Middle East. I believe that misguided souls in Europe, I believe that the misguided souls in the political brothel that is now the United Nations and sadly – and sadly even our own State Department will try once again to turn Israel into crocodile food. Winston Churchill said and I quote an appeaser is one who feeds a crocodile in the futile hope that it will eat him last [sic] – end of quote. In 1938 Czechoslovakia – Czechoslovakia's Sudetenland land [sic] was turned into crocodile food for Nazi Germany. The Nazi beast smelled the weakness in the appeasers, ate the food and marched and devoured most of Europe and systematically slaughtered 6,000,000 Jewish people.[37]

Hagee pulled no punches in his dramatic affirmation of the solidarity of millions of American Christian Zionists Israel:

There are millions of evangelical Christians across America who consider the Jewish people the apple of God's eye, who see you as the chosen people, a cherished people and a covenant people with an eternal covenant that will stand forever. Ladies and gentlemen of AIPAC it's a new day in America. The sleeping giant of Christian Zionism has awakened; there are 50 million Christians standing up and applauding the State of Israel. If a line has to be drawn, draw the line around both Christians and Jews; we are united; we are indivisible; we are bound together by the Torah – the roots of Christianity are Jewish. We are spiritual brothers and what we have in common is far greater than the things we've allowed to separate us over the years.[38]

Ominously, dispensationalist ideology claims that the USA is on an inevitable collision course with Russia, the Arab and Muslim world, and China. Contemporary Christian Zionists have neatly recast the nineteenth-century Great Game between the British and Russian empires into a twenty-first-century struggle between the USA and an evil axis of Russia, Arab allies, and China. Thus, the Eastern Question endures – remaining, as ever, a clash of interests and designs, and a clash in which Christian Zionism, just as in the nineteenth and twentieth centuries, plays a malevolent role in the service of imperialism. For a century and a half, Christian Zionism has insidiously twisted the American republic's traditional values of faith, hope, and charity into delusion, fear, and war.

Notes

Preface

1   René Albrecht-Carrié, *A Diplomatic History of Europe Since the Congress of Vienna* (New York: Harper and Brothers, 1958), p.671.
2   D. Edward Knox, *The Making of a New Eastern Question: British Palestine Policy and the Origins of Israel, 1917–1925* (Washington, DC: Catholic University of America Press, 1981).
3   For background and a listing of traditional Christian churches of the Middle East see the website of the Middle East Council of Churches at *http://www.mec-churches.org/*.
4   Robert D. Woodberry and Christian S. Smith, 'Fundamentalism et al: Conservative Protestants in America', *Annual Review of Sociology* 24 (1998), p.25.
5   Ibid.
6   Paul Charles Merkley, *Christian Attitudes towards the State of Israel* (Montreal: McGill-Queen's University Press, 2001), p.200.
7   See Stephen Sizer, *Christian Zionism: Road-map to Armageddon?* (Leicester: Inter-Varsity Press, 2004), p.265 (also glossary entry for 'amillennialism').
8   Ibid., p.268 (also glossary entry for 'preterism').
9   Ibid., p.268 (also glossary entry for 'postmillennialism').
10 For background see Ira V. Brown, 'Watchers for the Second Coming: the millenarian tradition in America', *The Mississippi Valley Historical Review* 39/3 (Dec. 1952), pp.441–58; James H. Moorehead, 'Between progress and apocalypse: a reassessment of millennialism in American religious thought, 1800–1880', *The Journal of American History* 71/3 (Dec. 1984), pp.524–42; Jean B. Quandt, 'Religion and social thought: the secularization of postmillennialism', *American Quarterly* 25/4 (Oct. 1973), pp.390–409; and Richard Wightman Fox, 'The culture of liberal protestant progressivism, 1875–1928', *Journal of Interdisciplinary History* 23/3 (winter 1993), pp.639–60.
11 B. Eugene Griessman, 'Philo-Semitism and Protestant Fundamentalism: the unlikely Zionists', *Phylon* 37/3 (1976), p.207.

12   For a useful treatment of the bi-national solution see Jenab Tutunji and Kamal Khalidi, 'A binational state in Palestine: the rational choice for Palestinians and the moral choice for Israelis', *International Affairs* 73/1 (Jan. 1997), pp.31–58.
13   Cathy Lynn Grossman, 'Some Protestant churches feeling "mainline" again', *USA Today*, available online at *http://www.usatoday.com/news/religion/2006-10-31-protestant-cover_x.htm*.
14   United States Religious Landscape Survey 2008, Pew Forum on Religion and Public Life. Available online at *http://religions.pewforum.org/*.
15   George Antonius, *The Arab Awakening: The Story of the Arab National Movement* (Beirut: Khayat's College Book Cooperative, 1955 [1938]), p.386.

Introduction

1   For background on imperialism see J.A. Hobson, *Imperialism* (Ann Arbor: University of Michigan Press, 1965); Parker Thomas Moon, *Imperialism and World Politics* (New York: The Macmillan Company, 1928); Raymond Leslie Buell, *International Relations* (New York: Henry Holt and Company, 1925); Frederick L. Schuman, *International Politics*, 2nd edn (New York: McGraw-Hill, 1937); Frank M. Russell, *Theories of International Relations* (New York: D. Appleton-Century, 1936).
2   Earl D. Huff, 'A study of a successful interest group: the American Zionist movement', *The Western Political Quarterly* 25/1 (Mar. 1972), pp.110. Huff follows the methodology established by David Truman in his book *The Governmental Process* (New York: Knopf, 1960). See also Norman J. Ornstein and Shirley Elder, *Interest Groups, Lobbying, and Policymaking* (Washington, DC: Congressional Quarterly Press, 1978).
3   For a general history of political Zionism see Walter Laqueur, *A History of Zionism* (New York: Holt, Rinehart and Winston, 1972). For an overview of American Zionism see Melvin I. Urofsky, *American Zionism from Herzl to the Holocaust* (Garden City: Anchor Press, 1975).
4   John J. Mearsheimer and Stephen M. Walt, *The Israel Lobby and US Foreign Policy* (New York: Farrar, Straus and Giroux, 2007), p.112.
5   Huff: 'A study', p.124.
6   Ibid.
7   Kevin Phillips, *American Theocracy: The Peril and Politics of Radical Religion, Oil, and Borrowed Money in the 21st Century* (New York: Viking, 2006), p.xii.
8   Ibid., pp.xiii–xiv.
9   John Danforth, 'In the name of politics', *New York Times*, 30 March 2005, available online at *http://www.nytimes.com/2005/03/30/opinion/30danforth.html?_r=1*.
10   Jimmy Carter, *Our Endangered Values* (New York: Simon and Schuster, 2005), p.39.
11   Ibid., pp.113–14.

12 E.A. Speiser, *The United States and the Near East* (Cambridge, MA: Harvard University Press, 1947), p.226.
13 Rami G. Khouri, 'Anti-Americanism as a form of resistance', *Agence Global*, 30 June 2007, available online at *http://www.agenceglobal.com/Article.asp?Id=1307*.

Part I   Chrisitan Zionism and Nineteenth-Century Imperialism

1. The Eastern Question and Imperialism

1 For an overview see David Fromkin, *A Peace To End All Peace: The Fall of the Ottoman Empire and the Creation of the Modern Middle East* (New York: Avon Books, 1990).
2 Take, for example, the activities of William Blackstone of Chicago in the 1880s and 1890s on behalf of Jewish resettlement to Palestine. See Kathleen Christison, *Perceptions of Palestine* (Berkeley: University of California Press, 2001), pp.23, 30.
3 For international public opinion research data and interpretation supporting this point see the Middle East/North Africa section on *http://worldpublicopinion.org*, a project of the The Program on International Policy Attitudes at the University of Maryland. Valuable public opinion data is also produced by the Pew Research Center for the People and the Press; see *http://people-press.org/*.
4 See Edward Gibbon, ed. Rev. H. R. Milman, *The History of the Decline and Fall of the Roman Empire*, Vol. II (New York: Harper, 1852).
5 Ibid., p.431.
6 Ibid., p.441.
7 Ibid., p.431.
8 Ibid., p.438.
9 See Karl A. Roider, *Austria's Eastern Question 1700–1740* (Princeton: Princeton University Press, 1982).
10 See, for example, D. Edward Knox, *The Making of a New Eastern Question: British Palestine Policy and the Origins of Israel, 1917–1925* (Washington, DC: Catholic University of America Press, 1981).
11 For an overview from an imperial Russian perspective see, 'Traités passés par la Russie avec sesvVoisins immédiats, la Suéde, la Pologne et la Turquie', Part 4 of A.M. Ouroussow, *Résumé Historique des Principaux Traités de Paix* (Evreux, France: Charles Hérissey, 1884), pp.366–440. For a still helpful overview of the European states system, see A.H.L. Heeren, *A Manual of the History of the Political System of Europe and its Colonies* (London: Henry G. Bohn, 1846).
12 For this period see Lavender Cassels, *The Struggle for the Ottoman Empire: 1717–1740* (London: John Murray, 1966) and John B. Wolf, 'The new balance

of power', in John B. Wolf (ed.), *The Emergence of the Great Powers. 1685–1715* (New York: Harper, 1951), pp.54–96.

13 Significantly, an able young German-born diplomat in the Russian service, Alexei Ivanovich Osterman (born Heinrich Johann Friedrich Ostermann, 1686–1747), assisted in the diplomatic negotiations at Pruth and did not forget the experience. After rendering important service negotiating the Treaty of Nystad (1721), which was exceptionally favorable to Russia, his star rose rapidly and he handled Russian foreign relations under three of Peter the Great's successors.

14 For background see Juan Cole, *Napoleon's Egypt: Invading the Middle East* (New York: Palgrave Macmillan, 2007); C.M. Watson, 'Bonaparte's expedition to Palestine in 1799', *Palestine Exploration Fund: Quarterly Statement for 1917* (London: Palestine Exploration Fund, 1917), pp.17–35.

15 For background see Wolf: *Emergence of the Great Powers*.

16 For a detailed study see François Charles-Roux, *Les Origines de l'Expédition d'Égypte* (Paris: Plon-Nourrit et Cie, 1910).

17 For a comprehensive treatment of Napoleon's relations with various Jewish populations see Robert Anchel, *Napoléon et les Juifs* (Paris: Les Presses Universitaires de France, 1928). See also Franz Kobler, *Napoleon and the Jews* (New York: Schocken, 1976).

18 The Balfour Declaration of 2 November 1917 was an official expression by the British government in support of a homeland for Jews in Palestine.

19 For background on Jews in Palestine in this period see Jacob Barnai, *The Jews in Palestine in the Eighteenth Century* (Tuscaloosa: University of Alabama Press, 1992) and Abraham David, *To Come to the Land: Immigration and Settlement in Sixteenth-Century Eretz-Israel* (Tuscaloosa: University of Alabama Press, 1999).

20 Nathan Schur, *Napoleon in the Holy Land* (London: Greenhill Books, 1999), pp.117–18.

21 For a view of Ottoman administration see Uriel Heyd, *Ottoman Documents on Palestine 1552–1615* (London: Oxford University Press, 1960).

22 Schur: *Napoleon*, p.117.

23 'Bonaparte a fait publier une proclamation, dans laquelle il invite tous les juifs de l'Asie et de l'Afrique à se ranger sous ses drapeaux pour rétablir l'ancienne Jèrusalem. Il en a déjà armé un grand nombre, et leurs batillons menacent Alep', as quoted in Philip Guedalla, *Napoleon and Palestine* (London: George Allen and Unwin, 1925), p.24.

24 'Ce n'est pas seulement pour render aux juifs leur Jérusalem que Bonaparte a conquis la Syrie; il avait de plus vastes dessins … de marcher sur Constantinople, pour jeter de là l'eprouvante dans Vienne et Petersbourg', as quoted in Guedalla: *Napoleon and Palestine*, p.24.

25 Schur: *Napoleon*, p.118.

26 Ibid., p.120.

27 Ibid., p.121.

28 Simon Schwarzfuchs, *Napoleon, the Jews and the Sanhedrin* (London: Routledge and Kegan Paul, 1979), p.27.
29 Ibid.
30 For an overview see René Albrecht-Carrié, *A Diplomatic History of Europe Since the Congress of Vienna* (New York: Harper and Bros, 1958). For detailed treatment of the Eastern Question see James A.B. Marriott, *The Eastern Question: An Historical Study*, 4th edn. (London: Oxford, 1940) and Harold W.V. Temperley, *England and the Near East: The Crimea* (London: Longmans, Green and Co., 1936).
31 See Jaspar Ridley, *Lord Palmerston* (London: Constable, 1970). For a detailed study see Charles Webster, *The Foreign Policy of Palmerston*, 2 vols. (London: G. Bell and Sons, 1969 [1951]).
32 Depending upon the transliteration system used Muhammad can also be spelt, for example, as Mohamed or Mehmet.
33 Ridley: *Palmerston*, p.208.
34 Ibid., pp.209–10.
35 See 'Mehmet Ali: the crisis of 1839', in Ridley: *Palmerston*, pp.208–24.
36 Ridley: *Palmerston*, p.239.
37 Ibid., p.233.
38 Barbara Tuchman, *Bible and Sword* (New York: Ballantine Books, 1984 [1956]), p. xiii.
39 Ibid., pp.163–4.
40 The Maronite religious tradition dates to the fifth century, considering itself an heir of Antioch. The Maronite patriarchate reaffirmed its connection to the papacy in the twelfth century.
41 Albert M. Hyamson, 'British projects for the restoration of Jews to Palestine', *Publications of the American Jewish Historical Society* 26 (1918), p.136.
42 Ibid.
43 Frederick Stanley Rodkey, 'Lord Palmerston and the rejuvenation of Turkey, 1830–41, Part II, 1939–41', *The Journal of Modern History* ii/2 (Jun. 1930), p.214; Part I is found in *The Journal of Modern History* i/4 (Dec. 1929).
44 Ibid.
45 Ridley: *Palmerston*, p.292.
46 Rodkey: 'Lord Palmerston', p.215.
47 Albert Hourani, 'Ottoman reform and the politics of notables', in William Polk and Richard Chambers (eds), *Beginnings of Modernization in the Middle East: The Nineteenth Century* (Chicago: University of Chicago Press, 1968), pp.41–68.
48 For analysis of this period see Alexander Schölch, 'Britain in Palestine, 1838–1882: the roots of the Balfour policy', *Journal of Palestine Studies* xxii/1 (autumn 1992), pp.39–56. See also Albert Hyamson, *The British Consulate in Jerusalem in Relation to the Jews of Palestine, 1838–1914* (London: Goldston, 1939–1940), Part I.

2. The Early American Republic and the Muslim World

1. For the best analysis of the early American foreign policy tradition see Samuel Flagg Bemis, *John Quincy Adams and the Foundations of American Foreign Policy* (New York: Alfred Knopf, 1949).
2. For Egyptian and Moroccan responses, for example, see *Muslim Public Opinion on US Policy, Attacks on Civilians and al Qaeda*, 24 April 2007, Program on International Policy Attitudes, University of Maryland, available online at *http://www.worldpublicopinion.org/pipa/pdf/apr07/START_Apr07_rpt.pdf*.
3. For background see James A. Field, Jr, *America and the Mediterranean World 1776–1882* (Princeton: Princeton University Press, 1969) and David J. Finnie, *Pioneers East: The Early American Experience in the Middle East* (Cambridge, MA: Harvard University Press, 1967).
4. For background see Peter Hopkirk, *The Great Game: The Struggle for Empire in Central Asia* (New York: Kodansha International, 1992) and Robert Johnson, *Spying for Empire: The Great Game in Central and South Asia, 1757–1947* (London: Greenhill, 2006).
5. See Edward Ingram, *Britain's Persian Connection 1798–1828: Prelude to the Great Game in Asia* (Oxford: Clarendon Press, 1992). For a later American perspective see W. Morgan Shuster, *The Strangling of Persia: A Personal Narrative* (New York: Century Company, 1912).
6. Finnie: *Pioneers East*, p.47, citing Walter Livingston Wright, Jr, 'American relations with Turkey to 1831', unpublished dissertation, Princeton University, 1928, pp.10–30.
7. From 1815 to 1848, the squadron's base was in the Balearic Islands at Port Mahon, Minorca, and was leased from Spain. From 1848 to 1861, the squadron's base was La Spezia, on the Ligurian coast, south of Genoa. In 1865 and 1866, it moved to Villefranche, France, and thence to Lisbon between 1866 and 1870. It returned to Villefranche between 1870 and 1883.
8. See James Curtis Ballagh (ed.), *The Letters of Richard Henry Lee*, 2 vols, (New York: Macmillan, 1911), Vol. 1.
9. See, Samuel Flag Bemis, *The Diplomacy of the American Revolution* (New York: D. Appleton-Century, 1935).
10. For background see Field: *America and the Mediterranean World* and Finnie: *Pioneers East*.
11. See, for example, *Seafaring in Colonial Massachusetts: a conference held by the Colonial Society of Massachusetts, November 21 and 22, 1975* (Boston: Colonial Society of Massachusetts, 1980); Arthur L. Jensen, *The Maritime Commerce of Colonial Philadelphia* (Madison, WI: State Historical Society of Wisconsin, 1963); and Samuel Eliot Morison, *Maritime History of Massachusetts* (Boston: Houghton Mifflin and Co., 1921).
12. On the matter of the corsairs of the Mediterranean see Salvatore Bono, *Les Corsaires en Mediterranée* (Rabat, Morocco: Éditions La Porte, 1998). The

original Italian edition is *Corsari nel Mediterraneo* (Milan: Arnoldo Mondadore Editorial, 1993).

13 Jerome B. Bookin-Weiner and Mohamed El Mansour, *The Atlantic Connection: 200 Years of Moroccan-American Relations 1786–1986* (Morocco: Edino Press, 1986).

14 The development of foreign commerce is emphasized in the early debates on the Constitution as reflected in the collection of newspaper columns in the Federalist papers, by James Madison, Alexander Hamilton, and John Jay. See, in particular, Federalist No. 11 by Hamilton. An excellent edition is Jacob E. Cooke (ed.), *The Federalist* (Middletown, CT: Wesleyan University Press, 1961).

15 For a full transcript see 'Washington's Farewell Address 1796', the Avalon Project at Yale Law School, available online at *http://avalon.law.yale.edu/18th_century/washing.asp*.

16 Field: *America and the Mediterranean World*, p.25.

17 William M. Malloy, *Treaties, Conventions, International Acts, Protocols and Agreements Between the United States of America and Other Powers 1776–1909*, Vol. 2 (Washington, DC: Government Printing House, 1909), p.1,794.

18 Frank Lambert, *The Barbary Wars: American Independence in the Atlantic World* (New York: Hill and Wang, 2005), p.8.

19 Finnie: *Pioneers East*, p.49, quoting E.D. Clarke, *Travels in Various Countries of Europe, Asia and Africa*, Vol. 3, 4th edn (London: Cadell and Davies, 1817), p.79.

20 Finnie, *Pioneers East*, p.73.

21 Ibid., p.89.

22 Quoted in ibid., p.77.

23 Ibid., p.81.

24 Joseph S. Nye, Jr, *Soft Power: The Means to Success in World Politics* (New York: Public Affairs, 2004).

25 Nasuh Uslu, Metin Toprak, Ibrahim Dalmis, and Ertan Aydin, 'Turkish public opinion toward the United States in the context of the Iraq Question', *The Middle East Review of International Affairs* ix/3 (Sep. 2005), available online at *http://meria.idc.ac.il/journal/2005/issue3/jv9no3a5.html*. See also, Rajan Meon and S. Enders Wimbush, 'Is The United States losing Turkey?', The Hudson Institute, 25 March 2007, available online at *http://www.hudson.org/files/pdf_upload/Turkey%20PDF.pdf*.

26 'Global unease with world major powers', Pew Global Attitudes Project, 27 June 2007, at *http://pewglobal.org/reports/display.php?ReportID=256*.

27 'Why Turks feel threatened by the US', World Public Opinion.org, University of Maryland, 5 September 2007, available online at *http://www.worldpublicopinion.org/pipa/articles/brmiddleeastnafricara/393.php?lb=brme&pnt=393&nid=&id=*.

28 See, for example, G. Bhagat, *Americans in India 1784–1860* (New York: New York University Press, 1970).

29 For a brief overview see Hermann Frederick Eilts, *A Friendship Two Centuries Old: The United States and the Sultanate of Oman* (Washington, DC: Sultan Qaboos Center, The Middle East Institute, 1990).
30 Sayyid Sa'id bin Sultan Al Bu Sa'id is the great-great-great grandfather of His Majesty, Sultan Qaboos bin Sa'id, the ruler of Oman today.
31 Eilts: *A Friendship*, p.13.
32 See the remarks by His Excellency Abdullah Bin Mohamad Al-Dhahb, *Washington Times*, special section on Oman, 21 December 1999.
33 'Global unease with world major powers', Pew Global Attitudes Project.
34 Elbert E. Farman, *Egypt and its Betrayal* (New York: Grafton Press,1908), p.280.
35 For background see William J. Burns, *Economic Aid and American Foreign Policy Toward Egypt 1855–1981* (Albany, NY: University of New York Press, 1985).
36 For President Carter's perspective see Jimmy Carter, *Palestine Peace Not Apartheid* (New York: Simon and Schuster, 2006).
37 On political Islam in Egypt see especially Richard P. Mitchell, *The Society of the Muslim Brothers* (New York: Oxford University Press, 1993).
38 For background on Chinese foreign policy see Suisheng Zhao (ed.), *Chinese Foreign Policy: Pragmatism and Strategic Behavior* (Armonk, NY: M.E. Sharpe, 2004).
39 For a specialized study see Joseph L. Grabill, *Protestant Diplomacy and the Near East: Missionary Influence on American Policy, 1810–1927* (Minneapolis: University of Minnesota Press, 1971).
40 On missionary activity see Finnie: *Pioneers East*.
41 For a contemporary treatment see Joseph Tracy, *The Great Awakening: A History of the Revival of Religion in the Time of Edwards and Whitefield* (Boston, MA: Tappan and Dennet, 1842). See also Alan Heimert and Perry Miller, *The Great Awakening: Documents Illustrating the Crisis and its Consequences* (Indianapolis: The Bobbs-Merrill Company, 1967).
42 'Religion and the American Revolution', June 1998, Library of Congress, Washington, DC, available online at *http://www.loc.gov/exhibits/religion/rel03.html*.
43 See William E. Strong, *The Story of the American Board: An Account of the First Hundred Years of the American Board of Commissioners for Foreign Missions* (Boston, MA: Pilgrim Press, 1910); Clifton Jackson Phillips, *Protestant America and the Pagan World: The First Half Century of the American Board of Commissioners for Foreign Missions, 1810–1860* (Cambridge, MA: East Asian Research Center of Harvard University, 1969).
44 Field: *America and the Mediterranean World*, p.93.
45 'Muslims believe US seeks to undermine Islam', World Public Opinion.org, University of Maryland, 24 April 2007, available online at *http://www.worldpublicopinion.org/pipa/articles/brmiddleeastnafricara/346.php?nid=&id=&pnt=346*.
46 Ibid.

3. Christian Zionism: Construction of an Ideology

1. For an Arab perspective see Abdul-Wahab Kayyali, 'Zionism and imperialism: the historical origins', *Journal of Palestine Studies* vi/3 (spring 1977), pp.98–112. For an overview see Richard Allen, *Imperialism and Nationalism in the Fertile Crescent: Sources and Prospects of the Arab-Israeli Conflict* (New York: Oxford University Press, 1974).
2. Barbara Tuchman, *Bible and Sword* (New York: Ballantine Books, 1984 [1956]), p.175.
3. Ibid., p.178.
4. Kevin Phillips, *American Theocracy: The Peril and Politics of Radical Religion, Oil, and Borrowed Money in the 21st Century* (New York: Viking, 2006), p.103.
5. Jimmy Carter, *Our Endangered Values: America's Moral Crisis* (New York: Simon and Schuster, 2005), p.115.
6. The best historical analysis of doctrinal issues is Ernest R. Sandeen, *The Roots of Fundamentalism: British and American Millenarianism 1800–1930* (Chicago, IL: University of Chicago Press, 1970).
7. B. Eugene Griessman, 'Philo-Semitism and Protestant Fundamentalism: the unlikely Zionists', *Phylon* xxvii/3 (fall 1976), p.198.
8. Jacob R. Marcus, *The Colonial Jew, 1492–1776* (Detroit: Wayne State University Press, 1970), p.413.
9. Robert H. Pfeiffer, 'The teaching of Hebrew in colonial America', *The Jewish Quarterly Review* xlv/4, tercentenary issue (Apr. 1955), p.364.
10. Pfeiffer: 'The teaching of Hebrew', pp.363–4. See also, Abraham I. Katsh, 'The teaching of Hebrew in American universities', *The Modern Language Journal* xxx/8 (Dec. 1946), pp.575–86 and Isidore S. Meyer, 'Hebrew at Harvard (1636–1760)', *Publications of the American Jewish Historical Society* 35 (1939), pp.145–70.
11. Its title reads: *The Whole Book of Psalmes Faithfully Translated into English Metre* (printed by Stephen Daye).
12. Griessman, 'Philo-Semitism', p.199.
13. Ibid., p.200. An early British writer speculating that American Indians were those tribes was Thomas Thorowgood, who wrote *Jews in America: or Probabilities that the Americans are of that Race* (1650).
14. For an overview of colonial cultural life see Louis B. Wright, *The Cultural Life of the American Colonies 1607–1763* (New York: Harper and Bros, 1957). For a specialized study in education see Lawrence A. Cremin, *American Education: The Colonial Experience 1607–1783* (New York: Harper and Row, 1970).
15. Nabil I. Matar, 'Protestantism, Palestine, and partisan scholarship', *Journal of Palestine Studies* xviii/4 (summer 1989), p.53. He discusses Peter Alix (1641–1717), Richard Baxter (1615–91), Hugh Broughton (1549–1612), Henry Danvers (1573–1644), Thomas Fuller (1608–61), Joseph Hall (1574–1656), Henry Hammond (1605–60), John Lightfoot (1602–75), and John Milton (1608–74).

16 Tuchman: *Bible and Sword*, p.160.
17 Stephen Sizer, *Christian Zionism: Road-map to Armageddon?* (Leicester: Inter-Varsity Press, 2004), pp.56–7.
18 See, Mayir Vereté, 'The restoration of Jews in English Protestant thought 1790–1840', *Middle Eastern Studies* viii/1 (Jan. 1972), pp.3–50.
19 Tuchman: *Bible and Sword*, p.219.
20 Samih K. Farsoun and Christina Zacharia, *Palestine and the Palestinians* (Boulder, CO: Westview Press, 1997), p.28.
21 Kathleen Christison, *Perceptions of Palestine: Their Influence on US Middle East Policy* (Berkeley: University of California Press, 1999), p.21. See Beshara Doumani, 'Rediscovering Ottoman Palestine: writing Palestinians into history', *Journal of Palestine Studies* 82 (winter 1992), p.8.
22 Sizer: *Christian Zionism*, p.55. For further background consult Sizer's bibliography and see Clarence Bass, *Backgrounds to Dispensationalism* (Grand Rapids, MI: Erdmans, 1960) and Donald E. Wagner, *Anxious for Armageddon* (Scottdale, PA: Herald Press, 1995). Rev. Wagner is a leading American expert on Christian Zionism.
23 For an overview of restorationism in British thought see Regina Sharif, 'Christians for Zion, 1600–1919', *Journal of Palestine Studies* v/3–4 (spring/summer 1976), pp.123–41.
24 Sizer: *Christian Zionism*, p.269.
25 Ibid., pp.267–69.
26 For a study on Hebrew thought and institutions (in the context of Mesopotamian and Egyptian cultures) see Eric Voegelin, *Order and History: Israel and Revelation* (Baton Rouge, LA: Louisiana State University, 1956).
27 See, for example, Joesph Bellamy's sermon 'The Millennium' (1758) in Alan Heimert and Perry Miller, *The Great Awakening: Documents Illustrating the Crisis and its Consequences* (Indianapolis: The Bobbs-Merrill Company, 1967), pp.609–35. Bellamy was a protégé of Jonathan Edwards.
28 Sizer: *Christian Zionism*, p.268.
29 There is a scholarly literature on this topic. See in particular Edwin S. Gaustad, 'The theological effects of the Great Awakening in New England', *The Mississippi Valley Historical Review* xl/4 (Mar. 1954), pp.681–706; Robert D. Rossel, 'The Great Awakening: an historical analysis', *The American Journal of Sociology*, lxxv/6 (May 1970), pp.907–25; and George W. Harper, 'Clericalism and revival: the Great Awakening in Boston as a pastoral phenomenon', *The New England Quarterly* lvii/4 (Dec. 1984), pp.534–66.
30 Joseph Tracy, *The Great Awakening: A History of the Revival of Religion in the Time of Edwards and Whitefield* (Boston, MA: Tappan and Dennet, 1842), p.420.
31 Ibid.
32 See Donald G. Mathews, 'The Second Great Awakening as an organizing process, 1780–1830: an hypothesis', *American Quarterly* xxi/1 (spring 1969), pp.23–43.

33 See sermon by Ezra Stiles (1727–95) and biographical sketch and editor's notes in John Wingate Thornton (ed.), *The Pulpit of the American Revolution: Or, the Political Sermons of the Period of 1776. With a Historical Introduction, Notes, and Illustrations* (Boston: Gould and Lincoln/New York: Sheldon and Company/Cincinnati: George S. Blanchard, 1860), pp.397–506.
34 Frank Lambert, *The Founding Fathers and the Place of Religion in America* (Princeton: Princeton University Press, 2003), p.8.
35 Cited in James A. Field, Jr, *America and the Mediterranean World 1776–1882* (Princeton: Princeton University Press, 1969), pp.9, 15.
36 See Gaillard Hunt, *The History of the Seal of the United States* (Washington, DC: Department of State, 1909).
37 Joseph L. Grabill, *Protestant Diplomacy and the Near East: Missionary Influence on American Policy, 1810–1927* (Minneapolis: University of Minnesota Press, 1971), p.38.
38 See, for example, studies by the Pew Forum on Religion and Public Life at *http://religions.pewforum.org/*.
39 Kelvin Crombie, *For the Love of Zion: Christian Witness and the Restoration of Israel* (London: Hodder and Stoughton, 1991) referenced in Sizer: *Christian Zionism*, p.35. On relief of the sick in Palestine see Yaron Perry and Efraim Lev, 'The medical activities of the London Jews' Society in nineteenth-century Palestine', *Medical History* xlvii/1 (Jan. 2003), pp.67–88, available online at *http://www.pubmedcentral.nih.gov/articlerender.fcgi?artid =1044765*.
40 See JewishEncyclopedia.com at *http://www.jewishencyclopedia.com/view.jsp?artid=61&letter=W*, accessed June 2007.
41 Tuchman: *Bible and Sword*, p.183.
42 Sizer: *Christian Zionism*, p.35.
43 Missionary Periodicals Database, University of Cambridge and Yale University, available online at *http://research.yale.edu:8084/missionperiodicals/viewdetail.jsp?id=707*.
44 A book by Way appeared in 1819 containing his memorandum to the Congress: *Mémoires sur l'Etat des Israélites Dédiés et Présentés à Leurs Majestés Impériales et Royales, Réunies au Congrès d'Aix-la-Chapelle* (Paris, 1819).
45 Sizer: *Christian Zionism*, p.36. For an overview, see also Don Wagner, 'For Zion's sake', *Middle East Report* 223 (summer 2002), pp.52–7.
46 See the website for Saint George's Anglican Parish, Paris, at *http://www.stgeorgesparis.com/history*.
47 For Napoleon's policy see Robert Anchel, *Napoléon et Les Juifs* (Paris: Les Presses Universitaires de France, 1928).
48 See Felix Henry Price Palmer, *Joseph Wolff: His Romantic Life and Travels* (London: Heath Cranton, 1935) and Hugh Evan Hopkins, *Sublime Vagabond: The Life of Joseph Wolff – Missionary Extraordinary*, foreword by Sir Fitzroy Maclean Bart (Worthing: Churchman, 1984).

194 Notes

49 Joseph Wolff's *Researches and Missionary Labours Among the Jews, Mohammedans, and Other Sects* (London: J. Nisbet and Co., 1835) was reprinted in an American edition published in Philadelphia by Rodgers in 1837. His *Narrative of a Mission to Bokhara, in the Years 1843–1845, to Ascertain the Fate of Colonel Stoddart and Captain Conolly* (London: J.W. Parker, 1845) was reprinted and published in New York by Harper and Bros in 1845.
50 See Charles Spurgeon's 'The restoration and conversion of the Jews', *Metropolitan Tabernacle Pulpit 10* (London: Passmore and Alabaster, 1862–1917), p.426, as cited in Sizer: *Christian Zionism*, p.426.
51 Yona Malachy, *American Fundamentalism and Israel: The Relation of Fundamentalist Churches to Zionism and the State of Israel,* (Jerusalem: Institute of Contemporary Jewry, Hebrew University of Jerusalem, 1978), p.125.
52 For an extensive analysis of prophetic interpretation consult LeRoy Edwin Froom, *The Prophetic Faith of Our Fathers: The Historical Development of Prophetic Interpretation*, 4 vols (Washington, DC: Review and Herald, 1946). On Irving see 'Irving's contribution marred by "utterances"', Vol. 4, chapter 27, pp.514–32.
53 Henry Drummond, *Dialogues on Prophecy*, 3 vols (London: James Nisbet, 1827–9).
54 Drummond: *Dialogues on Prophecy* (1828), pp.ii–iii as cited in Sizer: *Christian Zionism*, p.41.
55 Sizer: *Christian Zionism*, p.47.
56 Reflection on the Last Days, or End Times, generally draws on apocryphal books, the Book of Daniel, Zechariah 9–14, Ezekiel 38–9, Matthew 24, early Pauline letters (1 Thess 4:16–17; 5:1–11), and the Book of Revelation.
57 Froom: *The Prophetic Faith*, Vol. 4, pp.422–3.
58 Ibid.
59 Ibid., p.423.
60 Ibid.
61 See W.G. Turner, *John Nelson Darby* (London: C.A. Hammond, 1944) and W.B. Neatby, *A History of the Plymouth Brethren* (London: Hodder and Stoughton, 1901).
62 Sizer: *Christian Zionism*, p.52.

4. Christian Zionism on American Shores

1 Grace Halsell, *Journey to Jerusalem* (New York: Macmillan, 1981).
2 Grace Halsell, *Prophecy and Politics: Militant Evangelists on the Road to Nuclear War* (Westport, CT: Lawrence Hill and Co., 1986), p.15.
3 C. Norman Kraus, *Dispensationalism in America: Its Rise and Development* (Richmond, VA: John Knox, 1958), p.104.
4 Ernest R. Sandeen, *The Roots of Fundamentalism: British and American Millenarianism 1800–1930* (Chicago, IL: University of Chicago Press, 1970), pp.60–1.

5   Ibid., p.70.
6   Stephen Sizer, *Christian Zionism: Road-map to Armageddon?* (Leicester: Inter-Varsity Press, 2004), p.67.
7   James H. Brookes, *Till He Come*, 2nd edn (New York: Fleming H. Revell, 1895), pp.1–2, as cited in Sizer: *Christian Zionism*, p.68.
8   LeRoy Edwin Froom, *The Prophetic Faith of Our Fathers: The Historical Development of Prophetic Interpretation*, 4 vols (Washington, DC: Review and Herald, 1946), Vol. 4, p.424.
9   For a critical biography see James Findlay, *Dwight L. Moody: American Evangelist 1837–1899* (Chicago: University of Chicago Press, 1969).
10 Sandeen: *Roots of Fundamentalism*, p.176.
11 Sizer: *Christian Zionism*, p.75.
12 Craig A. Blaising, 'Dispensationalism, the search for definition', in Craig A. Blaising and Darrell I. Bock (eds), *Dispensationalism, Israel and the Church: The Search for Definition* (Grand Rapids, MI: Zondervan, 1992), cited in Sizer: *Christian Zionism*, pp.75–6.
13 Froom: *Prophetic Faith*, Vol. 4, pp.1,203–4.
14 William E. Blackstone, *Jesus is Coming* (Chicago, IL: F.H. Revel, 1908 [1887]).
15 Sizer: *Christian Zionism*, p.72, citing Beth M. Lindberg, *A God Filled Life* (Chicago, IL: American Messianic Fellowship, n.d.), pp.7–9.
16 Cited in Ruben Fink, *America and Palestine* (New York: American Zionist Emergency Council, 1945), pp.20–1.
17 See the discussion of Blackstone in Paul C. Merkley, *The Politics of Christian Zionism 1891–1948* (London: Frank Cass, 1998), pp.59–74.
18 Sandeen: *Roots of Fundamentalism*, p.132. Chapter 6 is called 'The Prophecy and Bible Conference Movement'.
19 See David O. Beale, *In Pursuit of Purity: American Fundamentalism Since 1850* (Greenville: Unusual Publications, 1986). See also L.W. Munhall, 'The Niagra Bible Conference', *Moody Bible Institute Bulletin XXII*, 1921–22, pp.1,104–05.
20 Stuart Grant Cole, *The History of Fundamentalism* (Hamden, CT: Archon Books, 1963 [c.1931]), pp.31–2. Conference proceedings are in Nathaniel West (ed.), *Premillennial Essays* (Chicago: Fleming H. Revell, 1879).
21 See conference report in Geo. C. Needham, *Prophetic Studies* (Chicago: Fleming H. Revell, 1886).
22 Sandeen: *Roots of Fundamentalism*, p.159.
23 Louis Gasper, *The Fundamentalist Movement* (The Hague: Mouton, 1963), p.11.
24 Cole: *History of Fundamentalism*, p.35.
25 The Scopes Trial was an important test case on the legality of teaching an unbiblical account of creation in any state-funded educational establishment. For an overview of the Scopes Trial see Wikipedia entry at *http://en.wikipedia.org/wiki/Scopes_Trial*.

26 See Nyack College website at *http://www.nyack.edu/*.
27 Cole: *History of Fundamentalism*, p.42. See Moody Institute website at *http://www.moodyministries.net/*.
28 See Northwestern College website at *http://nwc.nwc.edu/display/46*.
29 See BIOLA website at *http://www.biola.edu/about/history/*.
30 See Philadelphia Biblical University website at *http://www.pbu.edu/*.
31 See Dallas Theological Seminary website at *http://www.dts.edu/*.
32 Sizer: *Christian Zionism*, p.77. For a thorough analysis of the theology of premillennial dispensationalism see Chapter 2, 'The theological emphases of Christian Zionism', pp.106–201.

Part II   Christian Zionism and American Foreign Policy: 1917–48

5. Fundamentalism, the First World War, and Palestine

1 A.C. Dixon (ed.), *The Fundamentals* (Los Angeles: Bible Institute of Los Angeles, 1910–15).
2 For a view of Palestine in the late Ottoman period see David Kushner (ed.), *Palestine in the Late Ottoman Period: Political, Social and Economic Transformation* (Jerusalem: Yad Izhak Ben-Zvi, 1986).
3 For general background see 'The Mediterranean and the Middle East', in Royal Institute of International Affairs, *Political and Strategic Interests of the United Kingdom: An Outline* (London: Oxford University Press, 1938), pp.100–86.
4 See Edward Mead Earle, 'The Turkish Petroleum Company – a study in oleaginous diplomacy', *Political Science Quarterly* xxxix/1 (Jun. 1924), pp.265–79, and his 'The secret Anglo-German Convention of 1914 regarding Asiatic Turkey', *Political Science Quarterly* xxxviii (Mar. 1923), pp.24–44.
5 Contemporary insight on British Iraq policy is provided in B.H. Bourdillon, 'The political situation in Iraq', *Journal of the British Institute of International Affairs* iii/6 (Nov. 1924), pp.273–87.
6 On British naval policy during the interwar period see Stephen Roskill, *Naval Policy Between the Wars*, 2 vols (Annapolis, MD: Naval Institute Press, 1976).
7 On the question of the boundaries of Palestine see Gideon Biger, *The Boundaries of Modern Palestine, 1840–1947* (London: RoutledgeCurzon, 2004).
8 For insight on the transportation infrastructure and hydrocarbon issues see Morton B. Stratton, 'British railways and motor routes in the Middle East – 1918–1930', *Economic Geography* xx/2 (Apr. 1944), pp.116–29.
9 The text of the British Mandate for Palestine is reported in 'British Mandate for Palestine', *The American Journal of International Law* xvii/3, Supplement: Official Documents (Jul. 1923), pp.164–71, citing *League of Nations Official Journal*, August 1922, p.1,007. On the theory of the mandate system see J. Stoyanovsky, *La Théorie Générale des Mandats Internationaux* (Paris: Les

Presses Universitatires de France, 1925). See also David Hunter Miller, 'The origin of the mandate system', *Foreign Affairs* vi/2 (Jan. 1928).

10 For the specialized study, from a Palestinian perspective see Henry Cattan, *Jerusalem* (New York: St Martin's Press, 1981).

11 William Fitzgerald, 'The holy places of Palestine in history and in politics', *International Affairs*, xxvi/1 (Jan. 1950), p.1.

12 Kirsopp Lake, *The Religion of Yesterday and Today* (Boston, MA: Houghton Mifflin Company, 1926), p.60.

13 Ibid., pp.160–1.

14 Ibid.

15 William E. Blackstone, *Jesus is Coming* (Chicago, IL: F.H. Revel, 1908 [1887]).

16 The Acton Institute website is *http://www.acton.org/*.

17 William Martin, *With God on Our Side: The Rise of the Religious Right in America* (New York: Broadway Books, 1996), pp.9–10.

18 David O. Moberg, 'Religion and Society in the Netherlands and in America', *American Quarterly* xiii/2, part 1 (summer 1961), p.172.

19 The *Scofield Reference Bible* was first published in 1909 and has had numerous subsequent editions and revisions. For an overview see Wikipedia entry at *http://en.wikipedia.org/wiki/Scofield_Reference_Bible*. The 1917 edition Scofield notes are online at *http://www.studylight.org/com/srn/*.

20 Cole: *History of Fundamentalism*, p.53.

21 Ibid., pp.52–3.

22 Ibid., p.62.

23 For the proceedings see James M. Gray (ed.), *The Coming and Kingdom of Christ* (Chicago, IL: 1914).

24 Ernest R. Sandeen, *The Roots of Fundamentalism: British and American Millenarianism 1800–1930* (Chicago, IL: The University of Chicago Press, 1970), p.224–5.

25 Cole: *History of Fundamentalism*, p.230, n. 4.

26 For the proceedings for the New York conference see A.C. Gaebelein (ed.), *Christ and Glory* (New York: Publications Office 'Our Hope', 1918); for Philadelphia see W.L. Pettingill (ed.), *Light on Prophecy* (New York: Bible House Christian Herald, 1918).

27 On the relationship between Zionism and the October Revolution see Anita Shapira, 'Labour Zionism and the October Revolution', *Journal of Contemporary History* xxiv/4 (Oct. 1989), pp.623–56, and Henry Tobias, 'The Bund and Lenin until 1903', *Russian Review* xx/4 (Oct. 1961), pp.344–57. For contemporary context see Norman Davis, 'Great Britain and the Polish Jews, 1918–20', *Journal of Contemporary History*, col. 8, no. 2 (Apr. 1973), pp.119–42, and Henry Abramson, 'Jewish representation in the independent Ukrainian governments of 1917–1920', *Slavic Review* l/3 (autumn 1991), pp.542–50.

28 See for example V.H. Rothwell, 'Mesopotamia in British war aims, 1914–1918', *The Historical Journal*, xiii/2 (Jun. 1970), pp.273–94, and Aaron S. Klieman, 'Britain's war aims in the Middle East in 1915', *Journal of Contemporary History* iii/3 (Jul. 1968), pp.237–51.

29 The USA maintained a naval presence in the Eastern Mediterranean. See Henry P. Beers, 'United States naval detachment in Turkish waters, 1919–1924', *Military Affairs* vii/4 (winter, 1943), pp.209–20.

30 See William Yale, 'Ambassador Henry Morgenthau's special mission of 1917', *World Politics* i/3 (Apr. 1949), pp.308–20.

31 For French war aims see, C.M. Andrew and A.S. Kanya-Forstner, 'The French colonial policy and French colonial war aims, 1914–1918', *The Historical Journal* xvii/1 (Mar. 1974), pp.79–106. On the Italian factor see Frank E. Manuel, 'The Palestine Question in Italian diplomacy, 1917–1920', *The Journal of Modern History* xxvii/3 (Sep. 1955), pp.263–80. The complexities of managing interests in the region after the war are indicated in Martin Thomas, 'Bedouin tribes and the imperial intelligence services in Syria, Iraq and Transjordan in the 1920s', *Journal of Contemporary History* xxxviii/4 (Oct. 2003), pp.539–61.

32 See, Edward Peter Fitzgerald, 'France's Middle Eastern ambitions, the Sykes-Picot negotiations, and the oil fields of Mosul, 1915–1918', *The Journal of Modern History* lxvi/4 (Dec. 1994), pp.697–725. For general background on oil and strategy see William Engdahl, *A Century of War: Anglo-American Oil Politics and the New World Order*, rev. edn (London: Pluto Press, 2004) and John M. Blair, *The Control of Oil* (New York: Pantheon Press, 1976). For a detailed examination see Helmut Mejcher, *Die Politik und das Ol im Nahen Osten. I. Der Kampf der Mächte und Konzerne vor dem Zweiten Weltkrieg* (Stuttgart: Klett-Cotta Verlag, 1980).

33 See, Albert M. Hyamson, *Palestine Under the Mandate 1920–1948* (Westport: Greenwood Press, 1976 [1950]). On the matter of the borders of Palestine circa 1920 see John J. McTague, Jr, 'Anglo-French negotiations over the boundaries of Palestine, 1919–1920', *Journal of Palestine Studies* xi/2 (winter, 1982), pp.100–12. An early overview of the Palestine problem is presented in Quincy Wright, 'The Palestine Problem', *Political Science Quarterly* xli/3 (Sep. 1926), pp.384–412.

34 See G. Gareth Jones, 'The British government and the oil companies 1912–1924: the search for an oil policy', *The Historical Journal* xx/3 (Sep. 1977), pp.647–72. For a specialized study of British Petroleum (formerly the Anglo-Persian Oil Company) see J.R.L. Anderson, *East of Suez: A Study of Britain's Greatest Trading Company* (London: Hodder and Stoughton, 1969).

35 See Elie Kedourie, 'Cairo and Khartoum on the Arab Question, 1915–18', *The Historical Journal* vii/2 (1964), pp.280–97.

36 See Timothy J. Paris, 'British Middle East policy-making after the First World War: the Lawrentian and Wilsonian schools', *The Historical Journal* xli/3 (Sept. 1998), pp.773–93, and Helmut Mejcher, 'British Middle East policy 1917–21:

the inter-departmental level', *Journal of Contemporary History* viii/4 (Oct. 1973), pp.81–101.

37 On the Balfour Declaration see Leonard Stein, *The Balfour Declaration* (New York: Simon and Schuster, 1961); Mark Levene, 'The Balfour Declaration: a case of mistaken identity', *The English Historical Review* cvii/422 (Jan. 1992), pp.54–77; and Jehuda Reinharz, 'The Balfour Declaration and its maker: a reassessment', *The Journal of Modern History* lxiv/3 (Sep. 1992), pp.445–99. See also Isaiah Friedman, *Palestine: A Twice-Promised Land? The British, the Arabs, and Zionism 1915–1920* (New Brunswick, NJ: Transaction Publishers, 2000).

38 See Kenneth W. Stein, 'A historiographic review of literature on the origins of the Arab–Israeli conflict', *The American Historical Review* xcvi/5 (Dec. 1991), pp.1,450–65.

39 For insight from a participant see, James A. Malcolm, *Origins of the Balfour Declaration: Dr Weizmann's Contribution*, ff.12 [1944], The British Museum, cup.1,247, c.28.

40 For general background and British policy see James Parkes, *The Emergence of the Jewish Problem 1878–1939* (London: Oxford University Press, 1946) and Salo W. Baron, 'The Jewish Question in the nineteenth century', *The Journal of Modern History* x/1 (Mar. 1938), pp.51–65. There is, of course, an extensive literature on political Zionism. For a general history of political Zionism see Walter Laqueur, *A History of Zionism* (New York: Holt, Rinehart and Winston, 1972). There are some interesting insights in Richard J.H. Gottheil, *Zionism* (Philadelphia: Jewish Publications Society of America, 1914). See also, for documentation, Walid Khalidi (ed.), *From Haven to Conquest: Readings in Zionism and the Palestine Problem Until 1948* (Washington, DC: Institute for Palestine Studies, 1987).

41 On the Lloyd George government see Robert J. Scalley, *The Origins of the Lloyd George Coalition: The Politics of Social-Imperialism, 1900–1918* (Princeton, NJ: Princeton University Press, 1975).

42 Philip Guedalla, *Napoleon and Palestine* (London: George Allen and Unwin, 1925), p.12.

43 Quoted in ibid., pp.52–3.

44 Quoted in ibid., p.60.

45 Dov Gavish, 'An account of an unrealized aerial cadastral survey in Palestine under the British Mandate', *The Geographical Journal* cliii/1 (Mar. 1987), pp.93–8.

46 See Sahar Huneidi, 'Was Balfour policy reversible? The Colonial Office and Palestine, 1921–1923', *Journal of Palestine Studies* xxvii/2 (winter, 1998), pp.23–41; David Gilmour, 'The unregarded prophet: Lord Curzon and the Palestine Question', *Journal of Palestine Studies* xxv/3 (spring, 1996), pp.60–8; and John Fisher, *Curzon and British Imperialism in the Middle East, 1916–1919* (London: Frank Cass, 1999).

47 See Richard Ned Lebow, 'Woodrow Wilson and the Balfour Declaration', *The Journal of Modern History* xl/4 (Dec. 1968), pp.501–23. See also Paul Charles Merkley, *The Politics of Christian Zionism 1891–1948* (London: Frank Cass, 1998), pp.75–94.
48 Kathleen Christison, *Perceptions of Palestine: Their Influence on US Middle East Policy* (Berkeley, CA: University of California Press, 1999), p.43.
49 Ibid., p.33.
50 Ibid., p.39.
51 See the Official Documents supplement, *The American Journal of International Law*, xx/2 (Apr. 1926), pp.65–72, citing US Treaty Series No. 728. For a contemporary American assessment of the Turkish situation see Edward Mead Earle, 'The new constitution of Turkey', *Political Science Quarterly* xl/1 (Mar. 1925), pp.73–100.
52 On Herbert Samuels' political role see Bernard Wasserstein, 'Herbert Samuel and the Palestine Problem', *The English Historical Review* xci/361 (Oct. 1976), pp.753–75. For the Samuel family and its connections see Chaim Bermant, *The Cousinhood* (New York: Macmillan, 1971).
53 Mejcher, 'British Middle East policy', p.101.
54 See Michael J. Cohen, *Churchill and the Jews* (London: Frank Cass, 2003); Michael Makovsky, *Churchill and the Promised Land: Zionism and Statecraft* (New Haven, CT: Yale University Press, 2007); and Martin Gilbert, *Churchill and the Jews: A Lifelong Friendship* (New York: Henry Holt, 2007).
55 Winston S. Churchill, 'Zionism versus Bolshevism: a struggle for the soul of the Jewish people', *Illustrated Sunday Herald*, 8 February 1920, p.5.
56 Ibid.
57 Ibid.
58 Ernest R. Sandeen, *The Roots of Fundamentalism: British and American Millenarianism 1800–1930* (Chicago, IL: University of Chicago Press, 1970), p.234.
59 Ibid.
60 Stephen Gwynn (ed.), *The Letters and Friendships of Sir Cecil Spring Rice: A Record*, Vol. 2 (Boston: Houghton Mifflin Company, 1929), p.420.
61 Ibid.
62 Ibid., p.421.
63 Ibid. Opposition to political Zionism in the USA within the Jewish community is well documented in Stuart E. Knee, *The Concept of Zionist Dissent in the American Mind 1917–1941* (New York: Robert Speller and Sons, 1979).
64 See Eitan Bar-Yosef, 'The last crusade? British propaganda and the Palestine campaign, 1917–18', *Journal of Contemporary History* xxxvi/1 (Jan. 2001), pp.87–109.
65 Quoted in ibid., p.87.
66 Ibid., pp.88–89.
67 Ibid., p.89.
68 Ibid.

69 Ibid., p.90.
70 Ibid., p.100.
71 Ibid., p.105.
72 See Matthew Hughes, 'General Allenby and the Palestine campaign 1917–1918', *The Journal of Strategic Studies* ixx/4 (Dec. 1996), pp.58–88, and his *Allenby and British Strategy in the Middle East 1917–1919* (London: Frank Cass, 1999).
73 New Era Films (1923), directed and produced by H. Bruce Woolfe.

6. Christian Zionism from the First World War to the Second World War

1   The Scopes Trial was an important test case on the legality of teaching an unbiblical account of creation in any state-funded educational establishment. For an overview of the Scopes Trial see Wikipedia entry at *http://en.wikipedia.org/wiki/Scopes_Trial*.
2   For a gripping and controversial memoir of the period by a late friend of the author see Yitshaq Ben-Ami, *Years of Wrath, Days of Glory: Memoirs from the Irgun* (New York: Robert Speller and Sons, 1982).
3   Clyde Wilcox, 'The Christian Right in twentieth century America: continuity and change', *The Review of Politics* l/4 (fall 1988), pp.659–81.
4   Ibid., p.663.
5   Ibid., p.664.
6   Stuart Grant Cole, *The History of Fundamentalism* (Hamden, CT: Archon Books, 1963 [c.1931]), p.61.
7   For useful background see Elmer T. Clark, *The Small Sects in America*, rev. edn (New York: Abingdon-Cokesbury Press, 1949).
8   Louis Gasper, *The Fundamentalist Movement* (The Hague: Mouton, 1963), p.43.
9   Ibid.
10 See the discussion in Ernest R. Sandeen, *The Roots of Fundamentalism: British and American Millenarianism 1800–1930* (Chicago, IL: The University of Chicago Press, 1970), pp.260–4.
11 Cole: *History of Fundamentalism*, p.82.
12 The website of Western Seminary is at *http://www.westernseminary.edu/*. The website of Denver Seminary is at *http://www.denverseminary.edu/*.
13 See the discussion in Sandeen: *Roots of Fundamentalism*, pp.250–9.
14 Ibid., p 124.
15 The website of Westminster Theological Seminary is at *http://www.wts.edu/*.
16 The website of Wheaton College is at *http://www.wheaton.edu/*.
17 The website of Faith Theological Seminary is at *http://www.faiththeological.org/*.
18 Gasper: *Fundamentalist Movement*, p.20.
19 Ibid., p.24.
20 Quoted in ibid., p.25.

21 Ibid., p.27.
22 Ibid., p.30.
23 Curzon to Balfour, 20 August 1919, *Balfour MSS* 49734, British Museum, as cited in Helmut Mejcher, *Imperial Quest for Oil: Iraq 1910–1928*, St Antony's Middle East Monographs No. 6 (London: Ithaca Press, 1976), p.67.
24 Walid Khalidi, 'The Palestine problem: an overview', *Journal of Palestine Studies* xxi/1 (autumn, 1991), p.7.
25 H.S. Haddad, 'The biblical bases of Zionist colonialism', *Journal of Palestine Studies*, iii/4 (summer, 1974), p.97.
26 Ibid., p.98.
27 Ibid.
28 Ibid. See Moses Hess, *Rome and Jerusalem: A Study in Jewish Nationalism*, trans. Meyer Wasman (New York: Bloch Publishing Company, 1943).
29 Haddad: 'The biblical bases', p.103.
30 Ibid., p.98.
31 Eretz Israel is the term used by Jews and Zionists for the greater Israel that incorporates what they see as biblical Israel, including the West Bank area they call Judea and Samaria, rather than current national borders.
32 John Hagee, *Jerusalem Countdown* (Lake Mary, FL: Front Line), p.231.
33 Haddad: 'The biblical bases', pp.104–5.
34 Ibid., p.107.
35 Ibid., p.108.
36 Ibid.
37 Ibid., citing Marvin Lowenthal's translation of *The Diaries of Theodore Herzl* (New York: Dial Press, 1956), p.124.
38 Maoz Azaryahu and Aharon Kellerman, 'Symbolic places of national history and revival: a study in Zionist mythical geography', *Transactions of the Institute of British Geographers*, new series xxiv/1 (1999), p.112.
39 Jewish history can be divided into 'Commonwealth' eras. The First Commonwealth (the First Temple Period) covers the first temple built by Solomon and ends with its destruction in 586 BCE by the Babylonians. The Second Commonwealth spans the 165 BCE Maccabees Revolt to 135 CE (Roman rule) and the Third Commonwealth is said to have begun with the founding of the state of Israel in 1948.
40 Ibid.
41 See Michael J. Cohen, 'British strategy and the Palestine Question 1936–39', *Journal of Contemporary History* vii/3–4 (Jul.–Oct. 1972), pp.157–83, and Gabriel Sheffer, 'Appeasement and the problem of Palestine', *International Journal of Middle East Studies* xi/3 (May, 1908), pp.377–99.
42 Norman Rose, 'The Seventh Dominion', *The Historical Journal* xiv/2 (Jun. 1971), pp.397–416.
43 Arthur Koestler, *Promise and Fulfilment: Palestine 1917–1949* (London: Macmillan and Co., 1949), p.16.

44 J.C. Wedgwood, *The Seventh Dominion* (London: Labour Pub. Co., 1928), p.3, cited in Rose: 'The Seventh Dominion', p.400.
45 Rose, 'The Seventh Dominion', p.402.
46 Ibid., p.405.
47 Ibid., p.406.
48 On the internal situation in Arab Palestine see W.F. Abboushi, 'The road to rebellion: Arab Palestine in the 1930s', *Journal of Palestine Studies* vi/3 (spring, 1977), pp.23–46.
49 See Michael J. Cohen, 'Secret diplomacy and rebellion in Palestine, 1936–1939', *International Journal of Middle East Studies* viii/3 (Jul. 1977), pp.379–404.
50 Rose, 'The Seventh Dominion', p.411.
51 Ibid.
52 Koestler: *Promise and Fulfilment*, p.127
53 Ibid., p.126.
54 For a detailed treatment of this issue see, Aaron S. Klieman, 'The divisiveness of Palestine: Foreign Office versus Colonial Office on the issue of partition, 1937', *The Historical Journal* xxii/2 (Jun., 1979), pp.423–41.
55 For a detailed analysis see Michael J. Cohen, 'Appeasement in the Middle East: the British White Paper on Palestine, May 1939', *The Historical Journal* xvi/3 (Sep. 1973), pp.571–96.
56 For the situation in Egypt with respect to the Palestine issue see James Janikowski, 'Egyptian reponses to the Palestine problem in the interwar period', *International Journal of Middle East Studies* xii/1 (Aug. 1980), pp.1–38.
57 Michael J. Cohen: 'British strategy', p.179.
58 Ibid., p.182.
59 Ibid., p.183.
60 Paul Charles Merkley, *The Politics of Christian Zionism 1891–1948* (London: Frank Cass, 1998), p.114.
61 Ibid.
62 Quoted in ibid., p.102.
63 Cited in ibid.
64 Ibid., pp.106–14.
65 Ibid., pp.132–3. The Biltmore Program emerged from the Biltmore Conference; for an overview see Wikipedia entry at *http://en.wikipedia.org/wiki/Biltmore_Conference*.
66 Ibid., pp.142–3.

7. Zionism from the Second World War to 1948

1 George Kirk, *The Middle East in the War* (London: Oxford University Press, 1952), p.10.
2 Elmer T. Clark, *The Small Sects of America*, rev. edn (New York: Abingdon-Cokesbury Press, 1949), p.34.

204   Notes

3   Ibid., p.49.
4   Stuart E. Knee, *The Concept of Zionist Dissent in the American Mind 1917–1941* (New York: Robert Speller and Sons, 1979), p.113.
5   Kirk: *The Middle East in the War*, p.241.
6   *New York Times*, 27 January 1941, cited in Kirk: *The Midde East in the War*, p.242.
7   For the Arab response to the Palestine Questions see Leila S. Kadi, *Arab Summit Conferences and the Palestine Problem (1936–1950), (1964–1966)* (Beirut: Palestine Liberation Organization, Research Center, 1966).
8   *Zionist Review*, 4 April 1941, p.8, cited in Kirk: *The Middle East in the War*, p.242.
9   *Der Tag* (New York), 14 November 1941, cited in Kirk: *The Middle East in the War*, p.243.
10 *Zionist Review*, 12 September 1941, p.5, as cited in Kirk: *The Middle East in the War*, p.243.
11 Knee: *The Concept of Zionist Dissent*, p.115–16.
12 Ibid., pp.236–7.
13 Kirk: *The Middle East in the War*, p.244.
14 Cited in James L. Gelvin, *The Israel–Palestine Conflict: One Hundred Years of War* (Cambridge: Cambridge University Press, 2005), p.122.
15 Kirk: *The Middle East in the War*, p.248.
16 As cited in Kirk: *The Middle East in the War*, pp.310–11.
17 Kirk: *The Middle East in the War*, p.312.
18 Judge Bernard A. Rosenblatt in *Zionist Review*, 29 November 1946, p.3, cited in Kirk: *The Middle East in the War*, p.315.
19 Evan M. Wilson, 'The Palestine papers, 1943–1947', *Journal of Palestine Studies* ii/4 (summer, 1973), p.36.
20 For a detailed analysis see Michael J. Cohen, 'The British White Paper on Palestine, May 1939. Part II: The testing of a policy, 1942–1945', *The Historical Journal* xix/3 (Sep. 1976), pp.727–57.
21 For details and background see J. Bowyer Bell, *Terror Out of Zion: The Violent and Deadly Shock Troops of Israeli Independence 1929–1949* (New York: St Martin's Press, 1977).
22 Cohen: 'The British White Paper', Part II, p.741.
23 Wilson: 'Palestine papers', p.38.
24 Ibid.
25 Ibid., p.40.
26 William Phillips, *Ventures in Diplomacy* (London: John Murray, 1953), pp.276–7.
27 For Halifax in Washington see The Earl of Birkenhead, *Halifax: The Life of Lord Halifax* (London: Hamish Hamilton,1965).
28 Michael J. Cohen, 'The Genesis of the Anglo-American Committee on Palestine, November 1945: a case study in the assertion of American hegemony', *The Historical Journal* xxii/1 (Mar. 1979), p.187.

29 Churchill minute, 6 July 1945, in E4939/15/31, FO 371/45378, cited in Michael J. Cohen, 'The Genesis', p.187.
30 Cohen: 'The Genesis'.
31 Ibid.
32 Ibid., p.190.
33 For detailed background see Zvi Ganin, *Truman, American Jewry, and Israel 1945–1948* (New York: Holmes and Meier, 1979) and John Snetsinger, *Truman, the Jewish Vote and the Creation of Israel* (Stanford, CA: Hoover Institution Press, 1974). See also Fred Lawson, 'The Truman administration and the Palestinians', in Michael W. Suleiman (ed.), *US Policy on Palestine from Wilson to Clinton* (Normal, IL: Association of Arab-American University Graduates, 1995) and Kathleen Christison, *Perceptions of Palestine: Their Influence on US Middle East Policy* (Berkeley, CA: University of California Press, 1999).
34 Kenneth Harris, *Attlee* (New York: W.W. Norton and Co., 1982), p.390.
35 Ibid.
36 For Truman's explanation see Harry S. Truman, *Years of Trial and Hope*, Vol. 2 (Garden City, NY: Doubleday and Co., 1956), especially pp.143–69.
37 Harris: *Attlee*, pp.390–1.
38 Paul Charles Merkley, *American Presidents, Religion, and Israel: The Heirs of Cyrus*, p.3.
39 Wilson: 'Palestine papers', p.45.
40 Ibid.
41 Joseph A. Pika, 'Interest groups and the White House under Roosevelt and Truman', *Political Science Quarterly* cii/4 (winter, 1987–8), p.656.
42 Dean Acheson, *Present at the Creation* (New York: W.W. Norton, 1969), p.169.
43 Ibid.
44 Ibid.
45 Pika: 'Interest groups', p.656.
46 Ibid.
47 Harris: *Attlee*, p.391.
48 'Report to the United States Government and His Majesty's Government in the United Kingdom', Anglo-American Committee on Palestine, Lausanne, Switzerland, 20 April 1946, available online at the Avalon Project, Yale University, at *http://www.yale.edu/lawweb/avalon/anglo/angcov.htm*.
49 See the Israeli Declaration of Independence, 1948, available online at the Avalon Project, Yale University, at *http://www.yale.edu/lawweb/avalon/mideast/israel.htm*.
50 James G. McDonald, *My Mission in Israel* (New York: Simon and Schuster, 1951), p.6.
51 Gus Russo, *Supermob: How Sidney Korshak and his Criminal Associates became America's Hidden Power Brokers* (New York: Bloomsbury, 2006), p.107.

52 Paul Charles Merkley, *Christian Attitudes towards the State of Israel* (Montreal: McGill-Queen's University Press, 2001), pp.21–2.

53 For background see Edward W. Said and Christopher Hitchens (eds), *Blaming the Victims: Spurious Scholarship and the Palestine Question* (London: Verso, 1988); and Naseer Aruri, *Palestinian Refugees: The Right of Return* (London: Pluto Press, 2001). For an international legal perspective see W.T. Mallison, 'An international law appraisal of the juridical characteristics on the resistance of the people of Palestine', *Revue Egyptienne de Droit International* xxviii (1972), pp.1–19, and also in the same volume: A. Belkharroubi, 'Essai sur une théorie juridique des mouvements de liberation nationale', pp.20–43; H. Cattan, 'The Arab Israeli conflict', pp.44–55; and I. Sagay, 'International law relating to occupied territory', pp.56–64. See also Helena Cobban, *The Palestinian Liberation Organization: People, Power and Politics* (Cambridge: Cambridge University Press, 1984). For economic conditions as of 1945 see 'Palestine review of commercial conditions, February 1945' (London: HMSO, 1945).

54 Uri Bialer, *Between East and West: Israel's Foreign Policy Orientation 1948–1956* (Cambridge: Cambridge University Press, 1990), p.2. See also Samuel J. Roberts, *Survival or Hegemony* (Baltimore: Johns Hopkins University Press, 1973).

Part III Christian Zionism and American Foreign Policy, From the Cold War to Bush

8. The Christian Right in the Fifties and Sixties

1 For general background on imperialism from an American perspective see Parker Thomas Moon, *Imperialism and World Politics* (New York: Macmillan, 1928). On ancient Rome see William Stearns Davis, *The Influence of Wealth in Imperial Rome* (New York: Macmillan, 1910).

2 See Andrew Bacevich, *The New American Militarism: How Americans are Seduced by War* (New York: Oxford University Press, 2005).

3 See Chapter 9 in this volume.

4 For background see Douglas Little, 'The making of a special relationship: the United States and Israel, 1957–1968', *International Journal of Middle East Studies* xxv/4 (Nov. 1993), pp.563–85.

5 For background on this crisis see Hugh Thomas, *Suez* (New York: Harper and Row, 1966). For the Egyptian perspective see 'White Paper on the nationalisation of the Suez Maritime Canal Company' (Cairo: Government Press, 1956); The Selected Studies Committee, *The Suez Canal: Facts and Documents* (Cairo: The Selected Studies Committee, n.d.). For President Eisenhower's perspective see Dwight D. Eisenhower, *Mandate for Change 1953–1956* (New York: Doubleday, 1963), pp.150–9.

6   For the official US perspective as of 1955 see US Department of State, *United States Policy in the Near East, South Asia and Africa – 1955* (Washington, DC: GPO, May 1956).
7   See Grant F. Smith, *Foreign Agents: The American Israel Public Affairs Committee from the 1963 Fulbright Hearings to the 2005 Espionage Scandal* (Washington, DC: Institute for Research, 2007); J.J. Goldberg, *Jewish Power: Inside the American Jewish Establishment* (Reading, MA: Addison-Wesley, 1996); Edward Tivnan, *The Lobby: Jewish Political Power and American Foreign Policy* (New York: Simon and Schuster, 1987); and John J. Mearsheimer and Stephen M. Walt, *The Israel Lobby and US Foreign Policy* (New York: Farrar, Straus and Giroux, 2007).
8   Louis Gasper, *The Fundamentalist Movement* (The Hague: Mouton, 1963), p.146.
9   The website for the American Council of Christian Churches is at *http://www.amcouncilcc.org/*.
10 For a detailed examination of the origins of the ACCC and NAE, see 'The dual alignment of Fundamentalism', Chapter 2 in Gasper: *The Fundamentalist Movement*, pp.21–39.
11 Seymour Martin Lipset, 'The Radical Right: a problem for American democracy', *The British Journal of Sociology* vi/2 (Jun. 1955), pp.176–209.
12 For background see Michael W. Miles, *The Odyssey of the American Right* (New York: Oxford University Press, 1980) and William B. Hixson, Jr, *Search for the American Right Wing: An Analysis of the Social Science Record, 1955–1987* (Princeton, NJ: Princeton University Press, 1992).
13 Lipset: 'The Radical Right', p.186.
14 Ibid., p.189.
15 Ibid., p.190.
16 The website of the World Council of Churches is at *http://www.oikoumene.org/*.
17 See William Martin, *With God on Our Side: The Rise of the Religious Right in America* (New York: Broadway Books, 1996), pp.36–7.
18 Dr Carl McIntire, 'The coming great church', *Beacon*, 13 March 1952, pp.1, 8, cited in Gasper: *The Fundamentalist Movement*, p.156.
19 Gasper: *The Fundamentalist Movement*, p.53.
20 Martin: *With God on Our Side*, p.37.
21 The website for the International Council of Christian Churches is at *http://www.iccc.org.sg/*.
22 The website for the Christian Anti-Communist Crusade is at *http://www.schwarzreport.org/*.
23 The Summit Ministries website is at *http://www.summit.org/*.
24 Clyde Wilcox, 'The Christian Right in twentieth century America: continuity and change', *The Review of Politics* l/4 (fall, 1988), p.665.
25 For background see Gasper: *The Fundamentalist Movement*, pp.85–92.

26 As cited in Martin: *With God on Our Side*, p.27.
27 Ben Bagdikian, *Media Monopoly* (Boston, MA: Beacon Press, 2000), p.39.
28 W.A. Swanberg, *Luce and His Empire* (New York: Charles Scribner's Sons, 1972), p.291.
29 As quoted in George Seldes, *You Can't Do That* (New York: Modern Age Books, 1938), p.222.
30 Luce first placed Mussolini's portrait on the cover of the 6 August 1923 *Time* magazine. The July 1934 issue of *Fortune* magazine was dedicated to a positive overview of Italian Fascism.
31 For Salvemini's analysis of Italian Fascism see Gaetano Salvemini, *The Fascist Dictatorship in Italy* (New York: Henry Holt, 1927) and *The Origins of Fascism in Italy* (New York: Henry Holt, 1973), a penetrating study completed in 1942.
32 13th Plenum of the Executive Committee of the Communist International, Moscow 1933. For extensive consideration of the problem of fascism see Walter Laquer, *Fascism Past, Present, Future* (New York: Oxford University Press, 1996); Walter Laquer (ed.), *Fascism: A Reader's Guide. Analysis, Interpretations, Bibliography* (Berkeley, CA: University of California Press, 1976); and George L. Mosse (ed.), *International Fascism: New Thoughts and New Approaches* (London: Sage Publications,1979).
33 For background see Hans Rogger and Eugen Weber (eds), *The European Right: A Historical Profile* (Berkeley, CA: University of California Press, 1966); Ernst Nolte, *Der Faschismus in seiner Epoche: Action française, italienischer Faschismus, Nationalsozialismus,* (Munich: R. Piper, 1963); and Robert A. Brady, *The Spirit and Structure of German Fascism* (New York: Viking, 1937).
34 For valuable insight into the New Deal see Harold L. Ickes, *The Secret Diary of Harold L. Ickes: The First Thousand Days 1933–1936* (New York: Simon and Schuster, 1953).
35 For a comparative study of dictatorships in history see George W.F. Hallgarten, *Why Dictators? The Causes and Forms of Tyrannical Rule Since 600 BC* (New York: Macmillan, 1954). Part III expressing Hallgarten's concept of 'counter- and pseudo-revolutionary dictatorships' is of particular interest (pp.166–273).
36 For background see Charles Higham, *Trading with the Enemy: The Nazi-American Money Plot 1933–1949* (New York: Barnes and Noble, 1983); William C. McNeil, *American Money and the Weimar Republic: Economics and Politics on the Eve of the Great Depression* (New York: Columbia University Press, 1986).; and James Pool and Suzanne Pool, *Who Financed Hitler: The Secret Funding of Hitler's Rise to Power 1919–1933* (New York: The Dial Press, 1978).
37 George Seldes, *Facts and Fascism* (New York: In Fact, 1943), pp.122–3, quoting from Ambassador Dodd's interview with the Federated Press, 7 January 1938.
38 MacGuire was employed as a bond salesman by Robert Sterling Clark (1877–1956), Yale graduate and heir to the Singer Sewing Machine fortune and an

art collector who lived in Paris. MacGuire had been active in the American Legion, a First World War veterans' organization established by the Morgan interests.

39   The members of the committee were: John W. McCormack (Democrat – Massachusetts), Samuel Dickstein (Democrat – New York), Carl May Weideman (Democrat – Michigan), Charles Kramer (Democrat – California), Thomas A. Jenkins (Republican – Ohio), James Willis Taylor (Repubican – Tennessee), Ulysses Samuel Guyer (Republican – Kansas), and Thomas W. Hardwick, Counsel.

40   Special Committee on Un-American Activities Authorized to Investigate Nazi Propaganda and Certain Other Propaganda Activities, US House of Representatives, 74th Congress, 1st Session.

41   He was a director of the Guaranty Trust Company, Anaconda Copper, Chile Copper, Goodyear Tire, Bethlehem Steel, and the New York Transportation Company. He was decorated with the Crown of Italy by the Italian fascist regime.

42   As quoted in the journal of the National Education Association. See the Owsley-related website: *http://www.library.unt.edu/archives/Owsley/opening-page/index.htm* .

43   For background see George Wolfskill, *The Revolt of the Conservatives: A History of the American Liberty League 1934–1940* (Boston, MA: Houghton Mifflin, 1962).

44   For a study indicating how free governments have fallen 'by vote of the people' see Willis J. Ballinger, *By Vote of the People* (New York: Charles Scribner's Sons, 1946).

45   Arthur Schlesinger, Jr, *The Politics of Upheaval* (Boston, MA: Houghton Mifflin Company, 1960), p.16.

46   For background on the French Right see Eugen Weber, 'France', in Hans Rogger and Eugen Weber (eds), *The European Right: A Historical Profile* (Berkeley, CA: University of California Press, 1966), pp.71–127, and William D. Irvine, 'French Conservatives and the "New Right" during the 1930s', *French Historical Studies* viii/4 (autumn 1974), pp.534–62. See also Geoffroy de Charnay, *Synarchie: Panorama de 25 Années d'Activité Occulte* (Paris: Éditions Médicis, 1946) and Yann Moncomble, *Du Viol des Foules à la Synarchie ou le Complot Permanent* (Paris: Faits et Documents, 1983).

47   For Italian industrialists see Frank Hugh Adler, *Italian Industrialists from Liberalism to Fascism: The Political Development of the Industrial Bourgeoisie, 1906–1934* (Cambridge: Cambridge University Press, 1995). For German industrialists see Henry Ashby Turner, Jr, *German Big Business and the Rise of Hitler* (New York: Oxford, 1985); Joseph Borkin, *The Crime and Punishment of I.G. Farben* (New York: The Free Press, 1978); Richard Sasuly, *I.G. Farben* (New York: Boni Gaer, 1947); L. Wulfsohn and G. Wernle, *L'Évasion des Capitaux Alemands* (Paris: Société Anonyme d'Éditions, 1923); and P.F.

de Villemarest, *Les Sources Financières du Nazisme* (Cierrey, France: Éditions CEI, 1984).

48   'Business of empire', *Time*, 20 July 1936, available online at *http://www.time.com/time/magazine/article/0,9171,771837-1,00.html*.

49   See George Wolfskill, *The Revolt of the Conservatives: A History of the American Liberty League 1934–1940* (Boston, MA: Houghton Mifflin, 1962).

50   Lammot (1880–1952), Irene (1876–1963), and Pierre (1870–1954) duPont were the sons of Lammot duPont (1831–84) and Mary Belin (1839–1913), who was of Jewish ancestry. For background see Leonard Mosely, *Blood Relations: The Rise and Fall of the duPonts of Delaware* (New York: Atheneum, 1980).

51   See Wolfskill: *The Revolt*.

52   On Deterding see Glyn Roberts, *The Most Powerful Man in the World: The Life of Sir Henry Deterding* (New York: Covici Friede, 1938).

53   For notice of relations between Shell and the Worms group see, for example, Robert Henriques, *Marcus Samuel: First Viscount Bearsted and Founder of The 'Shell' Transport and Trading Company 1853–1927* (London: Barrie and Rockliff, 1960), pp.91, 95, 249.

54   The Crusaders organization was an anti-labor organization opposed to New Deal policies; the board included Albert D. Lasker, James P. Warburg, and John W. Davis, legal counsel for the Morgan interests and US Steel. Davis was the former Democratic Party presidential candidate in 1924 and lost to Republican Calvin Coolidge. Prior to this he had served as the US Ambassador in London (1918–21). Additional satellites of the Liberty League were the Southern Committee to Uphold the Constitution, the Farmers' Independence Council, and the Sentinels of the Republic.

55   Miles: *The Odyssey*, pp.44–5.

56   Ibid.

57   Richard Sanders, 'J. Howard Pew (1882–1971)', available online at *http://coat.ncf.ca/our_magazine/links/53/pew.html*.

58   Ibid., pp.45–6.

59   Gasper: *The Fundamentalist Movement*, p.139, quoting from Billy Graham, 'Why I must go to New York', *Christian Life*, February 1957, p.17.

60   Gasper: *The Fundamentalist Movement*, p.139.

61   For a revealing study of Vereide's organization, also called 'The Family', see Jeffrey Sharlet, *The Family: The Secret Fundamentalism at the Heart of American Power* (New York: HarperCollins, 2008); see also Jeffrey Sharlet, 'Jesus plus nothing', *Harpers*, March 2003, available online at *http://www.harpers.org/archive/2003/03/0079525?pg=1*.

62   Martin: *With God on Our Side*, p.40.

63   Ibid., p.41.

64   Ibid., pp.41–2.

65   Ibid., pp.95–6.

66   Ibid., p.97.

9. The Christian Right in the Seventies and Eighties

1. For an overview see Michael Lienesch, 'Right-wing religion: Christian conservatism as a political movement', *Political Science Quarterly* xcvii/3 (autumn, 1982), pp.403–25, and Mark J. Rozell and Clyde Wilcox, 'Second Coming: the strategies of the New Christian Right', *Political Science Quarterly* cxi/2 (summer 1996), pp.271–94..
2. For background see George H. Nash, *The Conservative Intellectual Movement in America Since 1945* (New York: Basic Books, 1976) and Paul Gottfried and Thomas Fleming, *The Conservative Movement* (Boston, MA: Twayne, 1988).
3. See Theodore H. White, *The Making of the President 1964* (New York: Atheneum, 1965) and his *The Making of the President 1960* (New York: Atheneum, 1961).
4. For background see Niels Bjerre-Poulson, *Right Face: Organizing the American Conservative Movement 1945–65* (Copenhagen: Museum Tusculanum Press, University of Copenhagen, 2002); on the New Right see Alan Crawford, *Thunder on the Right: The 'New Right' and the Politics of Resentment* (New York: Pantheon, 1980). Crawford was in the New York City based William F. Buckley circle.
5. For an overview of the Neoconservative movement see Jacob Heilbrunn, *They Knew They Were Right: The Rise of the Neocons* (New York: Doubleday, 2008). The best analysis of the foreign policy perspective of the Neoconservative movement is Stefan Halper and Jonathan Clarke, *America Alone: The Neo-Conservatives and the Global Order* (Cambridge: Cambridge University Press, 2004).
6. White: *1964*, pp.89–90. See Mary C. Brennan, *Turning Right in the Sixties: The Conservative Capture of the GOP* (Chapel Hill, NC: The University of North Carolina Press, 1995).
7. See Kevin Phillips, *The Emerging Republican Majority* (New Rochelle, NY: Arlington House, 1969).
8. White: *1964*, p.143.
9. On Taft see, William S. White, *The Taft Story* (New York: Harper and Brothers, 1954) and Robert A. Taft, *A Foreign Policy for Americans* (New York: Doubleday, 1951).
10. Jonathan Martin Kolkey, *The New Right, 1960–1968*, with epilogue 1969–1980 (Washington, DC: University Press of America, 1983).
11. See, for example, Dwight D. Eisenhower, address to the Republican National Conference, Washington, DC, 7 June 1957, available online at *http://www.presidency.ucsb.edu/ws/index.php?pid=10810*. See also David L. Stebenne, *Modern Republican: Arthur Larson and the Eisenhower Years* (Bloomington, IN: University of Indiana Press, 2006).
12. For an overview of the New Right ideology by its advocates see Robert W. Whitaker, *The New Right Papers* (New York: St Martin's Press, 1982). See also Amy E. Ansell (ed.), *Unraveling the Right: The New Conservatism in American*

Thought and Politics (Boulder, CO: Westview Press, 1998); Robert Brent Toplin, *Radical Conservatism: The Right's Political Religion* (Lawrence, KS: The University of Kansas Press, 2006); and Michael W. Miles, *The Odyssey of the American Right* (New York: Oxford University Press, 1980).

13 For background see Desmond S. King, 'New Right ideology, welfare state form, and citizenship: a comment on conservative capitalism', *Comparative Studies in Society and History* xxx/4 (Oct. 1988), pp.792–9. For data on the rightward turn in economic policy of business elites during the period see J. Craig Jenkins and Craig M. Eckert, 'The right turn in economic policy: business elites and the New Conservative economics', *Sociological Forum* xv/2 (Jun. 2000), pp.307–38.

14 The Free Congress Foundation website is at *http://www.freecongress.org/*.

15 See William Martin, *With God on Our Side: The Rise of the Religious Right in America* (New York: Broadway Books, 1996).

16 For background see the Sourcewatch entry at *http://www.sourcewatch.org/index.php?title=Arthur_S._DeMoss_Foundation*.

17 For important insights on Colson see Martin: *With God on Our Side*, pp.98, 99, 146, 149, 208.

18 Jeremy Scahill, *Blackwater: The Rise of the World's Most Powerful Mercenary Army* (New York: Nation Books, 2007).

19 Blackwater is a controversial private security company which provides private personnel to the US government for its operations in Iraq. For an overview see the entry in Wikipedia at *http://en.wikipedia.org/wiki/Blackwater_Worldwide*.

20 Scahill: *Blackwater*, p.19.

21 The Religious Right in the USA entered a new phase of activism in 1994 with the ECT document. This was the year of Republican Party triumph in the Congressional elections dubbed the 'Republican Revolution' by some. Polling data showed that evangelicals were an increasingly important group within the electorate and, in particular, a significant voting bloc in the Republican Party. Mitofsky International national exit polling data showed 27 per cent of all voters identified themselves as 'born-again' or evangelical Christians. This was up from 18 per cent in 1988 and 24 per cent in 1992. Republican House candidates outpolled Democrats among white evangelicals by a massive 52 points, 76 per cent to 24 per cent. (See 'United States House of Representatives Elections, 1994' at *http://en.wikipedia.org/wiki/U.S._House_election,_1994*.) According to data from a survey sponsored by the Christian Coalition, some 33 per cent of the 1994 voters were 'religious conservatives'. This was up from 24 per cent in 1992 and 18 per cent in 1988. In the 1994 Mitofsky exit poll, 38 per cent identified themselves as 'conservatives', compared with 30 per cent in 1992 (ibid.).

22 Scahill: *Blackwater*, pp.19–20. The ECT document is found in *First Things*, May 1994. For an online collection of documents relating to it to see the LeadershipU website at *http://www.leaderu.com/ect/ectmenu.html*.

23 Charles W. Colson, 'Biblical worldview crucial for the new millennium', *Religion & Liberty* ix/6 (Nov. and Dec. 1999), available online at *http://www.acton.org/publications/randl/rl_interview_325.php*.
24 Ibid.
25 Ibid.
26 For a critical view of the New Right from a feminist perspective see Rosalind Pollack Petchesky, 'Antiabortion, antifeminism, and the rise of the New Right', *Feminist Studies* vii/2 (summer, 1981), pp.206–46, and Zillah R. Eisenstein, 'The sexual politics of the New Right: understanding the "crisis of liberalism" for the 1980s', *Signs* vii/3 'Feminist Theory' (spring, 1982), pp.567–88.
27 Clyde Wilcox, 'The Christian Right in twentieth century America: continuity and change', *The Review of Politics* l/4 (fall 1988), pp.667–8.
28 The Christian Voice website is at *http://www.christianvoiceonline.com/*. For an overview see also the Wikipedia entry at *http://en.wikipedia.org/wiki/Christian_Voice_(USA)*.
29 For background on Jabotinsky and the Revisionist Zionist movement see a book by a late friend of the author, Yitshaq Ben-Ami, *Years of Wrath, Days of Glory: Memoirs from the Irgun* (New York: Robert Speller and Sons, 1982) and J. Bowyer Bell, *Terror Out of Zion: The Violent and Deadly Shock Troops of Israeli Independence, 1929–1949* (New York: St Martin's Press, 1977). See also Yaacov Shavit, *Jabotinsky and the Revisionist Movement, 1925–1948* (London: Frank Cass, 1988).
30 See the American Jewish Committee website at *http://www.ajc.org/*.
31 See a biographical sketch on the Proskauer Rose law firm's website at *http://www.proskauer.com/about_the_firm/proskauer*.
32 John Spivak, *New Masses*, 5 February 1935.
33 Heilbrunn: *They Knew They Were Right*, p.11.
34 Sara Diamond, *Roads to Dominion: Right-Wing Movements and Political Power in the United States* (New York: The Guilford Press, 1995), p.182.
35 Ibid., p.191.
36 Diamond: *Roads to Dominion*, p.195.
37 Ibid.
38 Ibid.
39 The Committee for the Present Danger website is at *http://www.committeeonthepresentdanger.org/*.
40 For background on President Carter's policy see Jimmy Carter, *Palestine: Peace Not Apartheid* (New York: Simon and Schuster, 2006). For the aftermath see William B. Quandt, *The Middle East: Ten Years after Camp David* (Washington, DC: The Brookings Institution, 1988.)
41 Irving Kristol, 'The political dilemma of American Jews', *Commentary* lxxviii/1 (Jul. 1984), pp.23–9.
42 Ibid., p.25.
43 Ibid.

44 Heilbrunn: *They Knew They Were Right*, p.167.
45 Connie de Boer, 'The polls: attitudes toward the Arab-Israeli crisis', *The Public Opinion Quarterly* xlvii/1 (spring 1983), p.121. See also Saad Ibrahim, 'American domestic forces and the October War', *Journal of Palestine Studies* iv/1 (autumn, 1974), pp.55–81.
46 See Duncan L. Clarke and Eric Flohr, 'Christian churches and the Palestine Question', *Journal of Palestine Studies* xxi/4 (summer 1992), pp.67–79, and B. Eugene Griessman, 'Philo-Semitism and Protestant fundamentalism: the unlikely Zionists', *Phylon* xxxvii/3 (1976), pp.197–211.
47 Donald Wagner, 'Beyond Armageddon, *The Link* (Americans for Middle East Understanding) xxv/4 (Oct.–Nov. 1992), p.5.
48 Foreword to George W. Ball, *Error and Betrayal in Lebanon: An Analysis of Israel's Invasion of Lebanon and the Implications for US–Israeli Relations* (Washington, DC: Foundation for Middle East Peace, 1984), p.15. See also Juliana S. Peck, *The Reagan Administration and the Palestinian Question: The First Thousand Days* (Washington, DC: Institute for Palestine Studies, 1984); Merle Thorpe, Jr, *Prescription for Conflict: Israel's West Bank Settlement Policy* (Washington, DC: Foundation for Middle East Peace, 1984).
49 Stephen Sizer, *Christian Zionism: Road-map to Armageddon?* (Leicester: Inter-Varsity Press, 2004), p.91.
50 Billy Graham, *Hope for the Future* (Minneapolis: Evangelical Literature Service, 1970), p.7.
51 See, for example, David D. Kirkpatrick, 'Club of the most powerful gathers in strict privacy', *New York Times*, 28 August 2004, and his 'Christian Right labors to find '08 candidate', *New York Times*, 27 February 2007. See also the entries for the Council for National Policy at Wikipedia at *http://en.wikipedia.org/wiki/Council_for_National_Policy* and at Sourcewatch at *http://www.sourcewatch.org/index.php?title=Council_for_National_Policy*.
52 Phyllis Bennis and Khaled Mansour, 'Praise God and pass the ammunition! The changing nature of Israel's US backers', *Middle East Report* 208, US Foreign Policy in the Middle East: Critical Assessments (autumn, 1988), p.18.
53 Kuttner quoted in Richard Curtis, *Stealth PACs: Lobbying Congress for Control of US Middle East Policy* (Washington, DC: The American Educational Trust, 1996), pp.81–2. See also Yossi Melman and Dan Raviv, *Friends in Deed: Inside the US–Israel Alliance* (New York: Hyperion, 1994).
54 Bennis and Mansour: 'Praise God', p.43.
55 For background on the Israeli political right see Mark Tessler, 'The political right in Israel: its origins, growth, and prospects', *Journal of Palestine Studies* xv/2 (winter 1986), pp.12–55, and Jonathan Mendilow, 'Party clustering in multiparty systems: the example of Israel 1965–1981', *American Journal of Political Science* xxvii/1 (Feb. 1983), pp.64–85.

56 Yona Malachy, *American Fundamentalism and Israel: The Relation of Fundamentalist Churches to Zionism and the State of Israel* (Jerusalem: Institute of Contemporary Jewry, Hebrew University of Jerusalem, 1978).
57 Israel Shahak and Norton Mezvinsky, *Jewish Fundamentalism in Israel* (London: Pluto Press, 2004), pp.74–5.
58 Grace Halsell, *Prophecy and Politics: Militant Evangelists on the Road to Nuclear War* (Westport, CT: Lawrence Hill and Co., 1986), p.118.
59 See the International Christian Embassy Jerusalem website at *http://www.icej.org/*.
60 Jason Vest, 'The men from JINSA', *The Nation*, 2 September 2002, available online at *http://www.thenation.com/doc/20020902/vest*.
61 The Center for Security Policy website is at *http://www.centerforsecuritypolicy.org/*.
62 The Zionist Organization of America website is at *http://www.zoa.org/*.
63 Levens has been a board member of JINSA, AIPAC, the National Council of Jewish Women, and the Republican Jewish Coalition. NUCI, a grass roots organization, emphasizes national mobilization based upon local outreach.
64 See Nicholas Laham, *Selling AWACS to Saudi Arabia: The Reagan Administration and the Balancing of America's Competing Interests in the Middle East* (Westport, CT: Praeger, 2002).
65 For some background on Helms and Israel, though lacking in detail and precision, see William A. Link, *Righteous Warrior: Jesse Helms and the Rise of Modern Conservatism* (New York: St Martin's Press, 2008), pp.318–19, 571 n. 52. Link does not take note of or account for the significant turn toward pro-Israel neoconservatism.
66 See, for example, Senator Helms' speech in the US Senate condemning the terrorist attack on TWA Flight 847, *Congressional Record*, 27 June 1985.
67 For example his speeches in the US Senate against Syrian sponsorship of terrorism, 'Syria and international terrorism', *Congressional Record*, 21 May 1986; and against Iranian sponsorship of terrorism, 'Iran: a terrorist state', *Congressional Record*, 7 February 1985.
68 The author participated, at the request of the Senator and his staff director Dr James P. Lucier, in the first such small luncheon meeting of influential New York based Israel lobby kingpins. It was held in Senator Helms' private office in the US Capitol Building in 1984. Roy Cohn sat to the author's right and Laurence A. Tisch, for example, was among the top level guests. Dr Lucier accompanied the Senator to New York City for a follow up meeting with influential New York Jewish leaders .
69 See a biography of US Senator Jacob Chic Hecht at *http://bioguide.congress.gov/scripts/biodisplay.pl?index=H000439*.
70 For background see the Jewish Sightseeing website at *http://www.jewishsightseeing.com/israel/jerusalem/hebrew_univ/19990507-hebrew_univ_hecht.htm*.

71 For background on the Council for National Policy see Wikipedia entry online at *http://en.wikipedia.org/wiki/Council_for_National_Policy*.

72 Daniel Pipes, 'Christian Zionism: Israel's best weapon?', *New York Post*, 15 July 2003.

73 I served on the professional staff of the Foreign Relations Committee from 1987 to 1992. I offered my resignation to Senator Helms in the fall of 1991. Our staff director, my friend Jim Lucier, was under pressure from Senator Helms' political operation in North Carolina and other dark forces. Jim, a staunch Roman Catholic from Detroit with a doctorate in medieval literature, had given much of the conservative intellectual foundation to Helms' positions. Jim had come to Senator Helms through Senator Strom Thurmond (Republican – South Carolina), who had given Senator Helms, the good-old-boy southern politician from rural North Carolina, a helping hand to start up his first office in the Senate in 1973. Senator Thurmond also recommended the late John Carbaugh, a hard-driving staffer from South Carolina and a controversial political operative. (See Carbaugh's obituary by Adam Bernstein, 'Helms foreign policy advisor John Carbaugh, 60', *Washington Post*, 24 March 2006.) Jim asked me to join the staff owing to my Cold War background in foreign policy and national security affairs and thus Senator Helms hired me.

74 For biographical data on Danielle Pletka see the Right Web website entry 'Danielle Pletka' at *http://rightweb.irc-online.org/profile/3273* and Source Watch website entry 'Danielle Pletka' at *http://www.sourcewatch.org/index.php?title=Danielle_Pletka*. For background on the Moon operation in the USA see Robert Boettcher, *Gifts of Deceit: Sun Myung Moon Tongusn Park and the Korean Scandal* (New York: Holt, Rinehart, and Winston, 1980).

75 For useful background and context on Churba, Likud, and the Christian Zionists see, Scott Thompson and Jeffrey Steinberg, 'Twenty-five year "shotgun marriage" of Israel's Likud and US fundamentalists exposed', *Executive Intelligence Review*, 29 November 2002, available online at *http://www.larouchepub.com/other/2002/2946likud_fundies.html*.

10. George W. Bush and the Dark Crusade

1 For Bush's commitment to Israel see Ron Hutcheson, 'Bush's attachment to Israel started with a trip to the Holy Land', Washington Bureau, McClatchy Newspapers (see *www.mcclatchydc.om*), 3 August 2006.

2 Jimmy Carter explained the dangers posed to American foreign policy in his 2005 book, *Our Endangered Values* (New York: Simon and Schuster, 2005).

3 Max Singer of the Hudson Institute, a Neoconservative think tank, suggested that the USA detach the oil-rich Eastern Province of Saudi Arabia from the Kingdom. See his paper 'Free the Eastern Province of Saudi Arabia', Hudson Institute, 16 May 2002, available online at *http://www.hudson.org/index.cfm?fuseaction=publication_details&id=1659*.

4   For background on early post-Second World War Middle East policy see George McGhee, *Envoy to the Middle World: Adventures in Diplomacy* (New York: Harper and Row, 1983) and Leonard M. Fanning, *Foreign Oil and the Free World* (New York: McGraw-Hill, 1954). For an overview of the geopolitics of energy see John M. Blair, *The Control of Oil* (New York: Pantheon, 1976) and William Engdahl, *A Century of War: Anglo-American Oil Politics and the New World Order* (London: Pluto, 2004).

5   For an example of elite perspective see Zbigniew Brzezinksi, *The Grand Chessboard: American Primacy and its Geostrategic Imperatives* (New York: Basic Books, 1997).

6   Clyde Wilcox, 'The Christian Right in twentieth century America: continuity and change', *The Review of Politics* 1/4 (fall, 1988), p.672.

7   Ibid., p.673.

8   Craig Unger, *The Fall of the House of Bush* (New York: Scribner, 2007), p.89.

9   William Martin, *With God on Our Side: The Rise of the Religious Right in America* (New York: Broadway Books, 1996), p.263.

10   Ibid.

11   Unger: *Fall of the House of Bush*, pp.94–5.

12   Ibid., p.95. Unger cites here a documentary film by Calvin Skaggs and David Van Taylor, *With God on Our Side: George W. Bush and the Rise of the Religious Right*, 2004.

13   Sarah Posner, *God's Profits: Faith, Fraud, and the Republican Crusade for Values Voters* (Sausalito, CA: PoliPoint Press, 2008).

14   See John Hagee, *Day of Deception* (Nashville, TN: Thomas Nelson, 1997).

15   Sarah Posner, *God's Profits: Faith, Fraud, and the Republican Crusade for Values Voters* (Sausalito, CA: PoliPoint Press, 2008).

16   Bush had brought Christian activist Michael J. Gerson into the White House as a key advisor and speech writer. Gerson laced Bush's speeches with coded religious language to appeal to the Christian Right. See Peter Baker, 'Bush's favorite author leaving the White House', *Washington Post*, 15 June 2006.

17   The group included: Elwood McQuaid, Executive Director of Friends of Israel; Reverend Jeff Snyder, Executive Director of the Apostolic Coalition; Donaldson Jones, head of the Baptist Black Ministries group; Mort Klein, President of the Zionist Organization of America; Rabbi Rafael Grossman, leader of the largest Orthodox synagogue in Memphis, TN; Joseph Farah, Christian Arab editor of WorldNetDaily.org; and Michael Little, President of Christian Broadcasting Network, Inc. See 'Jewish and Christian leaders at the White House', press release, Americans for a Safe Israel, 31 July 2001.

18   Bush has indicated he believes the USA is in the midst of a 'Third Awakening.' See Peter Baker, 'Bush tells group he sees a "Third Awakening"', *Washington Post*, 13 September 2006.

19   Julian Borger, 'Bush poll campaign courts Religious Right', *Guardian*, 3 July 2004. See also Rick Perlstein, 'The Jesus landing pad', *The Village Voice*, 18 May

2004. The Republican Party also made strong efforts to win over sections of the Jewish community. See, for example, Jim VandeHei, 'Future of Orthodox Jewish vote has implications for GOP', *Washington Post*, 3 August 2006.

20 Jane Lampman quoting Morton Klein in 'Mixing prophecy and politics', *Christian Science Monitor*, 7 July 2004.

21 On Perle see Akiva Eldar, 'Perles of wisdom for the Feithful', *Ha'aretz*, 1 October 2002. On Wolfowitz and the neoconservatives see Bill Keller, 'The sunshine warrior', *New York Times*, Magazine, 22 September 2002, available online at *http://query.nytimes.com/gst/fullpage.html?res=9C07E2DF1730F931A1575 AC0A9649C8B63*.

22 For background on Iraq see Christine Moss Helms, *Iraq: Eastern Flank of the Arab World* (Washington, DC: Brookings Institution, 1984) and the essential classic study, Stephen Hemsley Longrigg, *Iraq 1900 to 1950: A Political, Social, and Economic History* (London: Oxford University Press, 1953). See also Yitzhak Nakash, *The Shi'is of Iraq* (Princeton, NJ: Princeton University Press, 1995); and A.J. Abdulrahman, *Iraq*, World Bibliographical Series, Vol. 42 (Oxford: Clio Press, 1984).

23 See 'A clean break: a new strategy for securing the realm', June 1996, available online at the Institute for Advanced Strategic and Political Studies website at *http://www.iasps.org/strat1.htm*. Other such papers produced at this time include: 'Coping with crumbling states: a Western and Israeli balance of power strategy for the Levant', December 1996, and 'Succession in Saudi Arabia: the not so silent struggle', July 1997.

24 The Project for a New American Century website is at *http://www.newamericancentury.org/*.

25 See 'Rebuilding America's defenses: strategies, forces and resources for a new century', September 2000, Project for a New American Century, Washington, DC, available online at *http://www.newamericancentury.org/RebuildingAmericasDefenses.pdf*.

26 For background see Jason Vest, 'Beyond Osama: the Pentagon's battle with Powell heats up', AlterNet.org, 20 November 2001, available online at *http://www.alternet.org/story/11938/*, and Lawrence F. Kaplan, 'Cheney versus Powell, round two: containment', *The New Republic*, 5 February 2001.

27 See, for example, Alan Sipress, 'Policy divide thwarts Powell in Mideast effort', *Washington Post*, 26 April 2002; Dana Milbank, 'Who's pulling the foreign policy strings?', *Washington Post*, 14 May 2002; and Glenn Kessler and Peter Slevin, 'Cheney is fulcrum of foreign policy', *Washington Post*, 13 October 2002.

28 For background see Shadia B. Drury, *Leo Strauss and the American Right* (New York: St Martin's Press, 1997).

29 For archival materials relating to Goldwin's work in the Ford administration see 'Robert Allen Goldwin, special consultant: files, 1974–1976', Gerald R. Ford Library, Ann Arbor, Michigan. The files are summarized, with an in-

troduction, available online at *http://www.ford.utexas.edu/LIBRARY/guides/ Finding%20Aids/Goldwin,%20Robert%20-%20Files.htm*.

30 For a psychological study of George W. Bush see Justin A. Frank, MD, *Bush on the Couch: Inside the Mind of the President* (New York: Regan Books, 2004). For political background see Michael Lind, *Made in Texas: George W. Bush and the Southern Takeover of American Politics* (New York: Basic Books, 2003); Kevin Phillips, *American Dynasty: Aristocracy, Fortune, and the Politics of Deceit in the House of Bush* (New York: Viking, 2004); and James Moore and Wayne Slater, *Bush's Brain: How Karl Rove Made George W. Bush Presidential* (Hoboken, NJ: John Wiley, 2003).

31 James Mann, *Rise of the Vulcans: The History of Bush's War Cabinet* (New York: Viking, 2004).

32 See, for example, John K. Cooley, *An Alliance Against Babylon: The US, Israel, and Iraq* (London: Pluto Press, 2005).

33 Ron Suskind, *The Price of Loyalty: George W. Bush, the White House, and the Education of Paul O'Neill* (New York: Simon and Schuster, 2004), pp.71–2. For further detail of White House thinking see Suskind's *The One Percent Doctrine: Deep Inside America's Pursuit of its Enemies Since 9/11* (New York: Simon and Schuster, 2006). For the failure of the Bush administration with respect to international terrorism see Richard A. Clarke, *Against All Enemies: Inside America's War on Terror* (New York: Free Press, 2004). For a critical view of the Bush administration's Iraq policy see Scott Ritter, *Iraq Confidential: The Untold Story of the Intelligence Conspiracy to Undermine the UN and Overthrow Saddam Hussein* (New York: Nation Books, 2005) and Paul Sperry, *Crude Politics: How Bush's Oil Cronies Hijacked the War on Terrorism* (Nashville, TN: WND Books, 2003).

34 Quoted in Ron Suskind: *The Price of Loyalty*, p.72.

35 David Lamb, 'Israel's invasions, 20 years apart, look eerily alike', *Los Angeles Times*, 20 April 2002.

36 Janet Hook, 'Lawmakers press Bush to stand up for Israel', *Los Angeles Times*, 10 April 2002.

37 Ibid. For further reporting see Alan Cooperman, 'Bush stance pleases US Jewish groups', *Washington Post*, 4 April 2002; Tom Squitieri, 'Israel finds support in Congress', *USA Today*, 4 April 2002; Ronald Brownstein, 'Hawks dominate debate on US policy in region', *Los Angeles Times*, 18 April 2002; Gail Russell Chaddock, 'In Congress, support of Israel at peak pitch', *Christian Science Monitor*, 19 April 2002; Dan Morgan, 'Supporters consider how to increase military aid for Israel', *Washington Post*, 22 April 2002; Douglas Waller, 'Pro-Israel lobby takes a right turn', *TIME.com*, 23 April 2002; Thomas B. Edsall, 'GOP eyes Jewish vote with Bush tack on Israel', *Washington Post*, 30 April 2002; Mike Allen, 'White House and Hill state support for Israel', *Washington Post*, 23 April 2002; and Michael Lind, 'The Israel lobby', *Prospect* (London), April, September, October 2002.

38 Matthew E. Berger, 'AIPAC mounts offensive in Congress', Cleveland Jewish News.com, 24 April 2002. For further reporting see, Nick Anderson, 'Congress prepares to support Israel', *Los Angeles Times*, 2 May 2002; Juliet Eilperin and Mike Allen, 'Hill leaders plan votes on pro-Israel resolutions', *Washington Post*, 2 May 2002; Juliet Eilperin and Helen Dewar, 'Lawmakers endorse Israel's offensive', *Washington Post*, 3 May 2002; Romesh Ratnesar, 'The Right's new crusade', *TIME*, 6 May 2002; Nick Anderson, 'House panel increase aid for Israel, Palestinians', *Los Angeles Times*, 10 May 2002.

39 See, for example, Christopher Matthews, 'The road to Baghdad', *San Francisco Chronicle*, 24 March 2002.

40 Abraham McLaughlin and Gail Russell Chaddock, 'Christian Right steps in on Mideast', *Christian Science Monitor*, 16 April 2002.

41 Ibid.

42 Alison Mitchell, 'Israel winning broad support from US Right', *New York Times*, 21 April 2002.

43 Ibid.

44 Ibid.

45 Ibid.

46 For some background on Maher and the Egyptian position at this time see Secretary of State Colin Powell and His Excellency Ahmed Maher, 'Remarks with His Excellency Ahmed Maher Al-Sayeed, Minister of Foreign Affairs of the Arab Republic of Egypt, after their meeting', US Department of State, available online at *http://www.state.gov/secretary/former/powell/remarks/2001/6522.htm*, and his remarks at the Brookings Institution, 28 November 2001, available online at *http://www.brookings.edu/events/2001/1128middle-east.aspx*.

47 For the Palestinian perspective on these negotiations see Akram Hanieh, 'The Camp David papers', *Al-Ayyam* newspaper, Ramallah, Palestine, August 2000.

48 On the Taba Conference see the report by European Union envoy Miguel Moratinos summarizing the results, 'Taba negotiations – Moratinos non-paper', available online at *http://www.mideastweb.org/moratinos.htm*.

49 For example, see Godfrey Sperling, 'More wise words from Jimmy Carter', *Christian Science Monitor*, 30 April 2002 and Lynn Brezosky, 'Politics: Clinton lends support to Powell's peace efforts', Associated Press wire story, 28 April 2002.

50 For a detailed overview on Saddam Hussein and his senior leadership's perspective see Kevin M. Woods, Michael R. Pease, Mark E. Stout, Williamson Murray, and James G. Lacey, *The Iraqi Perspectives Report: Saddam's Senior Leadership on Operation Iraqi Freedom from Official US Joint Forces Command Report* (Annapolis, MD: Naval Institute Press, 2006). For background on the Gulf War see, Majid Khadduri and Edmund Ghareeb, *War in the Gulf 1990–1991: The Iraq–Kuwait Conflict and its Implications* (New York: Oxford University Press, 1997).

51 Brian Whitaker, 'Playing skittles with Saddam', *Guardian*, 3 September 2002. For further reporting see John Diamond, Judy Keen, Dave Moniz, Susan Page, and Barbara Slavin, 'Iraq course set from tight White House circle', *USA Today*, 10 September 2002; John Donnelly and Anthony Shadid, 'Iraq war hawks have plans to reshape entire Mideast', *Boston Globe*, 10 September 2002; Elisabeth Bumiller and Eric Schmitt, 'On the job and at home, influential hawks' 30-year friendship evolves', *New York Times*, 12 September 2002; Peter Grier, 'Larger aim in Iraq: alter Mideast', *Christian Science Monitor*, 17 September 2002; and James Bamford, 'Untested administration hawks clamor for war', *USA Today*, 17 September 2002.

52 For a convenient text of the resolution see C-span online at *http://www.c-span.org/resources/pdf/hjres114.pdf*.

53 The vote in the US Senate by Republicans was: Yea 48; Nay 1; Not voting 0. The Senate Democratic vote was: Yea 29; Nay 21; Not Voting 0. The vote in the Senate by Independents was: Yea 0; Nay 1; Not Voting 0. The Senate total was thus Yea 77 and Nay 23. In the House of Representatives the vote by Republicans was: Yea 215; Nay 6; Not Voting 2. The House Democratic vote was: Yea 81; Nay 126; Not Voting 1. The vote in the House by Independents was: Yea 0; Nay 1; Not Voting 0. The House total was thus Yea 296 and Nay 133 with 3 Not Voting.

54 William Pfaff, 'American policymakers awash in fantasy', *International Herald Tribune*, 17 October 2002.

55 Ibid.

56 Robert C. Byrd, *Losing America* (New York: Norton, 2004).

57 For background on the administration's foreign policy at this time see, Frances Fitzgerald, 'George Bush and the world', *The New York Review of Books*, 26 September 2002. One of the best accounts of the Bush administration's move toward war is George Packer, *The Assassins' Gate: America in Iraq* (New York: Farrar, Strauss and Giroux, 2005). For a voluminous tome with wide-ranging commentary and analysis see D.L. O'Huallachain and J. Forrest Sharpe (eds), *Neo-Conned Again: Hypocrisy, Lawlessness, and the Rape of Iraq* (Vienna, VA: HIS Press, 2005). For an interesting read see Tariq Ali, *Bush in Babylon: The Recolonisation of Iraq* (London: Verso, 2003).

58 The board of the US Committee for the Liberation of Iraq consisted of Mahdi al-Bassam, Carl Bildt, Barry Blechman, Eliot Cohen, Thomas A. Dine, Gen. Wayne Downing (AUS, ret.), Rend Rahim Francke, New Gingrich, Lt. Gen. Buster Glossom (USAF, ret.), Bruce P. Jackson, Howell Jackson, US Senator Bob Kerrey, Jeanne J. Kirkpatrick, William Kristol, Bernard Lewis, Gen. Barry McCaffrey (AUS, ret.), John McCain, Will Marshall, Richard N. Perle, Danielle Pletka, Randy Scheunemann, Gary Schmitt, George P. Shultz, Richard Shultz, Stephen Solarz, Ruth Wedgwood, Leon Wieseltier, Chris Williams, and R. James Woolsey. Source: SourceWatch online at *http://www.sourcewatch.org/index.php?title=Committee_for_the_Liberation_of_Iraq*.

59 Peter Slevin, 'New group aims to drum up backing for ousting Hussein', *Washington Post*, 4 November 2002.
60 Ibid. See also Kurt Nimmo, 'The Committee for the Liberation of Iraq: PR spinning the Bush doctrine', *Counterpunch*, 19 November 2002, available online at *http://www.counterpunch.org/nimmo1119.html*.
61 Slevin: 'New group aims'. The board of the US Committee for NATO consisted of Julie Finley, Tillie K. Fowler, Jeffrey Gedmin, Philip H. Gordon, Bruce P. Jackson, Robert Kagan, Will Marshall, Sally A. Painter, Richard N. Perle, Paige E. Reffe, Peter W. Rodman, David J. Rothkopf, Randy Scheunemann, Gary Schmitt, and Elaine Shocas. Source: SourceWatch.org online at *http://www.sourcewatch.org/index.php?title=U.S._Committee_on_NATO*. See comment on the USCN in John Laughland, 'The Prague racket', *Guardian*, 22 November 2002, available online at *http://www.guardian.co.uk/comment/story/0,,845129,00.html*.
62 Slevin: 'New group aims'.
63 'American Jewish Committee urges NATO expansion', American Jewish Committee, press release, 30 July 2002, carried on US Newswire online at *http://www.encyclopedia.com/doc/1G1-89856608.html*.
64 Steven R. Weisman, 'Bush names Iran-Contra figure his Mideast chief: Abrams' rise thrills Israel's supporters', *New York Times*, 7 December 2002.
65 Ibid.
66 Ibid.
67 Rosemary Hollis, 'Hawks won't stop with Baghdad', *Guardian*, 22 September 2002, available online at *http://www.guardian.co.uk/world/2002/sep/22/iraq.theworldtodayessays*.
68 Ibid.
69 Ibid.
70 Glenn Frankel, 'US, Europe divided over Middle East strategy', *Washington Post*, 10 November 2002.
71 Ibid.
72 Ibid.
73 Jean-Gabriel Fredet, 'Les croisés font la loi', *Le Nouvel Observateur*, 5–11 September 2002.

11. Christian Zionism and the Next War

1 Alec Russell, 'US evangelist leads the millions seeking a battle with Iran', *Daily Telegraph*, 5 August 2006. See also Sarah Posner, 'Pastor Strangelove', *The American Prospect*, 21 May 2006, available online at *http://www.prospect.org/cs/articles?articleId=11541*. Hagee urges war against Iran based upon his interpretation of biblical prophecy and offers what he calls ten prophetic signs of the 'End-Time World'. They are:

1) The knowledge explosion – Daniel 12:4;
2) Plague in the Middle East – Zechariah 14:12–13;
3) The rebirth of Israel – Isaiah 66:8–10;
4) The Jews will return home – Jeremiah 23:7–8;
5) Jerusalem no longer under Gentile control – Luke 21:24;
6) International instant communication – Revelation 11:3, 7–10;
7) Days of deception – Matthew 24:4;
8) Famines and pestilence – Matthew 24:7–8;
9) Earthquakes – Matthew 24:7–8;
10) 'As in the days of Noah...' – Matthew 24:36–9.

See John Hagee, *Jerusalem Countdown: A Prelude to War* (Lake Mary, FL: FrontLine, 2007), p.127. The Cornerstone Church website is at *http://www.sacornerstone.com*.

2   David D. Kirkpatrick, 'For evangelicals, supporting Israel is "God's foreign policy"', *New York Times*, 14 November 2006.
3   Hagee: *Jerusalem Countdown*, p.61.
4   See Stephen Sizer, *Christian Zionism: Road-Map to Armageddon?* (Leicester: Inter-Varsity Press, 2004), p.206.
5   For useful background on Hagee see Sarah Posner, *God's Profits: Faith, Fraud, and the Republican Crusade for Values Voters* (Sausalito, CA: PoliPoint Press, 2008).
6   The Citizens United for Israel website is at *http://www.cufi.org/site/PageServer*.
7   There is a growing academic literature on political Islam. For a calm and analytical view see, for example, R. Hrair Dekmejian, *Islam in Revolution: Fundamentalism in the Arab World* (Syracuse, NY: Syracuse University Press, 1985). See also John L. Esposito, *Political Islam: Revolution, Radicalism or Reform?* (Cairo: American University in Cairo Press, 1997); Olivier Carré and Paul Dumont, *Radicalismes Islamiques* vols 1 and 2 (Paris: Éditions L'Harmattan, 1986); and Graham E. Fuller, *The Future of Political Islam* (New York: Palgrave Macmillan, 2003).
8   John Hagee, *Jerusalem Countdown: A Prelude to War* (Lake Mary, FL: FrontLine, 2007).
9   See, for a sympathetic biography, Stephen Mansfield, *Derek Prince: A Biography* (Lake Mary, FL: Charisma House, 2005).
10 See S.D. Moore, 'Shepherding movement', in Stanley M. Burgess and Edouard van der Maas (eds), *New International Dictionary of Charismatic and Pentecostal Movements*, revised edn (Grand Rapids, MI: Zondervan, 2003).
11 The Intercessors for Israel website is at *http://www.ifij.org/all/*. See, for example, Christ Mitchell, 'Dividing the land, dishonoring God's Covenant', CBN News, available online at *http://www.cbn.com/cbnnews/news/050324a.aspx*.
12 Hagee: *Jerusalem Countdown*, p.3.

13 Ibid., p.70.
14 Samuel O. Huntington, *The Clash of Civilizations: Remaking of World Order* (New York: Simon and Shuster, 1996).
15 Ibid., p.318.
16 Hagee: *Jerusalem Countdown*, p.4.
17 Ibid., p.134.
18 Ibid.
19 Ibid., pp.134–5.
20 Ibid., p.137.
21 Ibid.
22 Ibid., pp.137–44, 154.
23 Ibid., pp.140–7.
24 Ibid., p.149.
25 Ibid., p.151.
26 Ibid., p.152.
27 Ibid., p.153.
28 Ibid.
29 See Max Blumenthal, 'Birth pangs of a New Christian Zionism', *The Nation*, 14 August 2006, available online at *http://www.thenation.com/doc/20060814/new_christian_zionism*.
30 Quoted in Bill Berkowitz, 'Christian Zionists gain Israel's inner sanctum', IPS News, 3 January 2008, available online at *http://ipsnews.net/news.asp?idnews=40670*.
31 The Stand for Israel website is at *http://standforisrael.blogs.com/*.
32 David Brog's website is at *http://davidbrog.com/index.php*. See, Schmuel Rosner, 'David Brog on why Christians support the Jewish state', *Ha'aretz*, 7 May 2006, available online at *http://www.haaretz.com/hasen/pages/rosnerGuest.jhtml?itemNo=713233*; YNetNews.com, 'A blessing or a curse? American evangelists explained', 5 May 2006, available online at *http://www.ynetnews.com/articles/0,7340,L-3323758,00.html*.
33 YNetNews.com: 'A blessing'.
34 Brian Wood, 'The Second Annual CUFI Conference, July 2007: The Christian Zionist coalition hits its stride', *Journal of Palestine Studies* xxxvii/1 (autumn, 2007), p.86.
35 Wood, 'Second Annual CUFI Conference', p.80. See also Bill Berkowitz, 'Defending Israel to the "End Times"', Media Transparency, 29 January 2008, available online at *http://www.mediatransparency.org/story.php?storyID=226*.
36 Pastor John Hagee, 'AIPAC policy conference, 11 March 2007', American Israel Public Affairs Committee (Washington, DC). Available online at *http://www.aipac.org/Publications/SpeechesByPolicymakers/Hagee-PC-2007.pdf*.
37 Ibid.
38 Ibid.

Select Bibliography

Books

Abdulrahman, A.J., *Iraq*, World Bibliographical Series, Vol. 42 (Oxford: Clio Press, 1984).

Acheson, Dean, *Present at the Creation* (New York: W.W. Norton, 1969).

Adler, Frank Hugh, *Italian Industrialists from Liberalism to Fascism: The Political Development of the Industrial Bourgeoisie, 1906–1934* (Cambridge: Cambridge University Press, 1995).

Albrecht-Carrié, René, *A Diplomatic History of Europe Since the Congress of Vienna* (New York: Harper and Bros, 1958).

Ali, Tariq, *Bush in Babylon: The Recolonisation of Iraq* (London: Verso, 2003).

Allen, Richard, *Imperialism and Nationalism in the Fertile Crescent: Sources and Prospects of the Arab–Israeli Conflict* (New York: Oxford University Press, 1974).

Ancel, Jacques, *Manuel Historique de la Question d'Orient (1792–1923)* (Paris: Delagrave, 1926).

Anchel, Robert, *Napoléon et Les Juifs* (Paris: Les Presses Universitaires de France, 1928).

Ansell, Amy E. (ed.), *Unraveling the Right: The New Conservatism in American Thought and Politics* (Boulder, CO: Westview Press, 1998).

Anderson, J.R.L., *East of Suez: A Study of Britain's Greatest Trading Company* (London: Hodder and Stoughton, 1969).

Antonius, George, *The Arab Awakening: The Story of the Arab National Movement* (Beirut: Khayat's College Book Cooperative, 1955 [1938]).

Aruri, Naseer, *Palestinian Refugees: The Right of Return* (London: Pluto Press, 2001).

Bacevich, Andrew, *The New American Militarism: How Americans are Seduced by War* (New York: Oxford University Press, 2005).

Bachrach, Bernard S., *Early Medieval Jewish Policy in Western Europe* (Minneapolis, MN: University of Minnesota Press, 1977).

Bachrack, Stanley D., *The Committee of One Million: 'China Lobby' Politics 1953–1971* (New York: Columbia University Press, 1976).

Bagdikian, Ben, *Media Monopoly* (Boston, MA: Beacon Press, 2000).

Ball, George W., *Error and Betrayal in Lebanon: An Analysis of Israel's Invasion of Lebanon and the Implications for US–Israeli Relations* (Washington, DC: Foundation for Middle East Peace, 1984).

Ballagh, James Curtis (ed.), *The Letters of Richard Henry Lee*, 2 vols (New York: Macmillan, 1911).

Ballesteros y Beretta and D. Antonio, *Historia de España y su Influencia en la Historia Universal*, Vol.2, part 2, 2nd edn (Barcelona: Salvat Editores, SA, 1944).

Ballinger, Willis J., *By Vote of the People* (New York: Charles Scribner's Sons, 1946).

Barnai, Jacob, *The Jews in Palestine in the Eighteenth Century* (Tuscaloosa, AL: The University of Alabama Press, 1992).

Bass, Clarence, *Backgrounds to Dispensationalism* (Grand Rapids, MI: Erdmans, 1960).

Beale, David O., *In Pursuit of Purity: American Fundamentalism Since 1850* (Greenville, SC: Unusual Publications, 1986).

Bell, J. Bowyer, *Terror Out of Zion: The Violent and Deadly Shock Troops of Israeli Independence 1929–1949* (New York: St Martin's Press, 1977).

Bemis, Samuel Flagg, *The Diplomacy of the American Revolution* (New York: D. Appleton-Century, 1935).

Bemis, Samuel Flagg, *John Quincy Adams and the Foundations of American Foreign Policy* (New York: Alfred Knopf, 1949).

Ben-Ami, Yitshaq, *Years of Wrath, Days of Glory: Memoirs from the Irgun* (New York: Robert Speller and Sons, 1982).

Bermant, Chaim, *The Cousinhood* (New York: Macmillan, 1971).

Bhagat, G., *Americans in India 1784–1860* (New York: New York University Press, 1970).

Bialer, Uri, *Between East and West: Israel's Foreign Policy Orientation 1948–1956* (Cambridge: Cambridge University Press, 1990).

Biger, Gideon, *The Boundaries of Modern Palestine, 1840–1947* (London: RoutledgeCurzon, 2004).

Birkenhead, The Earl of, *Halifax: The Life of Lord Halifax* (London: Hamish Hamilton, 1965).

Bjerre-Poulson, Niels, *Right Face: Organizing the American Conservative Movement 1945–65* (Copenhagen: Museum Tusculanum Press, University of Copenhagen, 2002).

Blackstone, William E., *Jesus is Coming* (Chicago: F.H. Revel, 1908 [1887]).

Blair, John M., *The Control of Oil* (New York: Pantheon Press, 1976).

Blaising, Craig A. and Darrell I. Bock (eds), *Dispensationalism, Israel and the Church: The Search for Definition* (Grand Rapids, MI: Zondervan, 1992).

Bohlen, Charles E., *Witness to History 1929–1969* (New York: W.W. Norton and Company, 1973).

Bono, Salvatore, *Les Corsaires en Mediterranée* (Rabat, Morocco: Éditions La Porte, 1998).
Bookin-Weiner, Jerome B. and Mohamed El Mansour, *The Atlantic Connection: 200 Years of Moroccan-American Relations 1786–1986* (Rabat: Edino Press, 1986).
Borkin, Joseph, *The Crime and Punishment of I.G. Farben* (New York: The Free Press, 1978).
Brady, Robert A., *The Spirit and Structure of German Fascism* (New York: Viking, 1937).
Brennan, Mary C., *Turning Right in the Sixties: The Conservative Capture of the GOP* (Chapel Hill, NC: University of North Carolina Press, 1995).
Brzezinksi, Zbigniew, *The Grand Chessboard: American Primacy and its Geostrategic Imperatives* (New York: Basic Books, 1997).
Buell, Raymond Leslie, *International Relations* (New York: Henry Holt and Co., 1925).
Burgess, Stanley M., and Edouard van der Maas (eds), *New International Dictionary of Charismatic and Pentecostal Movements*, rev. edn (Grand Rapids, MI: Zondervan, 2003).
Burns, William J., *Economic Aid and American Foreign Policy Toward Egypt 1855–1981* (Albany, NY: State University of New York Press, 1985).
Buzan, Barry, *The United States and the Great Powers: World Politics in the Twenty-First Century* (Cambridge: Polity, 2004).
Byrd, Robert C., *Losing America* (New York: W.W. Norton and Co., 2004).
Carré, Olivier and Paul Dumont, *Radicalismes Islamiques*, vols 1 and 2 (Paris: Éditions L'Harmattan, 1986).
Carter, Jimmy, *Our Endangered Values* (New York: Simon and Schuster, 2005).
Carter, Jimmy, *Palestine: Peace Not Apartheid* (New York: Simon and Schuster, 2006).
Cassels, Lavender, *The Struggle for the Ottoman Empire 1717–1740* (London: John Murray, 1966).
Cattan, Henry, *Jerusalem* (New York: St Martin's Press, 1981).
Charles-Roux, François, *Les Origines de L'Expédition D'Égypte* (Paris: Plon-Nourrit et Cie, 1910).
Charnay, Geoffroy de, *Synarchie: Panorama de 25 Années d'Activité Occulte* (Paris: Éditions Médicis, 1946).
Christison, Kathleen, *Perceptions of Palestine: Their Influence on US Middle East Policy* (Berkeley, CA: University of California Press, 1999).
Clark, Elmer T., *The Small Sects in America*, rev. ed. (New York: Abingdon-Cokesbury Press, 1949).
Clarke, Richard A., *Against All Enemies: Inside America's War on Terror* (New York: Free Press, 2004).
Cobban, Helena, *The Palestinian Liberation Organization: People, Power and Politics* (Cambridge: Cambridge University Press, 1984).
Cohen, Michael J., *Churchill and the Jews* (London: Frank Cass, 2003).

Cole, Juan, *Napoleon's Egypt: Invading the Middle East* (New York: Palgrave Macmillan, 2007).

Cole, Stuart Grant, *The History of Fundamentalism* (Hamden, CT: Archon Books, 1963 [c.1931]).

Cooley, John K., *An Alliance Against Babylon: The US, Israel, and Iraq* (London: Pluto Press, 2005).

Crawford, Alan, *Thunder on the Right: The 'New Right' and the Politics of Resentment* (New York: Pantheon, 1980).

Cremin, Lawrence A., *American Education: The Colonial Experience 1607–1783* (New York: Harper and Row, 1970).

Crombie, Kelvin, *For the Love of Zion: Christian Witness and the Restoration of Israel* (London: Hodder and Stoughton, 1991).

David, Abraham, *To Come to the Land: Immigration and Settlement in Sixteenth-Century Eretz-Israel* (Tuscaloosa, AL: University of Alabama Press, 1999).

Davis, William Stearns, *The Influence of Wealth in Imperial Rome* (New York: Macmillan, 1910).

Dean, John W., *Worse than Watergate: The Secret Presidency of George W. Bush* (New York: Little, Brown and Co., 2004).

Dekmejian, R. Hrair, *Islam in Revolution: Fundamentalism in the Arab World* (Syracuse, NY: Syracuse University Press, 1985).

Diamond, Sara, *Roads to Dominion: Right-Wing Movements and Political Power in the United States* (New York: The Guilford Press, 1995).

Diamond, Sara, *Not By Politics Alone* (New York: The Guilford Press, 1998).

Dixon, A.C. (ed.), *The Fundamentals* (Los Angeles: Bible Institute of Los Angeles, 1910–15).

Driault, Edouard, *La Question d'Orient depuis ses Origins jusqu'à la Paix de Sèvres* (Paris: F. Alcan, 1921).

Drummond, Henry, *Dialogues on Prophecy* (London: James Nisbet, 1827–9).

Drury, Shadia B., *Leo Strauss and the American Right* (New York: St Martin's Press, 1997).

Eilts, Hermann Frederick, *A Friendship Two Centuries Old: The United States and the Sultanate of Oman* (Washington, DC: Sultan Qaboos Center, The Middle East Institute, 1990).

Eisenhower, Dwight D., *Mandate for Change 1953–1956* (Garden City, NY: Doubleday and Co., 1963).

Engdahl, William, *A Century of War: Anglo-American Oil Politics and the New World Order*, rev. edn (London: Pluto Press, 2004).

Esposito, John L., *Political Islam: Revolution, Radicalism or Reform?* (Cairo: American University in Cairo Press, 1997).

Fall, Bernard B., *The Two Vietnams: A Political and Military Analysis*, 2nd rev. edn (New York: Frederick A. Praeger, 1967).

Fanning, Leonard M., *Foreign Oil and the Free World* (New York: McGraw-Hill, 1954).

Farman, Elbert E., *Egypt and its Betrayal* (New York: Grafton Press, 1908).
Farsoun, Samih K. and Christina Zacharia, *Palestine and the Palestinians* (Boulder, CO: Westview Press, 1997).
Field, James A., Jr, *America and the Mediterranean World 1776–1882* (Princeton, NJ: Princeton University Press, 1969).
Findlay, James, *Dwight L. Moody: American Evangelist 1837–1899* (Chicago: University of Chicago Press, 1969).
Fink, Ruben, *America and Palestine* (New York: American Zionist Emergency Council, 1945).
Finnie, David J., *Pioneers East: The Early American Experience in the Middle East* (Cambridge, MA: Harvard University Press, 1967).
Fisher, John, *Curzon and British Imperialism in the Middle East, 1916–1919* (London: Frank Cass, 1999).
Frank, Justin A., *Bush on the Couch: Inside the Mind of the President* (New York: Regan Books, 2004).
Frankel, Jonathan (ed.), *Jews and Messianism in the Modern Era: Metaphor and Meaning*, Studies in Contemporary Jewry VII, Institute of Contemporary Jewry, Hebrew University of Jerusalem (New York: Oxford University Press, 1991).
Friedman, Isaiah, *Palestine: A Twice-Promised Land? The British, the Arabs, and Zionism 1915–1920* (New Brunswick, NJ: Transaction Publishers, 2000).
Fromkin, David, *A Peace To End All Peace: The Fall of the Ottoman Empire and the Creation of the Modern Middle East* (New York: Avon Books, 1990).
Froom, LeRoy Edwin, *The Prophetic Faith of Our Fathers: The Historical Development of Prophetic Interpretation*, 4 vols (Washington, DC: Review and Herald, 1946).
Fuller, Graham E., *The West Bank of Israel: Point of No Return?*, prepared for the Office of the Secretary of Defense (Santa Monica, CA: RAND Corporation, August 1989).
Fuller, Graham E., *The Future of Political Islam* (New York: Palgrave Macmillan, 2003).
Gabrieli, F., *Arab Historians of the Crusades* (Berkeley, CA: University of California Press, 1984).
Gaddis, John Lewis, *The United States and the Origins of the Cold War 1941–1947* (New York: Columbia University Press, 1972).
Gaddis, John Lewis, *The United States and the End of the Cold War* (New York: Oxford University Press, 1992).
Gaebelein, A.C. (ed.), *Christ and Glory* (New York: Publications Office 'Our Hope', 1918).
Ganin, Zvi, *Truman, American Jewry, and Israel 1945–1948* (New York: Holmes and Meier, 1979).
Gasper, Louis, *The Fundamentalist Movement* (The Hague: Mouton, 1963).
Gelvin, James L., *The Israel–Palestine Conflict: One Hundred Years of War* (Cambridge: Cambridge University Press, 2005).

Gibbon, Edward, edited by Rev. H.R. Milman, *The History of the Decline and Fall of the Roman Empire* (New York: Harper and Bros, 1852).

Gilbert, Martin, *Churchill and the Jews: A Lifelong Friendship* (New York: Henry Holt, 2007).

Goldberg, J.J., *Jewish Power: Inside the American Jewish Establishment* (Reading, MA: Addison-Wesley, 1996).

Gorenberg, Gershom, *The End of Days: Fundamentalism and the Struggle for the Temple Mount* (New York: Simon and Schuster, 2001).

Gottfried, Paul and Thomas Fleming, *The Conservative Movement* (Boston, MA: Twayne, 1988).

Gottheil, Richard J.H., *Zionism* (Philadelphia: The Jewish Publications Society of America, 1914).

Goulden, Joseph C., *Korea: The Untold Story of the War* (New York: Times Books, 1982).

Grabill, Joseph L., *Protestant Diplomacy and the Near East: Missionary Influence on American Policy, 1810–1927* (Minneapolis, MN: University of Minnesota Press, 1971).

Graebner, Norman A., *Cold War Diplomacy 1945–1960* (New York: Van Nostrand Reinhold, 1962).

Graham, Billy, *Hope for the Future* (Minneapolis: Evangelical Literature Service, 1970).

Gray, James M. (ed.), *The Coming and Kingdom of Christ* (Chicago: 1914).

Grousset, P., *Histoire des Croisades*, 3 vols (Paris: Plon, 1934–6).

Guedalla, Philip, *Napoleon and Palestine* (London: George Allen and Unwin, 1925).

Gwynn, Stephen (ed.), *The Letters and Friendships of Sir Cecil Spring Rice: A Record*, Vol. 2 (Boston, MA: Houghton Mifflin Company, 1929).

Hagee, John, *Jerusalem Countdown: A Prelude to War* (Lake Mary, FL: FrontLine, 2007).

Hallgarten, George W.F., *Why Dictators? The Causes and Forms of Tyrannical Rule Since 600 BC* (New York: Macmillan, 1954).

Halper, Stefan and Jonathan Clarke, *America Alone: The Neo-Conservatives and the Global Order* (Cambridge: Cambridge University Press, 2004).

Halsell, Grace, *Journey to Jerusalem* (New York: Macmillan, 1981).

Halsell, Grace, *Prophecy and Politics: Militant Evangelists on the Road to Nuclear War* (Westport, CT: Lawrence Hill and Co., 1986).

Hanieh, Akram, *The Camp David Papers* (Ramallah, Palestine: *Al-Ayyam* newspaper, August 2000).

Harlow, Giles D. and George C. Maerz (eds), *Measures Short of War: The George F. Kennan Lectures at the National War College 1946–47* (Washington, DC: National Defense University Press, 1991).

Harris, Kenneth, *Attlee* (New York: W.W. Norton, 1982).

Hedges, Chris, *American Fascists: The Christian Right and the War on America* (New York: Free Press, 2006).

Heeren, A.H.L., *A Manual of the History of the Political System of Europe and its Colonies* (London: Henry G. Bohn, 1846).

Heilbrunn, Jacob, *They Knew They Were Right: The Rise of the Neocons* (New York: Doubleday, 2008).

Heimert, Alan and Perry Miller, *The Great Awakening: Documents Illustrating the Crisis and its Consequences* (Indianapolis, IN: Bobbs-Merrill Co., 1967).

Helms, Christine Moss, *Iraq: Eastern Flank of the Arab World* (Washington, DC: Brookings Institution, 1984).

Henriques, Robert and Marcus Samuel, *First Viscount Bearsted and Founder of The 'Shell' Transport and Trading Company 1853–1927* (London: Barrie and Rockliff, 1960).

Herzl, Theodore, *The Diaries of Theodore Herzl*, trans. Marvin Lowenthal (New York: Dial Press, 1956).

Hess, Moses, *Rome and Jerusalem: A Study in Jewish Nationalism*, trans. Meyer Wasman (New York: Bloch, 1943).

Heyd, Uriel, *Ottoman Documents on Palestine 1552–1615* (London: Oxford University Press, 1960).

Higham, Charles, *Trading with the Enemy: The Nazi-American Money Plot 1933–1949* (New York: Barnes and Noble, 1983).

Hillenbrand, C., *The Crusades: Islamic Perspectives* (Edinburgh: Edinburgh University Press, 1999).

Hixson, Jr, William B., *Search for the American Right Wing: An Analysis of the Social Science Record, 1955–1987* (Princeton, NJ: Princeton University Press, 1992).

Hobson, J.A., *Imperialism* (Ann Arbor, MI: University of Michigan Press, 1965).

Hopkins, Hugh Evan, *Sublime Vagabond: The Life of Joseph Wolff – Missionary Extraordinary*, foreword by Sir Fitzroy Maclean Bart (Worthing: Churchman, 1984).

Hopkirk, Peter, *The Great Game: The Struggle for Empire in Central Asia* (New York: Kodansha International, 1992).

Hourani, A.H., *Syria and Lebanon: A Political Essay* (London: Oxford University Press, 1946).

Hunt, Gaillard, *The History of the Seal of the United States* (Washington, DC: Department of State, 1909).

Huntington, Samuel P., *The Soldier and the State: The Theory and Politics of Civil–Military Relations* (New York: Vintage, 1964 [1957]).

Huntington, Samuel O., *The Clash of Civilizations: Remaking of World Order* (New York: Simon and Shuster, 1996).

Hyamson, Albert, *The British Consulate in Jerusalem in Relation to the Jews of Palestine, 1838–1914* (London: Goldston, 1939–40).

Hyamson, Albert M., *Palestine Under the Mandate 1920–1948* (Westport, CT: Greenwood Press, 1976 [1950]).

Ickes, Harold L., *The Secret Diary of Harold L. Ickes: The First Thousand Days 1933–1936* (New York: Simon and Schuster, 1953).

Ingram, Edward, *Britain's Persian Connection 1798–1828: Prelude to the Great Game in Asia* (Oxford: Clarendon Press, 1992).

Jensen, Arthur L., *The Maritime Commerce of Colonial Philadelphia* (Madison, WI: State Historical Society of Wisconsin, 1963).

Johnson, Chalmers, *Blowback: The Costs and Consequences of American Empire* (New York: Henry Holt, 2000).

Johnson, Chalmers, *The Sorrows of Empire: Militarism, Secrecy and the End of the Republic* (New York: Henry Holt, 2004).

Johnson, Robert, *Spying for Empire: The Great Game in Central and South Asia, 1757–1947* (London: Greenhill, 2006).

Kadi, Leila S., *Arab Summit Conferences and the Palestine Problem (1936–1950), (1964–1966)* (Beirut: Palestine Liberation Organization Research Center, 1966).

Kennan, George F., *At a Century's Ending: Reflections 1982–1995* (New York: Norton, 1996).

Khadduri, Majid and Edmund Ghareeb, *War in the Gulf 1990–1991: The Iraq–Kuwait Conflict and its Implications* (New York: Oxford University Press, 1997).

Khalidi, Walid (ed.), *From Haven to Conquest: Readings in Zionism and the Palestine Problem Until 1948* (Washington, DC: Institute for Palestine Studies, 1987).

Kirk, George, *The Middle East in the War* (London: Oxford University Press, 1952).

Kobler, Franz, *Napoleon and the Jews* (New York: Schocken, 1976).

Koestler, Arthur, *Promise and Fulfilment: Palestine 1917–1949* (London: Macmillan, 1949).

Kolkey, Jonathan Martin, *The New Right, 1960–1968 with Epilogue 1969–1980* (Washington, DC: University Press of America, 1983).

Knee, Stuart E., *The Concept of Zionist Dissent in the American Mind 1917–1941* (New York: Robert Speller and Sons, 1979).

Knox, D. Edward, *The Making of a New Eastern Question: British Palestine Policy and the Origins of Israel, 1917–1925* (Washington, DC: Catholic University of America Press, 1981).

Kraus, C. Norman, *Dispensationalism in America: Its Rise and Development* (Richmond, VA: John Knox, 1958).

Krock, Arthur, *Memoirs: Sixty Years on the Firing Line* (New York: 1968).

Kushner, David (ed.), *Palestine in the Late Ottoman Period: Political, Social and Economic Transformation* (Jerusalem: Yad Izhak Ben-Zvi, 1986).

Laham, Nicholas, *Selling AWACS to Saudi Arabia: The Reagan Administration and the Balancing of America's Competing Interests in the Middle East* (Westport, CT: Praeger, 2002).

Lake, Kirsopp, *The Religion of Yesterday and Today* (Boston, MA: Houghton Mifflin, 1926).

Laqueur, Walter, *A History of Zionism* (New York: Holt, Rinehart and Winston, 1972).

Laquer, Walter (ed.), *Fascism: A Reader's Guide. Analysis, Interpretations, Bibliography* (Berkeley, CA: University of California Press, 1976).

Lambert, Frank, *The Founding Fathers and the Place of Religion in America* (Princeton, NJ: Princeton University Press, 2003).
Lambert, Frank, *The Barbary Wars: American Independence in the Atlantic World* (New York: Hill and Wang, 2005).
Lauren, Paul Gordon, Gordon A. Craig and Alexander George, *Force and Statecraft: Diplomatic Challenges of Our Time*, 4th edn (New York: Oxford University Press, 2007).
Lind, Michael, *Made in Texas: George W. Bush and the Southern Takeover of American Politics* (New York: Basic Books, 2003).
Lindberg, Beth M., *A God Filled Life* (Chicago: American Messianic Fellowship, n.d.).
Link, William A., *Righteous Warrior: Jesse Helms and the Rise of Modern Conservatism* (New York: St Martin's Press, 2008).
Linker, Damon, *The Theocons: Secular America Under Siege* (New York: Doubleday, 2006).
Longrigg, Stephen Hemsley, *Iraq 1900 to 1950: A Political, Social, and Economic History* (London: Oxford University Press, 1953).
Makovsky, Michael, *Churchill and the Promised Land: Zionism and Statecraft* (New Haven, CT: Yale University Press, 2007).
Malachy, Yona, *American Fundamentalism and Israel: The Relation of Fundamentalist Churches to Zionism and the State of Israel* (Jerusalem: Institute of Contemporary Jewry, Hebrew University of Jerusalem, 1978).
Malloy, William M., *Treaties, Conventions, International Acts, Protocols and Agreements Between the United States of America and Other Powers 1776–1909*, Vol. 2 (Washington, DC: Government Printing House, 1909).
Mann, James, *Rise of the Vulcans: The History of Bush's War Cabinet* (New York: Viking, 2004).
Mansfield, Stephen, *Derek Prince: A Biography* (Lake Mary, FL: Charisma House, 2005).
Marcus, Jacob R., *The Colonial American Jew, 1492–1776* (Detroit, MI: Wayne State University Press, 1970).
Marriott, J.A.R., *The Eastern Question: An Historical Study in European Diplomacy* (London: Oxford, 1940).
Martin, James Stewart, *All Honorable Men* (Boston, MA: Little, Brown and Co., 1950).
Martin, William, *With God on Our Side: The Rise of the Religious Right in America* (New York: Broadway Books, 1996).
McAlister, Jr, John T. *Vietnam, The Origins of Revolution* (New York: Alfred Knopf, 1969).
McDonald, James G., *My Mission in Israel* (New York: Simon and Schuster, 1951).
McGhee, George, *Envoy to the Middle World: Adventures in Diplomacy* (New York: Harper and Row, 1983).

McNeil, William C., *American Money and the Weimar Republic: Economics and Politics on the Eve of the Great Depression* (New York: Columbia University Press, 1986).

Mearsheimer, John J. and Stephen M. Walt, *The Israel Lobby and US Foreign Policy* (New York: Farrar, Straus and Giroux, 2007).

Mejcher, Helmut, *Imperial Quest for Oil: Iraq 1910–1928*, St Antony's Middle East Monographs No. 6 (London: Ithaca Press, 1976).

Mejcher, Helmut, *Die Politik und das Ol im Nahen Osten. I. Der Kampf der Mächte und Konzerne vor dem Zweiten Weltkrieg* (Stuttgart: Klett-Cotta Verlag, 1980).

Melman, Yossi and Dan Raviv, *Friends in Deed: Inside the US–Israel Alliance* (New York: Hyperion,1994).

Merkley, Paul Charles, *The Politics of Christian Zionism 1891–1948* (London: Frank Cass, 1998).

Merkley, Paul Charles, *Christian Attitudes towards the State of Israel* (Montreal: McGill-Queen's University Press, 2001).

Merkley, Paul Charles, *American Presidents, Religion, and Israel: The Heirs of Cyrus* (Westport, CT: Praeger, 2004).

Miles, Michael W., *The Odyssey of the American Right* (New York: Oxford University Press, 1980).

Miller, William, *The Ottoman Empire and its Successors, 1801–1927* (Cambridge: Cambridge University Press, 1934).

Mitchell, Richard P., *The Society of the Muslim Brothers* (New York: Oxford University Press, 1993).

Moncomble, Yann, *Du Viol des Foules à la Synarchie ou le Complot Permanent* (Paris: Faits et Documents, 1983).

Moon, Parker Thomas, *Imperialism and World Politics* (New York: Macmillan, 1928).

Moore, James and Wayne Slater, *Bush's Brain: How Karl Rove made George W. Bush Presidential* (Hoboken, NJ: John Wiley, 2003).

Morison, Samuel Eliot, *Maritime History of Massachusetts* (Boston, MA: Houghton Mifflin and Co., 1921).

Mosely, Leonard, *Blood Relations: The Rise and Fall of the duPonts of Delaware* (New York: Atheneum, 1980).

Mosse, George L. (ed.), *International Fascism: New Thoughts and New Approaches* (London: Sage Publications, 1979).

Nakash, Yitzhak, *The Shi'is of Iraq* (Princeton, NJ: Princeton University Press, 1995).

Nash, George H., *The Conservative Intellectual Movement in America Since 1945* (New York: Basic Books, 1976).

Neatby, W.B., *A History of the Plymouth Brethren* (London: Hodder and Stoughton, 1901).

Nolte, Ernst, *Der Faschismus in seiner Epoche: Die Action française, der italienischer Faschismus, der Nationalsozialismus* (Munich: R. Piper, 1965).

Nye, Jr, Joseph S., *Soft Power: The Means to Success in World Politics* (New York: Public Affairs, 2004).
O'Huallachain, D.L. and J. Forrest Sharpe (eds), *Neo-Conned Again: Hypocrisy, Lawlessness, and the Rape of Iraq* (Vienna, VA: HIS Press, 2005).
Ornstein, Norman J. and Shirley Elder, *Interest Groups, Lobbying, and Policymaking* (Washington, DC: Congressional Quarterly Press, 1978).
Ouroussow, Le Prince A.M., *Résumé Historique des Principaux Traités de Paix* (Evreux, France: Charles Hérissey, 1884).
Packer, George, *The Assassins' Gate: America in Iraq* (New York: Farrar, Strauss and Giroux, 2005).
Palmer, Hurly Pring, *Joseph Wolff: His Romantic Life and Travels, etc* (London: Heath Cranton, 1935).
Parkes, James, *The Emergence of the Jewish Problem 1878–1939* (London: Oxford University Press, 1946).
Peck, Juliana S., *The Reagan Administration and the Palestinian Question: The First Thousand Days* (Washington, DC: Institute for Palestine Studies, 1984).
Pettingill, W.L. (ed.), *Light on Prophecy* (New York: Bible House, Christian Herald, 1918).
Phillips, Clifton Jackson, *Protestant America and the Pagan World: The First Half Century of the American Board of Commissioners for Foreign Missions, 1810–1860* (Cambridge, MA: East Asian Research Center of Harvard University, 1969).
Phillips, Kevin, *The Emerging Republican Majority* (New Rochelle, NY: Arlington House, 1969).
Phillips, Kevin, *American Dynasty: Aristocracy, Fortune, and the Politics of Deceit in the House of Bush* (New York: Viking, 2004).
Phillips, Kevin, *American Theocracy: The Peril and Politics of Radical Religion, Oil, and Borrowed Money in the 21st Century* (New York: Viking, 2006).
Phillips, William, *Ventures in Diplomacy* (London: John Murray, 1953).
Podhoretz, Norman, *World War IV: The Long Struggle Against Islamofascism* (New York: Doubleday, 2007).
Polk, William R., *The United States and the Arab World* (Cambridge, MA: Harvard University Press, 1965).
Polk, William and Richard Chambers (eds), *Beginnings of Modernization in the Middle East: The Nineteenth Century* (Chicago: University of Chicago Press, 1968).
Pool, James and Suzanne Pool, *Who Financed Hitler: The Secret Funding of Hitler's Rise to Power 1919–1933* (New York: The Dial Press, 1978).
Posner, Sarah, *God's Profits: Faith, Fraud, and the Republican Crusade for Values Voters* (Sausalito, CA: PoliPoint Press, 2008).
Prawer, Joshua, *The History of the Jews in the Latin Kingdom of Jerusalem* (Oxford: Oxford University Press, 1988).
Preble, Christopher, *John F. Kennedy and the Missile Gap* (DeKalb, IL: Northern Illinois University Press, 2004).

Purifoy, Lewis McCarroll, *Harry Truman's China Policy: McCarthyism and the Diplomacy of Hysteria, 1947–1951* (New York: New Viewpoints, 1976).

Ridley, Jaspar, *Lord Palmerston* (London: Constable, 1970).

Ritter, Scott, *Iraq Confidential: The Untold Story of the Intelligence Conspiracy to Undermine the UN and Overthrow Saddam Hussein* (New York: Nation Books, 2005).

Roberts, Glyn, *The Most Powerful Man in the World: The Life of Sir Henry Deterding* (New York: Covici Friede, 1938).

Roberts, Samuel J., *Survival or Hegemony* (Baltimore, MD: Johns Hopkins University Press, 1973).

Rogger, Hans and Eugen Weber (eds), *The European Right: A Historical Profile* (Berkeley, CA: University of California Press, 1966).

Roider, Karl A., *Austria's Eastern Question 1700–1740* (Princeton, NJ: Princeton University Press, 1982).

Roman, Peter, *Eisenhower and the Missile Gap* (Ithaca, NY: Cornell University Press, 1996).

Roskill, Stephen, *Naval Policy Between the Wars*, 2 vols (Annapolis, MD: Naval Institute Press, 1976).

Royal Institute of International Affairs, *Political and Strategic Interests of the United Kingdom: An Outline* (Oxford: Oxford University Press, 1938).

Rubinstein, Amnon, *The Zionist Dream Revisted: From Herzl to Gush Emunim and Back* (New York: Schocken Books, 1984).

Rugh, William A., *Arab Perceptions of American Foreign Policy During the October War* (Washington, DC: The Middle East Institute, 1976).

Runciman, S., *A History of the Crusades*, 3 vols (Cambridge: Cambridge University Press, 1952–1954).

Russell, Frank M., *Theories of International Relations* (New York: D. Appleton-Century, 1936).

Russo, Gus, *Supermob: How Sidney Korshak and his Criminal Associates became America's Hidden Power Brokers* (New York: Bloomsbury, 2006).

Said, Edward W. and Christopher Hitchens (eds), *Blaming the Victims: Spurious Scholarship and the Palestine Question* (London: Verso, 1988).

Salvemini, Gaetano, *The Fascist Dictatorship in Italy* (New York: Henry Holt, 1927).

Salvemini, Gaetano, *The Origins of Fascism in Italy* (New York: Henry Holt, 1973 [1942]).

Sandeen, Ernest R., *The Roots of Fundamentalism: British and American Millenarianism 1800–1930* (Chicago: The University of Chicago Press, 1970).

Sasuly, Richard, *I.G. Farben* (New York: Boni Gaer, 1947).

Scahill, Jeremy, *Blackwater: The Rise of the World's Most Powerful Mercenary Army* (New York: Nation Books, 2007).

Scalley, Robert J., *The Origins of the Lloyd George Coalition: The Politics of Social-Imperialism, 1900–1918* (Princeton, NJ: Princeton University Press, 1975).

Schlesinger, Jr, Arthur M., *The Politics of Upheaval* (Boston, MA: Houghton Mifflin Co., 1960).

Schlesinger, Jr, Arthur M., *The Imperial Presidency* (Boston, MA: Houghton Mifflin Co., 1973).

Schuman, Frederick L., *International Politics*, 2nd edn (New York: McGraw-Hill, 1937).

Schur, Nathan, *Napoleon in the Holy Land* (London: Greenhill Books, 1999).

Schwarzfuchs, Simon, *Napoleon, the Jews and the Sanhedrin* (London: Routledge and Kegan Paul, 1979).

Seafaring in Colonial Massachusetts: a conference held by the Colonial Society of Massachusetts, November 21 and 22, 1975 (Boston, MA: The Colonial Society of Massachusetts, 1980).

Seldes, George, *You Can't Do That* (New York: Modern Age Books, 1938).

Seldes, George, *Facts and Fascism* (New York: In Fact, 1943).

Shahak, Israel and Norton Mezvinsky, *Jewish Fundamentalism in Israel* (London: Pluto Press, 2004).

Sharlet, Jeffrey, *The Family: The Secret Fundamentalism at the Heart of American Power* (New York: HarperCollins, 2008).

Shavit, Yaacov, *Jabotinsky and the Revisionist Movement, 1925–1948* (London: Frank Cass, 1988).

Sheehan, Neil, Hedrick Smith, E.W. Kenworthy and Fox Butterfield, *The Pentagon Papers* (New York: Bantam Books, 1971).

Shuster, W. Morgan, *The Strangling of Persia: A Personal Narrative* (New York: Century Company, 1912).

Sizer, Stephen, *Christian Zionism: Road-Map to Armageddon?* (Leicester: Inter-Varsity Press, 2004).

Smith, Andrew F., *Rescuing the World: The Life and Times of Leo Cherne* (Albany, NY: State University of New York).

Smith, Grant F., *Foreign Agents: The American Israel Public Affairs Committee From the 1963 Fulbright Hearings to the 2005 Espionage Scandal* (Washington, DC: Institute for Research, 2007).

Snead, David L., *The Gaither Committee, Eisenhower, and the Cold War* (Columbus, OH: Ohio State University Press, 1999).

Snetsinger, John, *Truman, the Jewish Vote and the Creation of Israel* (Stanford, CA: Hoover Institution Press, 1974).

Speiser, E.A., *The United States and the Near East* (Cambridge, MA: Harvard University Press, 1947).

Sperry, Paul, *Crude Politics: How Bush's Oil Cronies Hijacked the War on Terrorism* (Nashville, TN: WND Books, 2003).

Stebenne, David L., *Modern Republican: Arthur Larson and the Eisenhower Years* (Bloomington, IN: University of Indiana Press, 2006).

Stein, Leonard, *The Balfour Declaration* (New York: Simon and Schuster, 1961).

Stoyanovsky, J., *La Théorie Générale des Mandats Internationaux* (Paris: Les Presses Universitaires de France, 1925).

Stoyanovsky, J., *The Mandate for Palestine: A Contribution to the Theory and Practice of International Mandates* (London: Longmans, Green, 1928).
Strong, William E., *The Story of the American Board: An Account of the First Hundred Years of the American Board of Commissioners for Foreign Missions* (Boston, MA: Pilgrim Press, 1910).
Suleiman, Michael W. (ed.), *US Policy on Palestine from Wilson to Clinton* (Normal, IL: Association of Arab-American University Graduates, 1995).
Suskind, Ron, *The Price of Loyalty: George W. Bush, the White House, and the Education of Paul O'Neill* (New York: Simon and Schuster, 2004).
Suskind, Ron, *The One Percent Doctrine: Deep Inside America's Pursuit of its Enemies Since 911* (New York: Simon and Schuster, 2006).
Swanberg, W.A., *Luce and His Empire* (New York: Charles Scribner's Sons, 1972).
Taft, Robert A., *A Foreign Policy for Americans* (New York: Doubleday, 1951).
Temperley, Harold W.V., *England and the Near East: The Crimea* (London: Longmans, Green, 1936).
Thomas, Hugh, *Suez* (New York: Harper and Row, 1966).
Thorpe, Jr, Merle, *Prescription for Conflict: Israel's West Bank Settlement Policy* (Washington, DC: Foundation for Middle East Peace, 1984).
Tivnan, Edward, *The Lobby: Jewish Political Power and American Foreign Policy* (New York: Simon and Schuster, 1987).
Toplin, Robert Brent, *Radical Conservatism: The Right's Political Religion* (Lawrence, KS: The University of Kansas Press, 2006).
Tracy, Joseph, *The Great Awakening: A History of the Revival of Religion in the Time of Edwards and Whitefield* (Boston, MA: Tappan and Dennet, 1842).
Truman, David, *The Governmental Process* (New York: Knopf, 1960).
Truman, Harry S., *Years of Trial and Hope*, Vol. 2 (Garden City, NY: Doubleday, 1956).
Tuchman, Barbara, *Bible and Sword: England and Palestine from the Bronze Age to Balfour* (New York: Ballantine Books, 1984 [1956]).
Turner, Jr, Henry Ashby, *German Big Business and the Rise of Hitler* (New York: Oxford, 1985).
Turner, W.C., *John Nelson Darby* (London: C.A. Hammond, 1944).
Unger, Craig, *The Fall of the House of Bush* (New York: Scribner, 2007).
Ure, P.N., *The Origin of Tyranny* (New York: Russell and Russell, 1962 [1922]).
Urofsky, Melvin I., *American Zionism from Herzl to the Holocaust* (Garden City, NY: Anchor Press, 1975).
Villemarest, P.F. de, *Les Sources Financières du Nazisme* (Cierrey, France: Éditions CEI, 1984).
Voegelin, Eric, *Order and History: Israel and Revelation* (Baton Rouge, LA; Louisiana State University, 1956).
Wagner, Donald E., *Anxious for Armageddon* (Scottdale, PA: Herald Press, 1995).
Watson, Adam, *The Evolution of International Society* (London: Routledge, 1992).

Watson, C.M., *Bonaparte's Expedition to Palestine in 1799*, Palestine Exploration Fund Quarterly Statement for 1917 (London: Palestine Exploration Fund, 1917).

Webster, Charles, *The Foreign Policy of Palmerston*, 2 vols (London: G. Bell and Sons, 1969 [1951]).

Wedgwood, J.C., *The Seventh Dominion* (London: Labour Pub. Co., 1928).

Whitaker, Robert W., *The New Right Papers* (New York: St Martin's Press, 1982).

White, F. Clifton and William J. Gill, *Suite 3505: The Story of the Draft Goldwater Movement* (New Rochelle: Arlington House, 1967).

White, Theodore H., *The Making of the President 1960* (New York: Atheneum, 1961).

White, Theodore H., *The Making of the President 1964* (New York: Atheneum, 1965).

White, William S., *The Taft Story* (New York: Harper and Bros, 1954).

Wilkinson, Mark F. (ed.), *The Korean War at Fifty: International Perspectives* (Lexington, VA: Virginia Military Institute, 2004).

Witcover, Jules, *Sabotage at Black Tom: Imperial Germany's Secret War in America 1914–1917* (Chapel Hill, NC: Algonquin Books, 1989).

Wolf, John B., *The Emergence of the Great Powers, 1685–1715* (New York: Harper and Bros, 1951).

Wolfskill, George, *The Revolt of the Conservatives: A History of the American Liberty League 1934–1940* (Boston, MA: Houghton Mifflin, 1962).

Woods, Kevin M., Michael R. Pease, Mark E. Stout, Williamson Murray and James G. Lacey, *The Iraqi Perspectives Report: Saddam's Senior Leadership on Operation Iraqi Freedom from Official US Joint Forces Command Report* (Annapolis, MD: Naval Institute Press, 2006).

Wright, Louis B., *The Cultural Life of the American Colonies 1607–1763* (New York: Harper and Bros, 1957).

Wulfsohn, L. and G. Wernle, *L'Évasion des Capitaux Alemands* (Paris: Sociètè Anonyme d'Éditions, 1923).

Zhao, Suisheng (ed.), *Chinese Foreign Policy: Pragmatism and Strategic Behavior* (Armonk, NY: M.E. Sharpe, 2004).

Articles

Abboushi, W.F., 'The road to rebellion: Arab Palestine in the 1930s', *Journal of Palestine Studies* vi/3 (spring, 1977), pp.23–46.

Abramson, Henry, 'Jewish representation in the independent Ukrainian governments of 1917–1020', *Slavic Review* l/3 (autumn, 1991), pp.542–50.

Adams, Michael, 'What Went Wrong in Palestine', *Journal of Palestine Studies* xviii/1, special issue: Palestine 1948 (autumn 1988), pp.71–82.

Andrew, C.M. and A.S. Kanya-Forstner, 'The French colonial policy and French colonial war aims, 1914–1918', *The Historical Journal* xvii/1 (Mar. 1974), pp.79–106.

Aruga, Tadashi, 'The problem of security treaty revision in Japan's relations with the United States: 1951–1960', *Hitotsubashi Journal of Law and Politics* xiii (Feb. 1985), pp.31–60.

Aruri, Naseer, 'The United States and Palestine: Reagan's Legacy to Bush', *Journal of Palestine Studies* xviii/36 (spring 1989), pp.3–21.

Azaryahu, Maoz and Aharon Kellerman, 'Symbolic places of national history and revival: a study in Zionist mythical geography', *Transactions of the Institute of British Geographers*, new series, xxiv/1 (1999), p.109–23.

Bar-Yosef, Eitan, 'The last crusade? British propaganda and the Palestine campaign, 1917–18', *Journal of Contemporary History* xxxvi/1 (Jan. 2001), pp.87–109.

Baron, Salo W., 'The Jewish Question in the nineteenth century', *The Journal of Modern History* x/1 (Mar. 1938), pp.51–65.

Beers, Henry P., 'United States naval detachment in Turkish waters, 1919–1924', *Military Affairs* vii/4 (winter, 1943), pp.209–20.

Belkharroubi, A., 'Essai sur une Théorie Juridique des Mouvements de Liberation nationale', *Revue Egyptienne de Droit International* xxviii (1972), pp.20–43.

Bennis, Phyllis and Khaled Mansour, '"Praise God and pass the ammunition!": the changing nature of Israel's US backers', *Middle East Report* 208 (US foreign policy in the Middle East: critical assessments) (autumn, 1998), pp.16–18, 43.

Boer, Connie de, 'The polls: attitudes toward the Arab–Israeli crisis', *The Public Opinion Quarterly* xlvii/1 (spring 1983), p.121–31..

Bourdillon, B.H., 'The political situation in Iraq', *Journal of the British Institute of International Affairs* iii/6 (Nov. 1924), pp.273–87.

Brinkley, Alan, 'The problem of American conservatism', *The American Historical Review* xcix/2 (Apr. 1994), pp.409–24.

Brown, Ira V., 'Watchers for the Second Coming: the millenarian tradition in America', *The Mississippi Valley Historical Review* xxxix/3 (Dec, 1952), pp.441–58.

Bruce, Steve, 'Modernity and fundamentalism: the New Christian Right in America', *The British Journal of Sociology* xli/4 (Dec. 1990), pp.477–96.

Cattan, H., 'The Arab Israeli Conflict', *Revue Egyptienne de Droit International* xxviii (1972), pp.44–55.

Clarke, Duncan L. and Eric Flohr, 'Christian churches and the Palestine Question', *Journal of Palestine Studies* xxi/4 (summer 1992), pp.67–79.

Cohen, Michael J., 'British strategy and the Palestine Question 1936–39', *Journal of Contemporary History* vii/3–4 (Jul.–Oct. 1972), pp.157–83.

Cohen, Michael J., 'Appeasement in the Middle East: the British white paper on Palestine, May 1939', *The Historical Journal* xvi/3 (Sep. 1973), pp.727–57.

Cohen, Michael J., 'The British white paper on Palestine, May 1939. Part II: The testing of a policy, 1942–1945', *The Historical Journal* xix/3 (Sep. 1976), pp.727–57.

Cohen, Michael J., 'Secret diplomacy and rebellion in Palestine, 1936–1939', *International Journal of Middle East Studies* viii/3 (Jul. 1977), pp.379–404.

Cohen, Michael J., 'The Genesis of the Anglo-American Committee on Palestine, November 1945: a case study in the assertion of American hegemony', *The Historical Journal* xxii/1 (Mar. 1979), p.187–207.

Conover, Pamela Johnston, 'The mobilization of the New Right: a test of various explanations', *The Western Political Quarterly* xxxvi/4 (Dec. 1983), pp.632–49.

Cunningham, Alan, 'Palestine – The Last Days of the Mandate', *International Affairs* xxiv/4 (Oct. 1948), pp.481–90.

Davis, Norman, 'Great Britain and the Polish Jews, 1918–20', *Journal of Contemporary History* viii/2 (Apr. 1973), pp.119–42.

Doumani, Beshara, 'Rediscovering Ottoman Palestine: writing Palestinians into history', *Journal of Palestine Studies* 82 (winter 1992), pp.5–28.

Earle, Edward Mead, 'The secret Anglo-German convention of 1914 regarding Asiatic Turkey', *Political Science Quarterly* xxxviii/1 (Mar. 1923), pp.24–44.

Earle, Edward Mead, 'The Turkish petroleum company – a study in oleaginous diplomacy', *Political Science Quarterly* xxxix/1 (Jun. 1924), pp.265–79.

Earle, Edward Mead, 'The new constitution of Turkey', *Political Science Quarterly* xl/1 (Mar. 1925), pp.73–100.

Eisenstein, Zillah R., 'The sexual politics of the New Right: understanding the "crisis of Liberalism" for the 1980s"', *Signs* vii/3, 'Feminist Theory' (spring 1982), pp.567–88.

Ferrari, Silvio, 'The Holy See and the postwar Palestine issue: the internationalization of Jerusalem and the protection of holy places', *International Affairs* lx/2 (spring 1984), pp.261–83.

Fitzgerald, Edward Peter, 'France's Middle Eastern ambitions, the Sykes–Picot negotiations and the oil fields of Mosul', *The Journal of Modern History* lxvi/4 (Dec. 1984), pp.697–725.

Fitzgerald, Edward Peter, 'France's Middle Eastern ambitions, the Sykes-Picot negotiations, and the oil fields of Mosul, 1915–1918', *The Journal of Modern History* lxvi/4 (Dec. 1994), pp.697–725.

Fitzgerald, William, 'The holy places of Palestine in history and in politics', *International Affairs* xxvi/1 (Jan. 1950), p.1–10.

Fox, Richard Wightman, 'The culture of liberal progressivism, 1875–1925', *Journal of Interdisciplinary History* xxiii/3 (winter 1993), pp.639–60.

Friedman, Robert I., 'Selling Israel to America', *Journal of Political Studies* xvi/4 (summer 1987), pp.169–79.

Gaustad, Edwin S., 'The theological effects of the Great Awakening in New England', *The Mississippi Valley Historical Review* xl/4 (Mar. 1954), pp.681–706.

Gavish, Dov, 'An account of an unrealized aerial cadastral survey in Palestine under the British mandate', *The Geographical Journal* cliii/1 (Mar. 1987), pp.93–8.

Gilmour, David, 'The unregarded prophet: Lord Curzon and the Palestine Question', *Journal of Palestine Studies* xxv/3 (spring 1996), pp.60–8.

Green, John C., 'The Christian Right and the 1994 elections: a view from the states', *PS: Political Science and Politics* xxviii/1 (Mar. 1995), pp.5–8.

Green, John C. and James L. Guth, 'The Christian Right in the Republican Party: the case of Pat Robertson's supporters', *The Journal of Politics* l/1 (Feb. 1988), pp.150–65.

Green, John C., James L. Guth and Kevin Hill, 'Faith and election: the Christian Right in congressional campaigns 1978–1988', *The Journal of Politics* lv/1 (Feb. 1993), pp.80–91.

Griessman, B. Eugene, 'Philo-Semitism and Protestant Fundamentalism: the unlikely Zionists', *Phylon* xxvii/3 (fall 1976), p.197–211.

Haddad, H.S., 'The biblical bases of Zionist colonialism', *Journal of Palestine Studies* iii/4 (summer 1974), pp.97–113.

Halperin, Morton H., 'The Gaither Committee and the policy process', *World Politics* xiii/3 (Apr. 1961), pp.360–84.

Halperin, Samuel, 'Ideology or philanthropy? The politics of Zionist fund-raising', *The Western Political Quarterly* xiii/4 (Dec. 1960), pp.950–73.

Harper, George W., 'Clericalism and revival: the Great Awakening in Boston as a pastoral phenomenon', *The New England Quarterly* lvii/4 (Dec. 1984), pp.554–66.

Huff, Earl D., 'A study of a successful interest group: the American Zionist movement', *The Western Political Quarterly* xxv/1 (Mar. 1972), pp.109–24.

Hughes, Matthew, 'General Allenby and the Palestine campaign 1917–1918', *The Journal of Strategic Studies* xix/4 (Dec. 1996), pp.58–88.

Huneidi, Sahar, 'Was Balfour policy reversible? The Colonial Office and Palestine, 1921–1923', *Journal of Palestine Studies* xxvii/2 (winter 1998), pp.23–41.

Hyamson, Albert M., 'British projects for the restoration of Jews to Palestine', *Publications of the American Jewish Historical Society* 26 (1918), pp.127–64.

Ibrahim, Saad, 'American domestic forces and the October War', *Journal of Palestine Studies* iv/1 (autumn 1974), pp.55–81.

Irvine, William D., 'French Conservatives and the "New Right" during the 1930s', *French Historical Studies* viii/4 (autumn 1974), pp.534–62.

Ishii, Osamu, 'China trade embargo and America's alliance management in the 1950s – the Japanese case', *Hitotsubashi Journal of Law and Politics* xx (Feb. 1992), pp.23–30.

Janikowski, James, 'Egyptian responses to the Palestine problem in the interwar period', *International Journal of Middle East Studies* xii/1 (Aug. 1980), pp.1–38.

Jelin, Ted G., 'The political consequences of religious group attitudes', *The Journal of Politics* xxxv/1 (Feb. 1993), pp.178–190.

Jenkins, J. Craig and Craig M. Eckert, 'The right turn in economic policy: business elites and the New Conservative economics', *Sociological Forum* xv/2 (Jun. 2000), pp.307–38.

Johnson, Nancy Jo, 'The Zionist organizational structure', *Journal of Palestine Studies* x/1 (autumn 1980), pp.80–93.

Jones, G. Gareth, 'The British government and the oil companies 1912–1924: the search for an oil policy', *The Historical Journal* xx/3 (Sep. 1977), pp.647–72.

Katsh, Abraham I., 'The teaching of Hebrew in American universities', *The Modern Language Journal* xxx/8 (Dec. 1946), pp.575–86.

Kaufman, Chaim, 'Threat inflation and the failure of the market place of ideas: selling the Iraq War', *International Security* xxix/1 (summer 2004), pp.5–48.

Kayyali, Abdul-Wahab, 'Zionism and imperialism: the historical origins', *Journal of Palestine Studies* vi/3 (spring 1977), pp.98–112.

Kedourie, Elie, 'Cairo and Khartoum on the Arab Question, 1915–18', *The Historical Journal* vii/2 (1964), pp.280–97.

Kedourie, Elie, 'The end of the Ottoman Empire', *Journal of Contemporary History* iii/4, '1918–1919: From War to Peace' (Oct. 1968), p.19–28.

Khalidi, Walid, 'The Palestine problem: an overview', *Journal of Palestine Studies* xxi/1 (autumn 1991), pp.5–16.

King, Desmond S., 'New Right ideology, welfare state form, and citizenship: a comment on conservative capitalism', *Comparative Studies in Society and History* xxx/4 (Oct. 1988), pp.792–9.

Klieman, Aaron S., 'Britain's war aims in the Middle East in 1915', *Journal of Contemporary History* iii/3, 'The Middle East' (Jul. 1968), pp.237–51.

Klieman, Aaron S., 'The divisiveness of Palestine: Foreign Office versus Colonial Office on the issue of partition, 1937', *The Historical Journal* xxii/2 (Jun. 1979), pp.423–41.

Klieman, Aaron S., 'The resolution of conflict through territorial partition: the Palestinian experience', *Comparative Studies – Society and History* xxiii/2 (Apr. 1988), pp.281–300.

Kristol, Irving, 'The political dilemma of American Jews', *Commentary* lxxviii/1 (Jul. 1984), pp.23–9.

Lebow, Richard Ned, 'Woodrow Wilson and the Balfour Declaration', *The Journal of Modern History* xl/4 (Dec. 1968), pp.501–23.

Levene, Mark, 'The Balfour Declaration: a case of mistaken identity', *The English Historical Review* cvii/422 (Jan. 1992), pp.54–77.

Lienesch, Michael, 'Right-wing religion: Christian conservatism as a political movement', *Political Science Quarterly* xcvii/3 (autumn 1982), pp.403–25.

Lipset, Seymour Martin, 'The Radical Right: a problem for American democracy', *The British Journal of Sociology* vi/2 (Jun. 1955), pp.176–209.

Little, Douglas, 'The making of a special relationship: the United States and Israel, 1957–68', *International Journal of Middle East Studies* xxv/4 (Nov. 1993), pp.563–85.

Mallison, W.T., 'An international law appraisal of the juridical characteristics on the resistance of the people of Palestine', *Revue Egyptienne de Droit International* xxviii (1972), pp.1–19.

Manuel, Frank E., 'The Palestine Question in Italian diplomacy, 1917–1920', *The Journal of Modern History* xxvii/3 (Sep. 1955), pp.263–80.

Matar, Nabil I., 'Protestantism, Palestine, and partisan scholarship', *Journal of Palestine Studies* xviii/4 (summer 1989), p.52–70.

Mathews, Donald G., 'The second Great Awakening as an organizing process, 1780–1830: an hypothesis', *American Quarterly* xxi/1 (spring 1969), pp.23–43.

McTague, Jr, John J., 'Anglo-French negotiations over the boundaries of Palestine, 1919–1920', *Journal of Palestine Studies* xi/2 (winter 1982), pp.100–12.

Mejcher, Helmut, 'British Middle East policy 1917–21: the inter-departmental level', *Journal of Contemporary History* viii/4 (Oct. 1973), pp.81–101.

Mendilow, Jonathan, 'Party clustering in multiparty systems: the example of Israel 1965–1981', *American Journal of Political Science* xxvii/1 (Feb. 1983), pp.64–85.

Meyer, Isidore S., 'Hebrew at Harvard (1636–1760)', *Publications of the American Jewish Historical Society* xxxv (1939), pp.145–70.

Miller, David Hunter, 'The origin of the mandate system', *Foreign Affairs* vi/2 (Jan. 1928), pp.277–89.

Moberg, David O., 'Religion and society in the Netherlands and in America', *American Quarterly* xiii/2, Part 1 (summer 1961), p.172–8.

Moen, Matthew, 'The evolving politics of the Christian Right', *PS: Political Science and Politics* xxix/3 (Sept. 1996), pp.461–4.

Moorehead, James H., 'Between progress and apocalypse: a reassessment of millennialism in American religious thought, 1800–1880', *The Journal of American History* lxxi/3 (Dec. 1984), pp.524–42.

Neff, Donald, 'Jerusalem in US policy', *Journal of Palestine Studies* xxiii/1 (autumn 1993), pp.20–45.

Overdale, Ritchie, 'The Palestinian policy of the British Labour government 1947: the decision to withdraw', *International Affairs* lvi/1 (Jan. 1980), pp.73–93.

Pallis, Elfi, 'The Likud Party: a primer', *Journal of Palestine Studies* xxi/2 (winter 1992), pp.41–60.

Paris, Timothy J., 'British Middle East policy-making after the First World War: the Lawrentian and Wilsonian schools', *The Historical Journal* xli/3 (Sep. 1998), pp.773–93.

Parra, Fredy, 'Historia y escatología en Manuel Lacunza. La temporalidad a través del milenarismo lacunziano', *Teología y vida* (Santiago) xliv (2003), pp.167–83.

Perry, Yaron and Efraim Lev, 'The medical activities of the London Jews' society in nineteenth-century Palestine', *Medical History* xlvii/1 (Jan. 2003), pp.67–88.

Petchesky, Rosalind Pollack, 'Antiabortion, antifeminism, and the rise of the New Right', *Feminist Studies* vii/2 (summer 1981), pp.206–46.

Pfeiffer, Robert H., 'The teaching of Hebrew in colonial America', *The Jewish Quarterly Review* (new series) xlv/4, tercentenary issue (Apr. 1955), p.353–73.

Pika, Joseph A., 'Interest groups and the White House under Roosevelt and Truman', *Political Science Quarterly* cii/4 (winter 1987–8), p.647–68.

Quandt, Jean B., 'Religion and social thought: the secularization of postmillennialism', *American Quarterly* xxv/4 (Oct. 1973), pp.390–409.

Regnerus, Mark D., David Sikkink and Christian Smith, 'Voting with the Christian Right: contextual and individual patterns of electoral influence', *Social Forces* lxxvii/4 (Jun. 1993), pp.1,375–401.

Reinharz, Jehuda, 'The Balfour Declaration and its maker: a reassessment', *The Journal of Modern History* lxiv/3 (Sep. 1992), pp.445–99.

Rodkey, Frederick Stanley, 'Lord Palmerston and the rejuvenation of Turkey, 1830–41, Part II, 1939–41', *The Journal of Modern History* ii/2 (Jun. 1930), p.193–225; Part I is in *The Journal of Modern History* i/4 (Dec. 1929), pp.570–93.

Rose, Norman, 'The seventh dominion', *The Historical Journal* xiv/2 (Jun. 1971), pp.397–416.

Rossel, Robert D., 'The Great Awakening: an historical analysis', *The American Journal of Sociology* lxxv/6 (May 1970), pp.907–25.

Rothwell, V. H., 'Mesopotamia in British war aims, 1914–1918', *The Historical Journal* xiii/2 (Jun. 1970), pp.273–94.

Rozell, Mark J. and Clyde Wilcox, 'Second Coming: the strategies of the New Christian Right', *Political Science Quarterly* cxi/2 (summer 1996), pp.271–94.

Rudolph, Frederick, 'The American Liberty League, 1934–1940', *The American Historical Review* lvi/1 (Oct. 1950), pp.19–33.

Sagay, I., 'International law relating to occupied territory', *Revue Egyptienne de Droit International* xxviii (1972), pp.56–64.

Schölch, Alexander, 'Britain in Palestine, 1838–1882: the roots of the Balfour policy', *Journal of Palestine Studies* xxii/1 (autumn 1992), pp.39–56.

Shahak, Israel, 'L'idee du 'transfert' dans la doctrine sioniste', *Revue d'etudes Palestiniennes* no. 29 (autumn 1988), pp.103–32.

Shapira, Anita, 'Labour Zionism and the October revolution', *Journal of Contemporary History* xxiv/4 (Oct. 1989), pp.623–56.

Sharif, Regina, 'Christians for Zion, 1600–1919', *Journal of Palestine Studies* v/3–4 (spring/summer 1976), pp.123–41.

Sheffer, Gabriel, 'Appeasement and the problem of Palestine', *International Journal of Middle East Studies* xi/3 (May 1908), pp.377–99.

Stein, Kenneth W., 'A historiographic review of literature on the origins of the Arab–Israeli conflict', *The American Historical Review* xcvi/5 (Dec. 1991), pp.1,450–65.

Stratton, Morton B., 'British railways and motor routes in the Middle East – 1918–1930', *Economic Geography* xx/2 (Apr. 1944), pp.116–29.

Tamney, Joseph and Stephen Johnson, 'Explaining support for the Moral Majority', *Sociological Forum* iii/2 (spring 1988), pp.234–55.

Tessler, Mark, 'The political Right in Israel: its origins, growth, and prospects', *Journal of Palestine Studies* xv/2 (winter 1986), pp.12–55.

Thomas, Martin, 'Bedouin tribes and the imperial intelligence services in Syria, Iraq and Transjordan in the 1920s', *Journal of Contemporary History* xxxviii/4 (Oct. 2003), pp.539–61.

Tobias, Henry, 'The Bund and Lenin until 1903', *Russian Review* xx/4 (Oct. 1961), pp.344–57.

Tutunji, Jenab and Kamal Khalidi, 'A binational state in Palestine: the rational choice for Palestinians and the moral choice for Israelis', *International Affairs* lxxiii/1 (Jan. 1997), pp.31–58.

Vereté, Mayir, 'The restoration of Jews in English Protestant thought 1790–1840', *Middle Eastern Studies* viii/1 (Jan. 1972), pp.3–50.
Wagner, Donald, 'Beyond Armageddon', *The Link* (Americans for Middle East Understanding) xxv/4 (Oct.–Nov. 1992), p.5.
Wagner, Donald, 'For Zion's sake', *Middle East Report* 223 (summer 2002), pp.52–7.
Wasserstein, Bernard, 'Herbert Samuel and the Palestine problem', *The English Historical Review* xci/361 (Oct. 1976), pp.753–75.
Watson, C.M., 'Bonaparte's expedition to Palestine in 1799', *Palestine Exploration Fund Quarterly Statement for 1917* (London: Palestine Exploration Fund, 1917), pp.17–35.
Wilcox, Clyde, 'Fundamentalists and politics: an analysis of the effects of differing operational definitions', *The Journal of Politics* xlviii/4 (Nov. 1986), pp.1,041–51.
Wilcox, Clyde, 'The Christian Right in twentieth century America: continuity and change', *The Review of Politics* l/4 (fall 1988), pp.659–81.
Wilcox, Clyde, 'Second Coming: the strategies of the New Christian Right', *Political Science Quarterly* cxi/2 (summer 1996), pp.271–94.
Wilson, Evan M., 'The Palestine papers, 1943–1947', *Journal of Palestine Studies* ii/4 (summer 1973), p.33–54.
Wood, Brian, 'The Second annual CUFI conference, July 2007: the Christian Zionist coalition hits its stride', *Journal of Palestine Studies* xxxvii/1 (autumn 2007), p.86.
Woodberry, Robert D. and Christian S. Smith, 'Fundamentalism et al: Conservative Protestants in America', *Annual Review of Sociology* xxiv (1998), p.25–56.
Wright, Quincy, 'The Palestine problem', *Political Science Quarterly* xli/3 (Sep. 1926), pp.384–412.
Yale, William, 'Ambassador Henry Morgenthau's special mission of 1917', *World Politics* i/3 (Apr. 1949), pp.308–20.

Dissertations

Wright, Jr, Walter Livingston, 'American relations with Turkey to 1831', unpub. dissertation, Princeton University, 1928, pp.10–30.

Index

A
Abrams, Elliott 146, 156, 170
Acheson, Dean 115–16
Acton Institute 75, 141
Adams, John 29, 31
Adams, John Quincy 33
Albury Circle 56, 58–9, 61
Ali, Muhammad 18–19, 23–4
Allenby, Edmund 74, 77, 82, 83–6
Alypius of Antioch 9
American Baptist Convention 90
American Bible and Prophetic
    Conference
    First 68
    Second 68
    Third 68
American Board of Commissioners of
    Foreign Missions 43
American Christian Palestine
    Committee (ACPC) 102, 105
American Coalition for Traditional
    Values 143
American Council of Christian
    Churches (ACCC) 70, 91–2, 122,
    124–5
American Enterprise Institute 144
American Israel Public Affairs Council
    (AIPAC) 40, 121, 137, 148–9,
    150, 163–4
    and John Hagee 180–1

American Jewish Committee
    (AJC) 107, 143, 169–70
American Liberty League 129–32, 143,
    148
American Palestine Council (APC) 101
American Zionist Emergency Council
    (AZEC) 102
Americans for a Safe Israel (AFSI) 159
amillennialism xii, 41, 49
Amway Corporation 139
Andover Theological Seminary 43,
    53–4
Anglo-American Commission of
    Inquiry 113–16, 117
Anglo-Persian Oil Company 73, 79
Anti-Revolutionaire Partij (Anti-
    Revolutionary Party, ARP) 75,
    140
Armageddon (1923 film) 86
Arvey, Jack 118
Attlee, Clement 112

B
Bainbridge, William 32
Balfour Declaration 79, 80–1, 82, 110
Baptist Bible Union of America 89–90
Baptist Missionary Society 42
Barbican Mission to the Jews 55
Barlow, Joel 29, 53
Barth, Karl 89

Index

Basle Program (1897) 1–2, 95, 104, 107
Bauer, Gary 140, 165, 179
Begin, Manachem 149
Bell, Daniel 143
Ben-Haim, Elyahu 176
Bible Institute of Los Angeles 69
Bible Institute of Philadelphia 69
Bible Presbyterian Church 91
Bible Protestant Church 91
Bible schools, institutes, seminaries 69–70
biblicism and Zionism 93–96
Biltmore Program (1942) 102, 104–8
Blackstone, William E. 61, 64, 66–7,
Blackwell, Morton 138
Bob Jones College 126
Brandeis, Louis 67
Bright, Bill 126, 139
British Society for the Propagation of the Gospel Among the Jews 55
Brog, David 179
Brookes, James H. 61, 64
Buckley, Jr, William F. 125
Business Plot 128–9
Bush, George H.W. 153, 157–8, 170
Bush, George W. 137, 153–4, 155
  and neoconservatives 160–3
Bush, Jeb 160
Buswell, J. Oliver 90
Byrnes, James F. 115

C

Calvin College 141
Campus Crusade for Christ 126, 133, 139
Canada 15
Carter, Jimmy 3, 39, 46–7, 135, 142, 145, 156
Cass, Lewis 37
Center for Security Policy (CSP) 150–1

Cheney, Richard 160–1, 162, 168–9
China xi, 9, 11, 35
  and dispensationalism 178, 181
Choiseul, Etienne François Duc de 14
Christian and Missionary Alliance 69
Christian Anti-Communist Crusade (CACC) 125
Christian Coalition 2, 143, 157, 179
Christian Council for Palestine (CCP) 102, 105
Christian Crusade (organization) 125
Christian Economic Foundation (CEF) 132
Christian Freedom Foundation (CFF) 132, 138
Christian Reformed Church 139
Christian Right 5
  and Middle East policy 164–6
Christian Voice 138, 143
Christian Zionism
  ideology 45–61
Christianity Today 133
Christians United for Israel (CUFI) 176, 179–80
Churba, Joseph 153
Church of the Holy Sepulchre 86
Church Missionary Society 25
Church of the Nativity 26
Churchill, Winston 80, 82, 110–12,
Coalition for a Democratic Majority (CDM) 145, 146
Cohn, Roy 125, 152
Cold War 11, 39, 77, 120–1, 133
Colson, Charles 139, 140, 141–2
Commentary 143, 145, 146, 169
Committee for the Liberation of Iraq (CLI) 168
Committee for the Present Danger (CPD) 146
Committee for the Survival of a Free Congress (CSFC) 138
Concerned Women for America 143

Conference of Presidents of Major
    Jewish Organizations 150
Congress of Vienna 18, 28
Conlan, John 139
Conservative Baptist Association 90
Conservative Baptist Theological
    Seminary (Denver Seminary) 90
Cooper, Anthony Ashley (seventh Earl
    of Shaftsbury) 22–5, 46–50
Coors, Joseph 138
Council for National Policy (CNP) 148,
    153
Crimean War 10, 25
Cyrus the Great 23

D
Dallas Theological Seminary 69–70
Danforth, John 3
Darby, John Nelson 4, 54, 55, 61
    and North America 63–4
Day of Deception 158
De Kay, George, C. 29
Democratic Party
    and neoconservatives 144
DeMoss, Arthur 139
    Arthur S. DeMoss Foundation 139
DeVoss, Richard 139
dispensationalism xiv, 4,
    ideology constructed 46–61
Dixon, Amzi 67
Djezzar, Ahmed 16
Dobson, James 140, 143
Dome of the Rock 10, 74
Drummond, Jr, Henry 56, 58
Dutch Reformed Church 75, 76, 139,
    140
Dwight, Timothy 53

E
Eckford, Harry 33
Eckstein, Yechiel 179
Edwards, Jonathan 42

Egypt 10, 18–19, 36–40, 156
    Khedive Ismail 38–40
    Napoleon in Egypt 15–18
    and Taba peace talks 166
Emergency Committee for Zionist
    Affairs (ECZA) 102
Erdman, Charles 67
Evangelical Theological College 70

F
Faith Theological Seminary 91
Falwell, Jerry 2, 138, 139, 153
    and George H.W. Bush 157
Falwell, Jonathan 179
Family Research Council 141, 143
Federal Council of Churches of
    Christ 91
Feith, Douglas 146, 156
Florida Bible Institute 126
Focus on the Family 143
Francis I 14
Franklin, Benjamin 31
Free Congress Foundation 138
French Institute of International
    Relations (IFRI) 172
Fuller, Charles E. 91
Fuller Theological Seminary 126
Fundamentalist Fellowship 89
Fundamentalist, The 90
Fundamentals, The 72, 75, 76

G
Gaffney, Frank 146, 150
George, Lloyd 79–80, 82
Gibbon, Edward 9–10
Glazer, Nathan 143
God's Candidate for America 159
Goldwater, Barry 137
Goldwin, Robert Allen 160
Gordon, Adoniram Judson 67
Gordon-Conwell Theological
    Seminary 132

Graham, Billy 69, 90, 122, 126–7, 132–5
  and Eisenhower 134
  and George H.W. Bush 158
  Hope for the Future 148
  New York crusade (1957) 133
  and Nixon 134–5
Grant, Robert 138, 143
Gray, James M. 83
Great Awakening
  First 42, 52
  Second 42, 52
Great Britain 8, 11, 14–15, 25
  and the First World War 72–4
  and interwar period 96–100
  and the Second World War 108–16

H
Hagee, John 5, 156, 174
  AIPAC 2007 speech 180–1
  Armageddon scenario 175–8
  calls for war against Iran 176–8
  Day of Deception 158
  God's Candidate for America 159
  Jerusalem Countdown 176
  launches CUFI 176, 179–80
  opposes Middle East peace 174–5
Hargis, Billy James 125
Hearst, William Randolph 126–7
Hechler, William H. 95
Hecht, Jacob 'Chic' 152
Helms, Jesse 151–3
Heritage Foundation 138
Herzl, Theodore 95
Hess, Moses 94
Hodgson, William Brown 33
Hourani, Albert 25
Hunt family 123, 148

I
Institute for Advanced Strategic and Political Studies (IASPS) 160

Intercessors for Israel 176
International Christian Embassy Jerusalem (ICEJ) 150
International Christian Leadership 134
International Council for Religious Education 91
International Fellowship of Christians and Jews (IFCJ) 179
Iran (Persia) xi, 29, 30
  Hagee calls for war against 177
Irving, Edward 4, 57

J
Jabotinsky, Vladimir 143
Jackson, Henry 'Scoop' 145
Jarmin, Gary 143
Jefferson, Thomas 29, 31
Jewish Agency 108, 179
Jewish Institute for National Security Affairs (JINSA) 150–1
Jewish Question 10
Julian the Apostate 9–10

K
Kagan, Robert 160, 169
Khouri, Rami 4,
Kristol, Irving 143, 146
Kristol, William 160, 165
Kuyper, Abraham 75, 90, 123, 139, 140, 142

L
LaHaye, Beverly 143
LaHaye, Tim 148, 153
Larkin, Clarence 94
League of Nations 11
Levens, Esther 151
Liberty College 139
Liberty National Insurance Company 139
Lindsay, Alexander William Crawford (Lord Lindsay) 23

Lindsay, Hal 148
Lipset, Seymour Martin 143
London Jews' Society (LJS) 54,
London Missionary Society 42
London Society for Promoting Christianity Amongst the Jews 25, 54
Luce, Henry 126, 127

M

Machen, J. Gresham 90
Magnes, Judah 108
mandate system (League of Nations) 11
    Iraq 78
    Palestine 78, 81, 99
Massachusetts Missionary Society 43
McCarthy, Joseph 91, 122, 125, 152
McDonald, James G. 117
McIntire, Carl 70, 91–2, 122, 124–6, 133
McTeer, Edward 159
Mildmay Mission to the Jews 55
Mildmay Second Advent Conference 67
Missionary Society of Connecticut 43
Missionary Society of Rhode Island 43
Moody Bible Institute 69, 72, 77, 122
Moody, Dwight L. 61, 64–6,
Moorehead, William 67
Moral Majority 2, 139, 147, 153
Morocco 30–1

N

Napoleon 8, 13, 15, 49, 80
    Battle of Acre 17
    Battle of the Nile 17
    Egyptian Campaign 14
    and Jews 15–18
National Association of Evangelicals (NAE) 92, 122, 124
    supports Iraq War 156
National Council of the Churches of Christ in America 91, 132
National Unity Coalition for Israel (NUCI) 150, 151, 179–80
Neo-Calvinism 90
neoconservatives 137, 143–6
    European concern over 171–3
New Christian Right 88, 91, 137
New Right 121, 137, 145
    and Christian Right 142–3
New York Missionary Society 43
Niagara Bible Conferences 64, 67, 68
Niles, David K. 115–6
Noebel, David 125
Norris, J. Frank 90
North Atlantic Treaty Organization (NATO) 14, 161
Northern Baptist Convention 89
Northern New York Missionary Society 43
Northwestern Bible Training School 69
Northwestern College 126

O

Obama administration 174
Ocean Spray Corporation 139
Old Fashioned Bible Hour 91
Oman 35–6
Ormsby-Gore, William 97
Ottoman Empire 8, 10–11, 13, 16, 46, 73
    and British imperial policy 18–26
    Conference of London 81
    and the First World War 77–82
    San Remo Conference 81
    Sultan 10–11
    Treaty of Lausanne 81
    Treaty of Sèvres 81
    and USA 29

P

Palestine Question 73, 104

Palmerston, Viscount (*see* Temple, Henry John)
Passfield White Paper 97
Peace of Westphalia 13
Peel Commission (Palestine Royal Commission) 98–9
Perle, Richard 146, 150, 156, 169
Pew, J. Howard 130, 132–3, 138–9
Philadelphia Biblical University 69
Philadelphia School of the Bible 69
Plymouth Brethren 61
Podhoretz, Norman 143, 145
Political Zionism
    American Israel Public Affairs Council (AIPAC) 40, 121, 137, 148–9, 150, 163–4
    American Jewish Committee (AJC) 107, 143, 169–70
    Americans for a Safe Israel (AFSI) 159
    American Zionist Emergency Council (AZEC) 102
    Basle Program (1897) 1–2, 95, 104, 107
    Biltmore Program (1942) 102, 104–8
    Conference of Presidents of Major Jewish Organizations 150
    Emergency Committee for Zionist Affairs (ECZA) 102
    and geography 94–6
    Jewish Agency 108, 179
    Second World War 100–3
Porter, David 33
postmillennialism xii, 41, 51
Powerscourt Prophetic Conferences 59–60, 61
Presbyterian Church 90
    Lane Theological Seminary 90
    Omaha Theological Seminary 90
    Princeton Theological Seminary 90
Presidential prayer breakfast 134
preterism xiii
Prince, Edgar 140
Prince, Erik 140
Prince, Peter Derek Vaughan 176
Prison Fellowship 139
Pro-Palestine Federation of America (PPF) 102, 105
Project for a New American Century (PNAC) 160
Prophetic Bible Conference Movement 67–9
Proskauer, Joseph Meyer 143

R
Reed, Ralph 143, 157, 179
Reformed Church in the Netherlands 75
Religious Right 76, 120–2, 132–3
Religious Roundtable 159
Republican Party (GOP) 2–3, 144
    and Christian Right 165
    and Iraq War 161–2
Rhodes, Foster 33–4
Roberts, Edmund 35
Robertson, Pat 2, 143, 157
Robinson, Edward 54
Rumsfeld, Donald 160–1
Russia xi, 11, 13, 18, 22
    Bolshevik Revolution 77
    and British imperial policy 18–21
    and dispensationalism 88, 178, 181
    Russo-Turkish Wars 11

S
Sadat, Anwar 39
St James Conference 99
Samuel, Herbert 82
Saudi Arabia 156
    arms sale (1981) 151
Schaeffer, Francis August 91, 126, 158
Schmitt, Gary 169
Schwartz, Fred C. 125

Scofield, Cyrus 61, 64, 65–6, 69, 70
    Scofield Bible 5, 76,
Scopes Trial 70, 87, 120
Seven Years War 14
Sheldon, Louis 143
Shepherding Movement 176
Shultz, George 162, 168
Simeon, Charles 55, 56
Six Day War (1967) 5, 77, 121
Southern Baptist Convention 69, 90
Southwestern School of the Bible 70
Spring-Rice, Cecil 83–4
Spurgeon, Charles 55–6
Stand for Israel 179
Standing Committee on Missions of the Dutch Reformed Church 43
Standing Committee on Missions of the Presbyterian Church 43
Stephens, John Lloyd 29
Stewart, Lyman 69, 75
Stewart, Milton 75
Stiles, Ezra 52–3
Stone, Charles P. 38–40
Suez Crisis 121, 151
Suleiman the Magnificent 14
Sunday, Billy 75
Sykes, Percy 86
Syrian Question 10

T

Talcott, John 139
Taylor, James Hudson 67
Temple, Henry John (third Viscount Palmerston) 8
    and Christian Zionism 21–5
    and imperial policy 18–21
    and Palestine 21–5
Third Century Publishers 138–9
Toronto Bible Training School 69
Treaty of London (1840) 21
Treaty of Unkiar Skelessi (1833) 19, 21

Truman, Harry 116–9, 143
    Truman Letter 116–8

U

Union Oil Company (UNOCAL) 69
United Nations Special Committee on Palestine (UNSCOP) 117
United Palestine Appeal 107
United States of America 11, 26
    Barbary Wars 32
    Congress and Iraq War 166–8
    early Republic and the Muslim world 28–9
    Mediterranean Squadron 29
    missionaries 41–4
United States Committee on NATO (USCN) 169
United States Religious Landscape Survey 2008 xv
Unity Coalition for Israel (UCI) 150

V

Van Prinsterer, Guillaume Groen 140
Van Til, Cornelius 90
Vereide, Abraham 133
    Presidential prayer breakfast 134

W

Walvoord, John F. 70
Way, Lewis 55–6,
Wead, Doug 157–9
    and John Hagee 158–9
Wedgewood, Josiah 97
Weizman, Chaim 107
Western Baptist Theological Seminary (Western Seminary) 90
Western Missionary Society 43
Westminster Theological Seminary 90
Weyrich, Paul 138
Wheaton College 69, 90, 91, 126
Wilson, Woodrow 80–1
Wolff, Joseph 55, 56

Wolfowitz, Paul 146, 156,
Woodbury, Levi 35
Woodhead Commission 99
World Bible Conference 77
World Council of Churches
    (WCC) 124
World Jewish Congress (WJC) 107
World's Christian Fundamentals
    Association 77

Y
Youth for Christ (YFC) 126, 133

Z
Zakheim, Dov 146
Zionist Organization of America
    (ZOA) 107
Zweibon, Herbert 159

www.ingramcontent.com/pod-product-compliance
Ingram Content Group UK Ltd.
Pitfield, Milton Keynes, MK11 3LW, UK
UKHW021857060326
468729UK00008B/3553